# MEASURING MENTAL ILLNESS: PSYCHOMETRIC ASSESSMENT FOR CLINICIANS

# Clinical Practice
Number 8

*Judith H. Gold, M.D., F.R.C.P. (C)*
*Series Editor*

# MEASURING MENTAL ILLNESS: PSYCHOMETRIC ASSESSMENT FOR CLINICIANS

*Edited by*

**SCOTT WETZLER, Ph.D.**

Assistant Professor of Psychiatry
Albert Einstein College of Medicine/
Montefiore Medical Center
Bronx, New York

American Psychiatric Press, Inc.
1400 K Street, N.W.
Washington, DC 20005

Copyright © 1989 American Psychiatric Press, Inc.
ALL RIGHTS RESERVED
Manufactured in the United States of America
First Edition

89   90   91   92   4   3   2   1

**Library of Congress Cataloging-in-Publication Data**

Measuring mental illness: psychometric assessment for
  clinicians / edited by Scott Wetzler.—1st ed.
      p.      cm.—(The Clinical practice series; 8)
   Includes bibliographies.
   ISBN 0-88048-179-X
   1. Mental illness—Diagnosis.   2. Psychometrics.
3. Psychological tests.   I. Wetzler, Scott,
1955-      .  II. Series: Clinical practice series
(Washington, D.C.); no. 8.
   [DNLM: 1. Mental Disorders—diagnosis.
2. Psychometrics.   WM 145 M484]
RC473.P79M43 1989
616.89′075—dc19
DNLM/DLC                                          88-39232
for Library of Congress                           CIP

# Contents

CONTRIBUTORS     vii

INTRODUCTION TO THE CLINICAL PRACTICE
SERIES     xi

### Introduction

**1** Introduction: The Contemporary Parameters     3
of Assessment in Psychopathology
*Scott Wetzler, Ph.D.*

**2** Use of Research Instruments in     21
Psychopathological Assessment:
Some Historical Perspectives
*Joseph Zubin, Ph.D.*

**3** Use of Structured Interviews for Diagnosis     43
*Eileen P. Rubinson, M.S.W.*
*Gregory M. Asnis, M.D.*

### Assessment of Psychopathological Disorders

**4** Assessment of Depression     69
*Scott Wetzler, Ph.D.*
*Herman M. van Praag, M.D., Ph.D.*

**5** Clinical Assessment in Schizophrenia     89
*John A. Sweeney, Ph.D.*
*Gretchen L. Haas, Ph.D.*
*Peter J. Weiden, M.D.*

**6** Assessment of Anxiety Disorders     113
*M. Katherine Shear, M.D.*
*Janet Klosko, Ph.D.*
*Minna R. Fyer, M.D.*

**7** Assessment of DSM-III Personality   *139*
Disorders

*Lawrence B. Jacobsberg, M.D.*
*Scott Goldsmith, M.D.*
*Thomas Widiger, Ph.D.*
*Allen J. Frances, M.D.*

**8** Assessment of Alcoholism and   *161*
Substance Abuse

*Leslie C. Morey, Ph.D.*
*Peter R. Martin, M.D.*

**9** Assessment of Organic Mental Disorders   *183*

*Robert M. Bilder, Ph.D.*
*John M. Kane, M.D.*

### Related Topics in Assessment

**10** Instruments for the Assessment   *211*
of Family Malfunction

*John F. Clarkin, Ph.D.*
*Ira D. Glick, M.D.*

**11** Ethnocultural Issues in the Assessment of   *229*
Psychopathology

*Anthony J. Marsella, Ph.D.*
*Velma A. Kameoka, Ph.D.*

**12** Assessment of Psychopathology   *257*
in Minorities

*Bruce L. Ballard, M.D.*

**13** Legal and Ethical Aspects of Psychometric   *267*
Assessment

*Robert D. Miller, M.D., Ph.D.*

Appendix: List of 100 Assessment   *289*
Instruments

# Contributors

**Gregory M. Asnis, M.D.**
Associate Professor of Psychiatry, Albert Einstein College of
Medicine/Montefiore Medical Center

**Bruce L. Ballard, M.D.**
Associate Professor of Clinical Psychiatry, New York
Hospital–Cornell University Medical College

**Robert M. Bilder, Ph.D.**
Chief, Clinical Neuropsychology, Long Island Jewish Medical
Center–Hillside Division

**John F. Clarkin, Ph.D.**
Professor of Clinical Psychology in Psychiatry, New York
Hospital–Cornell University Medical College

**Allen J. Frances, M.D.**
Professor of Psychiatry, New York Hospital–Cornell
University Medical College

**Minna R. Fyer, M.D.**
Assistant Professor of Psychiatry, New York Hospital–Cornell
University Medical College

**Ira D. Glick, M.D.**
Professor of Psychiatry, New York Hospital–Cornell
University Medical College

**Scott Goldsmith, M.D.**
Instructor of Clinical Psychiatry, New York Hospital–Cornell
University Medical College

**Gretchen L. Haas, Ph.D.**
Assistant Professor of Psychology in Psychiatry, New York Hospital–Cornell University Medical College

**Lawrence B. Jacobsberg, M.D., Ph.D.**
Instructor of Psychiatry, New York Hospital–Cornell University Medical College

**Velma A. Kameoka, Ph.D.**
Associate Professor of Social Work, University of Hawaii

**John M. Kane, M.D.**
Chairman and Professor of Psychiatry, Long Island Jewish Medical Center, School of Medicine–SUNY Stony Brook

**Janet Klosko, Ph.D.**
Research Assistant, Department of Psychiatry, New York Hospital–Cornell University Medical College

**Anthony J. Marsella, Ph.D.**
Vice-President of Academic Affairs, University of Hawaii

**Peter R. Martin, M.D.**
Associate Professor of Psychiatry, Vanderbilt University School of Medicine

**Robert D. Miller, M.D., Ph.D.**
Clinical Associate Professor of Psychiatry, Medical College of Wisconsin, Milwaukee

**Leslie C. Morey, Ph.D.**
Associate Professor of Psychology, Vanderbilt University

**Eileen P. Rubinson, M.S.W.**
Head, Diagnostics, Anxiety and Depression Clinic, Albert Einstein College of Medicine/Montefiore Medical Center

**M. Katherine Shear, M.D.**
Associate Professor of Clinical Psychiatry, New York
Hospital–Cornell University Medical College

**John A. Sweeney, Ph.D.**
Assistant Professor of Psychology in Psychiatry, New York
Hospital–Cornell University Medical College

**Herman M. van Praag, M.D., Ph.D.**
Silverman Professor and Chairman of Psychiatry, Albert
Einstein College of Medicine/Montefiore Medical Center

**Peter J. Weiden, M.D.**
Instructor of Psychiatry, New York Hospital–Cornell
University Medical College

**Scott Wetzler, Ph.D.**
Assistant Professor of Psychiatry (Psychology), Albert
Einstein College of Medicine/Montefiore Medical Center

**Thomas Widiger, Ph.D.**
Associate Professor of Psychology, University of Kentucky

**Joseph Zubin, Ph.D.**
Distinguished Research Professor of Psychiatry, University of
Pittsburgh Medical School

# Introduction
## to the Clinical Practice Series

O ver the years of its existence the series of monographs entitled *Clinical Insights* gradually became focused on providing current, factual, and theoretical material of interest to the clinician working outside of a hospital setting. To reflect this orientation, the name of the Series has been changed to *Clinical Practice.*

The Clinical Practice Series will provide readers with books that give the mental health clinician a practical clinical approach to a variety of psychiatric problems. These books will provide up-to-date literature reviews and emphasize the most recent treatment methods. Thus, the publications in the Series will interest clinicians working both in psychiatry and in the other mental health professions.

Each year a number of books will be published dealing with all aspects of clinical practice. In addition, from time to time when appropriate, the publications may be revised and updated. Thus, the Series will provide quick access to relevant and important areas of psychiatric practice. Some books in the Series will be authored by a person considered to be an expert in that particular area; others will be edited by such an expert who will also draw together other knowledgeable authors to produce a comprehensive overview of that topic.

Some of the books in the Clinical Practice Series will have their foundation in presentations at an annual meeting of the American Psychiatric Association. All will contain the most recently available information on the subjects discussed. Theoretical and scientific data will be applied to clinical situations, and case illustrations will be utilized in order to make the material even more relevant for the practitioner. Thus, the Clinical Practice Series should provide educational reading in a compact format especially written for the mental health clinician–psychiatrist.

Clinicians in practice often require psychological testing to assist in both diagnosis and treatment of patients. This book provides a concise and current review of the tests available today. It discusses their appropriate use and their advantages and disadvantages for the clinician. The clinician will find this publication to be of great usefulness in daily work with patients.

Judith H. Gold, M.D., F.R.C.P.(C)
*Series Editor,*
*Clinical Practice Series*

# Introduction

# Chapter 1

# *Introduction: The Contemporary Parameters of Assessment in Psychopathology*

**SCOTT WETZLER, Ph.D.**

# Chapter 1

# *Introduction: The Contemporary Parameters of Assessment in Psychopathology*

**M**easurement of components of mental illness is of crucial importance to all mental health professionals. Psychiatrists and psychologists are confronted daily with difficult clinical situations that require careful evaluation and assessment. Is this patient dangerous or suicidal? Is he or she manic or schizophrenic? Or demented or depressed? Is the severity of the depression great enough to warrant a particular type of treatment? Has the patient improved since the beginning of a treatment intervention? Will the patient be able to function independently and without supervision? Does the family situation contribute to the psychiatric difficulties? How intelligent is he or she? What sort of interpersonal relationships does the patient have? After this acute crisis resolves, what can be expected regarding premorbid personality? How much of the symptomatic presentation may be attributed to the patient's particular ethnic or demographic status? One could construct an endless list of hypothetical clinical situations that require thorough evaluation.

This book is intended to help clinicians find methods to answer many of these and other assessment questions. At present, the typical clinician tends to rely on his or her own idiosyncratic means of evaluation such as an open-ended interview and an informal mental status examination. By standardizing assessment, all practitioners may be able to utilize the same methods and know that their evaluations would be identical to those of other professionals. In fact, clinicians rarely use standardized assessment instruments; they leave these tools to the researcher in psychopathology. This is a glaring and destructive separation of functions, which unnecessarily limits advances in clinical work.

The basic premise of this book is to encourage a dialogue between clinicians and researchers. That the fields of psychology and psychiatry have permitted such a fragmentation of roles as exists today between the clinician and the researcher is particularly unfortunate. It seems these two kinds of professionals have no common language or domain of study, when in fact they share a common interest in psychopathology. And the individual who tries to combine both roles leads a strange life composed of two separate, split-off identities. Better integration within the field will lead to more scientific, standardized assessment and to more practical and useful research investigations.

Because clinicians are frequently confronted with the same problem that the researchers must face—how to assess psychopathology in a standardized fashion—they can take advantage of the advances in research methodology over the last 20 years (although standardized assessment does have a tradition dating back at least to Sir Francis Galton's day). In an effort to define homogeneous patient populations and to determine relevant outcome variables, researchers have spent an enormous amount of time developing and refining measurement instruments. The technologies that have been developed in the course of studies include structured interviews, observational rating scales, and self-report inventories. These methods do have a place in daily clinical practice. This book considers the value of utilizing these new tools for the clinical assessment of psychopathology. The more knowledgeable the clinician is about the strengths and limitations of these instruments, the more he or she will be able to effectively and appropriately use them.

During the last 20 years there has been an avalanche of clinical assessment methodologies. Recent reviews identify over 100 widely used tests (Carr 1985; Endicott and Spitzer 1980) (see Appendix). These tests range from the well-known Hamilton Rating Scale for Depression, the Symptom Checklist 90 (SCL-90), and the Schedule for Affective Disorders and Schizophrenia (SADS), to the lesser-known Buss-Durkee Hostility Inventory, Katz Adjustment Scale, or Personality Disorder Examination. That such instruments may be used for clinical assessment purposes represents a major breakthrough for these research tools.

The large repertoire of instruments gives clinicians greater flexibility. They can select the particular method or instrument that suits their particular assessment needs. However, such a large quantity of tests can only leave the naive clinician feeling overwhelmed and uncertain about which test should be used in any given clinical situation. An introduction to the general principles of how to use research instruments in clinical settings is necessary, along with some examples of how they may be used and a historical review of the changes in psychiatry that have permitted this development.

Until recently, nonpsychologists were reluctant to use standardized assessment instruments in their practices. When they required a standardized assessment they referred the patient to a clinical psychologist who administered a standard battery of psychological tests consisting of Rorschach, Thematic Apperception Test (TAT), and Wechsler Adult Intelligence Scale (WAIS). Similarly, it was rare for a psychologist to administer any psychological tests to a patient he or she was treating psychotherapeutically. By no longer restricting assessment to a particular technology (i.e., projective tests), standardized assessment is accessible to all disciplines. For the most part, the research methods included under the rubric of clinical assessment do not require years of training as the traditional psychological tests had. Most assessment tools now require only a few hours of introduction, training in administration and interpretation, and reliability testing. The most important feature remains good clinical judgment. For the few assessment tools that continue to require specialized training, a referral to a psychologist or neuropsychologist is still in order.

For research instruments to actually make any inroads into clinical practice, they must be useful. In order for the instruments to be useful, the clinician must learn the value of the data generated by the tests. These tests must not be additional forms burdening the clinician who conducts his or her typical evaluation. They are most valued when they offer new data that may otherwise have been ignored by the clinician.

## Standardized Assessment

Standardized assessment is the formal and rigorous measurement of clinical psychopathology using scientific principles of behavioral observation. Its goal is the same as an informal psychiatric or psychological evaluation. Nonetheless, this broad definition covers many different forms of data collection. Multiple sources of information may be tapped depending on the appropriateness of one or another vantage point. Different vantages include: a patient's self-report inventory (i.e., Minnesota Multiphasic Personality Inventory) or questionnaire (i.e., Derogatis Sexual Functioning Inventory or Alcohol Use Questionnaire), a psychiatrist's or psychologist's structured interview (i.e., SADS), an observer's behavioral rating by a nurse on an inpatient unit (i.e., Psychotic Inpatient Profile) or by a family member from home (i.e., Katz Adjustment Scale), and other more direct measures of performance such as cognitive testing (i.e., Wechsler Memory Scale) or motor speed testing (i.e., Finger Tapping Test). Each assessment instrument may also measure different domains of psychopathology ranging from symptomatic descriptions, to level of functioning in various spheres of life (i.e., social, occupational), to gross dimensions of behavior and affect (i.e., hostility, anxiety). In addition, assessment instruments differ according to the time frame over which the clinical phenomena are being measured (from immediate to 1 day to 1 week to a lifetime) and according to the way severity is measured (intensity or frequency).

To improve the reliability of an evaluation, the conditions of assessment must be standardized and psychometrically proven. The units of data must be clearly manifest, operationally defined, and require minimal inference for interpretation. Behavioral and symptomatic constructs are typically preferred to more abstract psychological constructs (Hymowitz and Sweeney 1985). Despite its reliance on quantifiable methods, standardized assessment still requires good clinical judgment for interpretation. The most skilled assessor is one who can interpret the quantitative data in an elegant humanistic framework. Quantitative approaches may still be idiographic and need not lose the richness and individuality of an informal assessment. The most clinically useful assessment is one that describes an individual patient. In that sense, numbers must be absorbed and translated into a narrative description of the patient. Numbers alone will never substitute for an individualized evaluation. In my opinion, the greater the application of standardized approaches, the greater the opportunity for more accurate, well-differentiated, and relevant evaluations. By carefully choosing which standardized assessment instrument to use and taking advantage of the flexibility of this approach, the particular evaluation issue may be responded to.

Standardized assessment offers the opportunity to measure a wide variety of relevant psychopathological components. Each test is a specialized instrument designed to cover a focal area of psychopathology. The focus may range from broad (i.e., all psychiatric symptoms) to narrow (i.e., a specific kind of behavior such as alcohol use). For example, depending on the area of functioning to be assessed one may choose a rating scale to evaluate depressive symptomatology or an interview about sexual dysfunction. The test data are concrete and descriptive, requiring a low level of interpretation. They tend to focus on surface symptoms and behavior that may be assessed in a reliable, often quantifiable, way. They are administered in a standard format with clearly defined criteria for scoring. Normative data on clinical populations are usually available, and the rigorous process of research planning has demanded thorough validation and refinement of the instrument. In light of this scientific foundation, standardized assessment is frequently more valid and therefore more effective than an informal assessment.

The psychometric concepts of reliability and validity are fundamental to a critical review of measurement instruments in psychiatry. Reliability is the dependability or reproducibility of measurement and is typically assessed in three ways: *interrater reliability*, reflecting the likelihood that two or more raters will agree on their judgments; *test-retest reliability*, referring to the stability of measurement at different points in time; and *internal consistency*, referring to the homogeneity of certain scales, whether all items measure the same construct. Once reliability has been established, then we know that the measurement is reproducible. But we do not know what it measures.

Validity refers to truth or accuracy: does this instrument measure what it purports to measure? Whereas an instrument may be reliable without being valid, it cannot be valid without being reliable. If a measurement is not reproducible, then one cannot be clear about what is being measured. Validity is assessed in several ways: *internal validity*, referring to intrinsic properties of the instrument and their impact on the subject; *external validity*, referring to the generalizability of results; *face or content validity*, referring to whether the content of items is representative of the construct being measured; *criterion validity*, referring to the relationship of one measure to other measures either concurrently or predictively; and *construct validity*, referring to how well one measure converges with other similar measures and diverges from other unrelated measures based on a preexisting theory regarding the construct being measured. In general, standardized assessment instruments display better reliability and validity than nonstandardized instruments.

## The Need for Changes in Assessment

The innovative use of research methodology for clinical assessment is long overdue. The parameters of psychiatric treatment and the modes of conceptualization have been revolutionized (Blain and Barton 1979). As these radical changes have occurred, an opportunity has developed to introduce assessment technology suited to these changes. Diagnostic systems, types of psychiatric and psychological treatments, lengths of treatment (especially in an inpatient setting), and theoretical orientations have all changed dramatically. What was appropriate to the profession during the 1930s, 1940s, and 1950s is no longer appropriate.

The most noteworthy change in psychiatry over the last 40 years is the drastic reduction in length of hospitalizations (Mattes 1982). At present, the main goal is to return the patient to the community as soon as possible (Barofsky and Budson 1983). Economic and legal factors have mandated that psychiatric patients deserve treatment in the least restrictive setting rather than in an institution. Cost-cutting and deinstitutionalization are the overriding issues of the day (Talbott 1979; Williamson et al. 1982). Hospital utilization and review committees and peer-review organizations oversee inpatient treatment with an accountant's vigilant eye. These concerns have all helped to create a policy of minimizing the length of hospitalization. Similarly, in outpatient settings less frequent and briefer treatments are preferred. In many instances, third-party payers will not reimburse for intense and lengthy outpatient therapies.

Today's treatment is conducted within this limited time frame. The efficacy of pharmacological interventions has permitted the shortening of inpatient stays and the successful maintenance of psychiatric patients in the community with less intensive contact. Hence, medications play the central role in most treatment decisions. Psychotherapy in this context frequently takes an adjunctive role. It has become short-term, and under such conditions aimed at focal problems. It is more eclectic and tends to focus on more narrow and reality-based issues. Treatment planning decisions reflect this time frame and these treatment alternatives. Therefore, the most useful assessment is one that keeps pace with such changes.

The language of psychiatry has changed as well. The diagnostic system has been revamped in recent years in order to be more descriptive and symptom-based (Spitzer et al. 1980). At the same time, hospital utilization and review committees, quality assurance committees, local peer-review organizations, and the like have introduced a problem-focused nomenclature (Langsley 1980). Standardization of diagnosis goes hand in hand with the introduction of objective measures to document changes in the patient's clinical condition. Such objective measures identify problems and goals of treatment, and track the success or failure of any treatment over time. The changes in the language of psychiatry are a reality that is here to stay. Being compatible with this new language, standardized assessment is naturally suited to assist in this diagnostic and evaluative process.

The developments in the field of psychiatry stand in stark contrast to the climate before the discovery of psychopharmacology (Blain and Barton 1979). At that time, inpatient treatment was measured in months rather than weeks, and outpatient treatments in years rather than months; psychotherapy and clinical conceptualizations were psychoanalytic in nature; diagnosis was less reliable because it was based more on theoretical assumptions than phenomenologic data; and the need to document the clinical condition of each patient in concrete, behavioral terms was nonexistent. Insofar as assessment does not conform to the new parameters and expectations, it is outdated and anachronistic.

When a talking cure is the only treatment alternative, then intensive personality assessment is the most important evaluation question. A psychoanalytically oriented assessment considers the patient's psychic structure, predominant defenses, ego strength, ego boundaries, object relations, self-other differentiation, reality testing and psychodynamics. In general this evaluation is made through an unstructured, nondirective interview, and the conclusions drawn from it are subjective and unreliable. Consequently, during the psychoanalytic era, traditional psychological assessment flourished using the Rorschach and other projective tests. Rapaport et al. (1945) developed an ego psychological assessment approach that focused on these rather abstract and overarching issues. However, in the last 20 years, the value of the traditional psychological assessment strategy has diminished in most treatment settings. Psychiatrists complain that test findings are no longer relevant to their clinical needs and entail overly lengthy time delays (Berg 1984; Lewandowski and Saccuzzo 1976; Smyth and Reznikoff 1971). Requests for traditional psychological testing appear to be down (Berg 1986; Garfield and Kurtz 1976). The reason for the decline is that psychiatry has changed dramatically.

The traditional psychological assessment approach was never designed to address contemporary issues. It has limited usefulness for making a syndromal diagnosis or for objectively describing the patient's clinical condition (Korchin and Schuldberg 1981). Its psychoanalytic language is not compatible with the DSM-III and problem-focused nomenclature. And certainly, the traditional battery of psychological tests offers no guidance with medication decisions.

In contrast, standardized assessment is particularly appropriate to the parameters of contemporary treatment in psychiatry. Since many of the standardized instruments do not require the practitioner's time for administration, they permit a rapid and efficient assessment procedure, in many cases reducing the time for an evaluation. Standardized testing suits a brief, cost-effective time frame.

Since medication decisions require a descriptive diagnosis based on identification of target symptoms and a syndromal diagnosis, the clarity and concreteness of standardized tests make them valuable aids. Rating scales and self-report inventories define specific problems which may then be the focus of a particular short-term therapy or crisis intervention. The reliability of these tools coincides with the standardization of diagnosis and the current emphasis on objective measures to track clinical change. Many tests permit weekly serial measures on a patient and are easy to administer in such a fashion. They may guide treatment planning by identifying problems and defining measurable goals, and then mark the relative success of treatment over time. Specific choices of treatments and dispositions will clearly follow from a standardized assessment. Furthermore, these tests generate data compatible with a problem-focused nomenclature.

Another notable advantage of standardized assessment is its flexibility. The practitioner can select the appropriate test based on the particular clinical question raised and the clinical context within which the evaluation is being conducted. The most important rule is that the standardized assessment be well-suited to and coordinated with the needs and context of the clinical service (e.g., inpatient ward, outpatient clinic, private practice). Inpatient services have much different needs than outpatient services, private settings differ from public clinics, and state-run facilities differ from city hospitals. Services catering to specialized populations also have idiosyncratic assessment needs. Therefore, the specific strategy of standardized assessment depends on the unique parameters and base rates of psychopathology in that particular service and setting.

## Examples of Standardized Assessment

In this book, we are defining a process of assessing psychopathology rather than a specific strategy. The strategy depends on the questions of interest to the practitioner. The process of assessment may be further clarified by giving a few illustrations.

**Case 1.** Ms. A. was a 29-year-old woman hospitalized for the first time. On admission she was given a series of self-report tests including the SCL-90, Millon Clinical Multiaxial Inventory (MCMI), and Profile of Mood States (POMS); a SADS interview; and was rated by the nursing staff on the Affective Disorders Rating Scale (ADRS). The self-report findings indicated that she was in an acute state of distress with multiple nonspecific complaints including disturbed sleep; feeling down, worried, restless, and angry; and periods of paranoid referential thinking. Her long-term functioning was characterized by unstable work and social patterns suggestive of a personality disorder with borderline and infantile features. The structured interview was able to clarify this ambiguous diagnostic picture. Ms. A. appeared to have a major depression, without psychotic features, of fairly high severity considering the extracted Hamilton Rating Scale for Depression score of 32. The nursing ratings confirmed the impression of major depression and found no indication of a psychotic process. On the basis of these test results collected during the first 2 days of hospitalization, target symptoms were identified and differentiated from her underlying characterological difficulties (including ego weakness leading to poor control and integration of affect). She was started on antidepressant medication. Follow-up assessment at 3 weeks detected significant clinical improvement in all symptomatology and a current Hamilton score of 8. When the hospital utilization and review committee reviewed this patient's chart, they initially questioned the 3.5-week length of stay. But close inspection of the weekly nursing rating scales indicated that the patient had had a delayed response to the medication and that she was ready to be discharged only by the 3rd week of treatment.

**Case 2.** Ms. B. was a 24-year-old woman who appeared at a walk-in outpatient psychiatric clinic. She was given an SCL-90, which indicated a significant depression. On the basis of these scores she was given the Beck Suicide and Hopelessness scales. Her score elevations reflected great hopelessness, ruminations about death, and suicidal intent. In light of these findings, the screening psychiatrist interviewed her carefully about her suicidal behavior and recommended admission to an inpatient ward. The treatment team decided to place Ms. B. on a restrictive status. The self-report scales helped the treatment team to complete the Multidisciplinary Treatment Plan since they identified several measurable problems including suicidal ideation and hopelessness. The treatment team was later able to detect change in these problems by a sharp decrease in her scale scores.

**Case 3.** Mr. C. was a 79-year-old man who lived alone. His children requested a consultation with a psychiatrist because the patient's functioning had been deteriorating gradually over the last 2 years. On the basis of an interview, the psychiatrist rated the patient on the Hamilton Rating Scale for Depression, giving him a moderate score of 20. Considering the complaint of poor concentration the psychiatrist tested the patient's cognitive functioning with a Wechsler Memory Scale, Trailmaking Test, and the Shipley Institute of Living Scale. These test findings indicated a moderate level of dementia with significant memory problems, visual-spatial difficulties, and executive deficits. On reconsideration the psychiatrist determined that the Hamilton score could be attributed to these primary cognitive deficits and recommended placement in a health-related facility. At that facility, the psychiatrist instructed the nursing staff on how to rate the patient's weekly functioning using the Geriatric Rating Scale in order to detect any further decline in the patient's level of functioning.

**Case 4.** Johnny D. was a 16-year-old high school student who had been having serious academic difficulties over the past 4 years and was becoming more and more socially withdrawn. He was admitted to a private psychiatric hospital for the first time in an acutely psychotic state where it was determined that he was a paranoid schizophrenic. During the first 2 weeks of hospitalization, the primary therapist interviewed Johnny D.'s parents about their reactions to his illness. On the basis of these interviews the primary therapist was able to rate the level of "expressed emotion" in this family. It became clear that the amount of strife within the family had played a significant contributing role in the development of Johnny D.'s illness. Were he to return to this environment, the primary therapist could predict a quick relapse. Therefore, the treatment team identified this family situation as a primary problem and decided to intervene with an aggressive psychoeducational approach with family sessions and multiple family groups. The family sessions focused on lowering the amount of expressed hostility in the family unit.

## Changes in Role and Training

The introduction of standardized and quantitative assessment into daily clinical practice represents a major change in role for many practitioners. Psychiatrists or psychologists must learn to integrate these data into their clinical judgments. Initially many professionals are resistant to such approaches since the standardization is typically antithetical to what they have done throughout their careers. After gaining some familiarity with these techniques, the assessor is frequently surprised by how easy it is to administer the tests and how useful they are. Nonetheless, standardized assessment does change the way people think of psychiatric or psychological evaluation.

This book has been written to increase awareness of standardized assessment, to educate practitioners about these instruments, and to illustrate how useful they are for daily clinical work in almost all settings. By developing expertise in the clinical use of standardized approaches, we will be improving training in the mental health field. Ultimately we hope to define a new curriculum. This book represents a first step in that direction. It provides an overview of how to measure mental illness.

As a way to introduce the issues of psychopathological assessment, Joseph Zubin describes the ancient history of standardized approaches, and Eileen P. Rubinson and Gregory M. Asnis focus on the important role of structured interviewing in diagnosis. The next section reviews the most effective ways of measuring different psychopathological syndromes including depression (Scott Wetzler and Herman M. van Praag), schizophrenia (John A. Sweeney, Gretchen L. Haas, and Peter

J. Weiden), anxiety (M. Katherine Shear, Janet Klosko, and Minna R. Fyer), personality disorders (Lawrence B. Jacobsberg, Scott Goldsmith, Thomas Widiger, and Allen J. Frances), alcohol abuse (Leslie C. Morey and Peter R. Martin), and neuropsychiatric disorders (Robert M. Bilder and John M. Kane). The third section considers related issues for the measurement of psychopathology: family malfunction (John F. Clarkin and Ira D. Glick), cultural factors (Anthony J. Marsella and Velma A. Kameoka), ethnic factors (Bruce L. Ballard), and the legal and ethical problems of using quantitative and actuarial approaches for psychopathological assessment (Robert D. Miller). The Appendix provides a list of 100 popular assessment instruments.

## References

Barofsky I, Budson RD (eds): The Chronic Psychiatric Patient in the Community: Principles of Treatment. New York, S.P. Medical & Scientific Books, 1983

Berg M: Teaching psychiatric residents about psychological testing. Professional Psychology: Research and Practice 15:343–352, 1984

Berg M: Toward a diagnostic alliance between psychiatrist and psychologist. Am Psychol 41:52–59, 1986

Blain D, Barton D: The History of American Psychiatry: A Teaching and Research Guide. Washington, DC, American Psychiatric Association, 1979

Carr A: Psychological testing of personality, in Comprehensive Textbook of Psychiatry IV. Edited by Kaplan H, Sadock B. Baltimore, Williams & Wilkins, 1985, pp 514–535

Endicott J, Spitzer R: Psychiatric rating scales, in Comprehensive Textbook of Psychiatry III. Edited by Kaplan H, Freedman A, Sadock B. Baltimore, Williams & Wilkins, 1980, pp 2391–2409

Garfield SR, Kurtz R: Clinical psychologists in the 1970s. Am Psychol 31:1–9, 1976

Hymowitz P, Sweeney JA: Focal diagnostic psychological testing. The Psychiatric Hospital 16:91–95, 1985

Korchin S, Schuldberg D: The future of clinical assessment. Am Psychol 36:1147–1158, 1981

Langsley DG: Quality assurance in psychiatric treatment. Journal of the National Association of Private Psychiatric Hospitals 11:13, 1980

Lewandowski D, Saccuzzo D: The decline of psychological testing. Professional Psychology 7:177–184, 1976

Mattes JA: Optimal length of hospitalization for psychiatric patients: a review of the literature. Hosp Community Psychiatry 33:824–828, 1982

Rapaport D, Gill M, Schafer R: Diagnostic Psychological Testing, Vols 1 and 2. Chicago, Yearbook Publishers, 1945

Smyth R, Reznikoff M: Attitudes of psychiatrists toward the usefulness of psychodiagnostic reports. Professional Psychology 2:283–288, 1971

Spitzer RL, Williams JBW, Skodol AE: DSM-III: the major achievements and an overview. Am J Psychiatry 137:151–164, 1980

Talbott JA: Deinstitutionalization: avoiding the disasters of the past. Hosp Community Psychiatry 30:621–624, 1979

Williamson JW, Hudson JI, Nevins MN: Teaching Quality Assurance and Cost Containment in Health Care. San Francisco, Jossey-Bass, 1982

## Chapter 2

# Use of Research Instruments in Psychopathological Assessment: Some Historical Perspectives

**JOSEPH ZUBIN, Ph.D.**

# Chapter 2

# Use of Research Instruments in Psychopathological Assessment: Some Historical Perspectives

*T*he beginnings of classification, assessment, and measurement of human behavior including psychopathological behavior are hidden in the dawn of history. There are, however, bits of cultural evidence in customs and laws indicating that at least deviant behavior was recognized and sanctioned early in the development of civilization. But even more than recognizing the presence of the deviant behavior, tests to establish the deviation were also applied quite early, e.g., the Shibboleth test (The Holy Bible) at the fords of the Jordan in which the Ephraimite escapees were identified by their inability to pronounce Shibboleth correctly, and thereupon were slain; and the Talmudic test for mental competence consisting of the placement of a nut and a shaving of wood in front of the suspect to determine which would be selected. If the suspect chose the latter, he or she would be judged as incompetent.

Before quantitative assessment began, poets and literary phenomenologists were the assessors of human personality and

The preparation of this paper was supported by the Medical Research Service of The Veterans Administration.

life experience. Ovid, Cicero, St. Augustine, Shakespeare, Milton, and Freud have provided descriptions of personality that even our best instruments today cannot yet reach. The objectivity we relish today has its price in the loss of the rich content of the poet's descriptions.

Perhaps the earliest quantitative assessment of personality, including psychopathology, was through astrology dating back 25 centuries in Mesopotamia. Palmistry began 3,000 years ago in China. Handwriting analysis came much later, and phrenology came in the middle of the 18th century in France—pioneered by Gall. These pseudosciences are still part of folklore and have left scientific impacts. Thus, astrology was probably the forerunner for the studies of Locus of Control; palmistry and handwriting analysis were the forerunners of identification of individuals through palm prints, fingerprints, and signatures; and phrenology was the forerunner of brain localization. Divining personality through animal entrail examination, cloud reading, and flame inspection were the forerunners of projective techniques.

Assessment based on handwriting analysis is another art that goes back to earliest times. Quite a literature has developed describing the meanings to be attached to various elements in a handwriting specimen, including such characteristics as length of the middle zone of the letters, width, slant, curvature, and pressure on the writing instruments, which was usually interpreted as reflecting instinctual drive.

As for handwriting, I undertook to evaluate it at the behest of Dr. Nolan D. C. Lewis, then the Director of the New York State Psychiatric Institute, because a graphologist named Thea Stein Lewinson had analyzed the handwriting of some of her patients and reported apparently to his satisfaction their personality characteristics based only on the inspection of the handwriting samples. As a result, we developed some objective measures of handwriting characteristics of high reliability, but could not establish their validity (Lewinson and Zubin 1942).

How did classification, assessment, and measurement of

behavior get their start? Classification is the way infants get a handle on the blooming confusion that the world presents. To live in the world, they must classify, identify, and evaluate their surroundings, just as the anthropologist entering a new culture must learn how the natives perceive and organize their world. The classification of the tribal connections in the form of kinships is one of the first classifications of human beings. As for objects, Aristotle was one of the first to establish categories for the classification of objects and insisted that each category had an essence that must have been shared by the members in the category. This establishment of qualitative categories permitted comparison between objects in the form of the positive, comparative, and superlative levels of adjectives, e.g., red, redder, reddest.

But how did the categories of objects arise, and how was class membership determined? Perhaps the judgments of similarity and difference were the underpinnings of the classification system. The judgment of similarity between objects may have rested on the criterion of whether the two objects served the infant equally well for the task at hand. If the string and the long-handled fork were equally good for fetching a toy, the judgment of similarity applied. If only one of two objects suited the purpose of the individual, the objects were regarded as different. However, as development continued, the self-referred criterion of similarity gradually was replaced by more objective external criteria independent of whether the objects under scrutiny depended on self-reference as a basis. Thus, an ounce of gold and an ounce of coal are regarded as equal in weight even though self-reference would make one prefer the gold.

As a matter of interest, the psychological rationale for sorting tests, such as the Goldstein and Scheerer Sorting Test used in differentiating schizophrenic subjects from normal subjects, may have arisen on the basis of infantile self-reference, which the adult schizophrenic may regress to when the disorder develops (Zubin and Thompson 1941).

But how did the categorical qualitative judgment of similarity and difference lead to measuring scales? Here again, history has no record of the development. However, we can safely assume that even before the scales for measuring such physical characteristics as warmth, weight, and length developed, they were measured subjectively. There are no data to substantiate this suggestion, but we can use our imagination in describing how it may have happened.

Let us look at the measurement of subjective warmth. Because there is no documentary evidence for initial attempts by human beings at gauging the cause and degree of subjective warmth, we shall resort to fantasy. Come with me to a cave in some prehistoric ice age, before Prometheus, and listen to a symposium on the origin of the experience of subjective warmth. One savant declares that warmth depends on the number of skins covering the body. Another claims that it depends on duration of exposure to the sun. A third postulates swift running as the source of warmth and the distance covered as a measure. The medicine man in their midst raises a controversy because of his claim that his patients often report experiencing warmth without the benefit of skins, sunshine, and running. The symposium ends without a resolution. But Prometheus later discovers fire, and it becomes possible to demonstrate that by adding faggots to the fire, the experience of warmth is raised in all the inhabitants of the cave and, by the same process, removal of faggots reduces it. The first breakthrough has occurred. Humans can manipulate an external agent to raise and lower subjective warmth at will. But this is still far from measurement.

The first known historical breakthrough occurred in ancient Egypt, where after the linguistic development of ratings in the grammatical form of positive, comparative, and superlative adjectives (warm, warmer, warmest) took place, rating scales were developed for measuring warmth in four steps, with warmth anchored at one extreme to the hottest day of summer and at the other extreme to the coldest day of winter.

Eventually, the expansion of mercury with increase of experienced warmth was noted, and the thermometer was born, and finally, humidity and air pressure were recognized as important factors, and the present-day discomfort index emerged.

What were the essential steps in the process? First, the discovery of means of inducing changes in a sensory experience by external control (fire). Second, the development of an external criterion for measurement independent of the self-referred subjective experience (mercury). The same process, no doubt, held true of the other measures such as weight and length, which have attained great objectivity. Pain is still a subjective phenomenon without an external criterion, and without measurable ways of inducing it, though recent efforts along these lines show considerable promise. Intelligence tests became objective when mental age scales were substituted for teachers' subjective impressions. Anxiety, depression, and elation are still in the rating stage. In my fantasy, I sometimes imagine that we may find a life-bearing planet, somewhere in space, where anxiety has already been measured, but where warmth or length are still on the intuitive level (Zubin 1965a).

## Early Development of Modern Rating Scales, Tests, and Interviews

Two traditions have developed in assessment: the psychometric and clinical traditions. These two trends differ essentially in the contrast between the dimensional and categorical approaches. The dimensional approach arose from the psychometric tradition and the categorical from the clinical tradition.

It might be best to pause here for a moment and inquire as to which approach—the categorical (typological) or the dimensional—is the truest. By the dimensional approach I mean the assumption that types do not exist and instead the hyperspace of personality variables has continuous hypersurfaces without hills or valleys, or multimodal distribution, or discontinuities.

I had raised this question in 1968 (Zubin 1968) and as a result of the heated discussion which ensued, could not fall asleep that night. I turned on the TV and caught the Farmer's Hour with a program on pomology. The reporter indicated that historically apple knockers would test apples by applying their knuckles to the surface of the apple to test for maturity and water core. This typological approach of separating good from bad apples has been replaced by a conveyor belt that passes the apples under two sets of double monochromatic lights, and the amount of light transmission determines whether the apples pass as acceptable or nonacceptable. Thus, the typological test has been replaced by a dimensional test. However, when one considers that the genes of the apple may determine its acceptability we again return to a typology of alleles. But since the alleles secrete some amino acids, we can measure their quantity and return to dimensional tests again. However, the amino acids consist of patterns of molecules and these again yield a typological basis for discrimination and so on ad infinitum. Apparently, the struggle between typology and dimensionality is based on a pseudoproblem dependent on the state of the art at any given time.

### Rating Scales and Personality Inventories

Following the pattern of the ancient Egyptians in providing a rating scale for the measurement of warmth, similar attempts form the basis for the ratings of human behavior. Thus, ordinal rating scales were the initial steps. The first recorded attempt was by Heymans and Wiersma (1909) who drew up an inventory of symptoms through a self-reporting instrument. The early history of the development of rating scales and personality inventories can be found in McReynolds and Ludwig (1987, 1984). These early inventories paralleled the attempts by Adolf Meyer at describing patient behavior (Zubin and Zubin 1977). This effort at describing and rating eventually led to the Woodworth Personal Data Sheet (Zubin

1948), the forerunner of modern personality inventories, which finally led up to the Minnesota Multiphasic Personality Inventory (MMPI).

Jung introduced measurement of emotional complexes through the Word Association Test, and Kraepelin introduced psychological testing to help in diagnosis in the following words:

> As soon as our methodology has sufficiently proved itself through experience with healthy individuals, it would be possible to approach the actual ultimate goal of these efforts, the investigation of the sick personality, especially of the inborn pathological disposition.... We, therefore, have first of all to investigate whether it is possible by means of psychological tests to determine individual deviations, which cannot be recognized by ordinary observation. If that succeeds, we would be in the position through the quantitative determinations at our disposal, to establish the borderline between health and disease much more precisely and more validly than has been possible so far. (Kraepelin 1896, p. 77)

Measurement of psychopathology lagged behind the measurement of psychometric traits primarily because the changes in patient behavior were not sufficiently large to observe. Patients stagnated for the most part, and static description of their behavior did not require rating or measurement. However, with the arrival of somatic therapies, changes in behavior were so striking and rapid that a demand arose for providing such measures.

The speed of the behavioral changes under the influence of drugs was so dramatic that it challenged the therapist to provide measures of the degree of change and the corresponding relation to dosage. For the first time in psychiatric history, psychotic behavior could be altered before one's eyes, and the need for measurement and evaluation became apparent. This caught the measurement experts—mostly psychologists—unprepared, since all the available clinical tests and tools provided only static descriptive measurements like intelligence tests or projective techniques geared to constant-trait rather than varying-state measurement. Rating scales had to be produced practically overnight by such pioneers as Lorr, Wittenborn, and Malamud. There is a story, probably apocryphal, about the physiologist Hudson Hoagland, who found some biochemical change in Malamud's patients at the Worcester State Hospital and asked to see Malamud's data on the same patients. Malamud, who was a leading clinical psychiatrist, handed Hoagland his voluminous case histories. "Are there no numbers here on their behavior," Hoagland inquired, to which Malamud cried, "No, but if you want numbers I'll make them up for you." That night, with the help of a colleague named Sands, he converted his descriptions of behavior into rating scales (Malamud et al. 1946; Malamud and Sands 1947).

The success of drug therapies also required better classification of patients in order to obtain more homogeneous groups. To fill this need, the free-floating clinical interview had to be converted from a blunderbuss into a sharpshooting rifle. Systematic semistructured and structured interviews resulted. Their use in the United States–United Kingdom (U.S.-U.K.) Diagnostic Project and in the World Health Organization (WHO) International Pilot Study of Schizophrenia were the proving grounds in which these instruments were fire tested. These projects aroused diagnosis from its academic lethargy and finally led to the development of such instruments as the Schedule for Affective Disorders and Schizophrenia (SADS), the Diagnostic Interview Schedule (DIS), Research Diagnostic Criteria (RDC), and the Diagnostic and Statistical Manual of Mental Disorders, Third Edition (DSM-III) classification system.

It must be pointed out, however, that the revolution in psychopathology was not due to pharmacological intervention alone. Even before the drug era, the opening of the doors in European hospitals, especially in England, had brought about better outcome results (Shepherd 1988). But, the dramatic effect of the drugs electrified the field.

## Tests

Perhaps the best example of measurement in human behavior is the intelligence test. Before Binet, attempts were made to rate intelligence through adjectival ratings. Eugen Bleuler, at the turn of the century, would ask his residents to assess the intelligence of a new patient. One resident began his questioning by asking a female patient where she came from and how she got to the clinic. Bleuler interrupted scoldingly with "never ask a lady about geography, she has no sense of it." (Remember that this was 1900 in Switzerland, a country that even now has denied women votes in some cantons.) Apparently Bleuler laid down the first requisite of a test: it should deal with knowledge that the patient possesses or should possess. As in my discussion of the development of temperature scales, it is important to ask, what are the criteria that the test would satisfy? There has to be some way in which we can manipulate the trait under investigation. We cannot, of course, vary intelligence through manipulation but can instead use variation in chronological age as a quasi-manipulation, since it is clear that intelligence, at least during the developmental period, varies with age. That is how the concept of mental age was born. Thus, instead of varying the subjective experience, as was the case with subjective warmth, the natural variation in intelligence with age was used to manipulate the degree of intelligence. The external criterion for intelligence corresponding to the expansion of the mercury column in the case of subjective warmth, was school progress, which presumably varied with intelligence and thus served the ends of construct validity.

## The Interview

I have pointed out elsewhere that the clinical interview is the psychiatric tool par excellence for arriving at a diagnosis and the conduct of psychotherapy (Zubin et al. 1985). None-

31

theless, until the 1960s little research effort had been directed at investigating the reliability, validity, and usefulness of this basic tool. The interview dates back to antiquity (Zubin 1965b; Mattarazzo 1965). Interview-like conversations consisting of questions and answers are found in the Bible. The Socratic method of interviewing in the search for truth is well known. Soranus formulated rules for conversing with mental patients, recommending that laborers should be engaged in conversation about cultivation, sailors about navigation, and so on (Zilboorg and Henry 1941). Interviewing techniques have varied with the zeitgeist. The ancient Greeks regarded mental disorder as due to either perversity, possession, or drug-induced states, and verbal utterances were regarded as random effects that were of little or no interest to the physician. Interest in interviewing languished during this period. During the Moorish period in Spain, diagnosis was based on mystical and intuitive approaches, and the patient's utterances were interpreted by seers on the basis of these criteria rather than on the basis of the patient's needs and difficulties. Interest in the patient's attitudes and beliefs rose in the Western Caliphate (Seville and Cordova) when the problem of personal responsibility came to the fore. During the Spanish Inquisition the accused were interrogated to establish their heresy, and the guide for enticing heretics to admit guilt was formulated as perhaps the first systematic interview (Lea 1888). With the rise of the idea of personal responsibility, implying that only those who are mentally competent can be punished, there arose a need to interview the patient in order to assess thoughts and feelings. In the early seventeenth century, Bacon inquired whether the patient knew his own age and name, thereby initiating interviewing with regard to time and orientation. Freud first introduced suggestion and hypnosis to induce patients to speak more freely before developing the psychoanalytical interview, in which all constraints on the conversation were removed and free associations were encouraged, thus permitting unconscious as well as conscious communication.

Certain criteria separate the interview from ordinary conversation or communication. For the purposes of this chapter, we can differentiate it from other types of human encounter as follows: 1) it consists of a meeting of at least two individuals, the interlocutors, face to face; 2) it is directed at a particular purpose by either one or all interlocutors; 3) it employs conversation and observation; and 4) it involves a hierarchical relation between the interlocutors, insofar as one is the interviewer and the other the interviewee.

For a long time the psychiatric interview remained a free-floating conversation between clinician and patient, and though this is still the vogue today, the increasing use of the interview for research purposes has led to a considerable metamorphosis of this communication technique. The impetus for improving the interview was provided by several factors, including the need for yardsticks to assess the rapid changes due to pharmacological treatment, and by individual studies like the binational U.S.-U.K. Diagnostic Project (Cooper et al. 1972) and the International Pilot Study of Schizophrenia (World Health Organization 1973).

The aims of the psychiatric interview are fourfold; first, to elicit (as far as possible) information about presenting symptoms and the antecedents of current episodes in order to cast light on possible causes; second, to determine the patient's feelings and attitudes about his or her current status and symptoms; and, third, to note the pertinent nonverbal behavior, which can help establish the nature of the problems. In addition, because an episode of mental illness reflects a disturbance in interpersonal relationships, the behavior sampled during the interview offers information on the nature of the disturbance. The degree to which the interview taps these main sources of information is a measure of its success, which is why psychiatric interviewing cannot be left to the novice or be based on computers alone. While sophisticated systematic interviewing can elicit factual information, the more subtle attitudinal factors, the assessment of interpersonal relationships, and the detection of abnormal nonverbal signs require a flexible give-and-take possessed only by experienced clinicians.

The proven unreliability of the early interviews prompted attempts to develop self-rating inventories and scales designed to be filled out by the patient, and checklists and rating scales to be completed by the interviewer. Self-reporting instruments have the advantage of eliminating interviewer bias and interpretation by putting the onus on the individual's response rather than on the response of the interviewer to the patient's behavior. This strategy does not, of course, guarantee a better result, and obvious self-reporting inventories have generally not been found to be useful for the classification of inpatients, although they have been found quite useful in dealing with minor disorders encountered primarily among student populations and in surveys of the general population. In a notable study, Dohrenwend and his colleagues (1979) found that the common denominator in such self-reports seems to be related more to Frank's (1973) demoralization factor than to clinical psychopathology, a factor which related more to personality deviation than to clinical psychopathology.

The checklists and rating scales used by interviewers did not utilize standardized methods for obtaining the information needed for the ratings, and consequently results were not always comparable from patient to patient. To obtain a more systematic method for the collection of the information, a new clinical interview with a systematic structured format was developed. This began with an attempt to use a checklist for the Mental Status Examination used by the residents and staff of the New York State Mental Hygiene Department. This "redbook," as it came to be called, underwent a series of revisions by each succeeding Director of the New York State Psychiatric Institute, and when Dr. Nolan D. C. Lewis became director, he invited me to help with the revision. I introduced a systematic checking schedule for recording the presence of the symptoms observed during the course of the examination. World War II interfered with its application, but soon after the end of the war, Drs. Burdock and Hardesty took over this task and in 1964 with the help of two of their trainees—Robert Spitzer and Joseph Fleiss—prepared the first in the series of systematic semistructured interviews from which the SADS finally emerged. The revision of DSM and provision of RDC followed. A first step was to standardize the usual mental status examination (Spitzer et al. 1964). The questions to be asked of the patient were then specified in a proper sequence and directions for coding the responses were laid down. Thus, the loose mental status examination, formerly the psychiatrist's mainstay, was converted into a systematic, structured interview which yielded high reliability in the scoring of items and carried some degree of validity.

This technique has undergone a series of modifications (Zubin et al. 1985). Three types of interviews were developed: 1) the nonprobing Structured Clinical Interview (SCI) (Burdock and Hardesty 1969); 2) the medium-probing schedules, the Mental Status Schedule (MSS) (Spitzer et al. 1964) and the Psychiatric Status Schedule (PSS) (Spitzer et al. 1970), and 3) a deep-probing Present State Examination (PSE) (Wing et al. 1967). These interviewing methods have demonstrated their value in the two major international studies mentioned previously.

The U.S.-U.K. project was initiated to determine why the national statistics show such disproportionate frequencies of affective disorders in the United Kingdom and of schizophrenia in the United States. When the newly developed systematic interviews (Gurland, cited in Zubin et al. 1975) were applied to samples of patients admitted to hospitals in the two countries, the cross-national differences turned out to reflect different diagnostic practices of psychiatrists rather than differing characteristics of patients in the two countries. Whereas the U.S.-U.K. project limited itself to two cultures but investigated a spectrum of mental disorders, the WHO study of schizophrenia limited itself to one disorder but examined its incidence, form, and course in nine different cultures. The WHO study found specific syndromes of schizophrenia ubiquitously distributed in both developing and advanced cultures from Ibadan, Nigeria, to Washington, D.C.

Wing (1978) has pointed out that, as a result of these two international studies, the clinical symptoms associated with schizophrenia can be categorized in two syndromes, positive and negative. The positive syndrome consists of delusions, hallucinations, incoherent speech, and other florid and productive phenomena. These symptoms tend to be responsive to treatment and to remit at the end of the episode. The negative syndrome (including the so-called clinical poverty syndrome) is composed of the symptoms of social withdrawal, emotional apathy, slowness of thought and movement, underactivity, lack of drive, and poverty of speech. These more often characterize the chronic state and are not generally affected by drugs. Strauss and co-workers (1974) have added a third syndrome category, disorders of relating, which seem to be of ontogenetic origin and may reflect such deviations as absence of intimacy in schizophrenics' premorbid friendship patterns during adolescence (Kreisman 1970). The contrast between positive and negative symptoms reflects a striking comparison in the behavior of patients and normal individuals. Positive symptoms denote behaviors in which patients engage (hallucinations, delusions) but normal individuals do not, while the negative symptoms denote behaviors that normal individuals engage in (social interaction, emotional warmth) but patients do not (Zubin 1985a).

## Personality

Following the paradigm described for the development of measurement in the physical sciences and psychological tests, attempts were made to devise techniques for measuring personality and psychopathology. Unfortunately, means for utilizing the first procedure described earlier in measuring subjective experience—manipulation of the subjective or internal phenomena—was not always available for personality as it was in the case of temperature and intelligence. The second procedure, that of establishing an independent criterion (the expansion of mercury in the case of subjective warmth, chronological age for intelligence), was also rarely available. For these reasons, progress in tests for personality and in psychopathology has been slow. Perhaps the most successful test for psychopathology is the MMPI. The varying of the degree of the subjective phenomena under measurement was accomplished by studying contrasting groups of diagnostic categories including normalcy. The difficulties presented by this approach inhere in the fact that the clinical categories were based on interviewing, which at the time of the preparation of the MMPI was in a low state of reliability and validity. Perhaps a restandardization based on Research Diagnostic Criteria might help. Construct validity (corresponding to the expansion of mercury) is also problematical, and very little research has been done along these lines, because we do not have any consensus on what the constructs might be. The problems of developing tests of personality suffer from the same difficulties facing tests of psychopathology, and we are reduced to returning to interviewing as our mainstay.

One of the reasons for the failure of the Rorschach to qualify as a diagnostic instrument is the fact that in the last analysis the scoring of the responses and their clinical significance was originally based on the interview by means of which a clinical diagnosis was reached. We have already pointed out that the clinical interview in Rorschach's day was a weak rod to lean on. However, if the Rorschach protocols themselves are regarded as interviews and analyzed for their content, the resulting dimensions have been shown to correlate with diagnoses because both the Rorschach protocols and the diagnoses are based on interview content (Zubin et al. 1965).

### Reliability

It is well known that the greatest advances in science come not from new theories but from new technological inventions.

The development of audiotaping and videotaping have had the most important impact on the study of reliability. I recall that I was once asked by Clarence P. Oberndorf, a noted psychoanalyst, to help him evaluate psychoanalysis. I suggested that he pick out one of his analysands and record several interviews with the patient so that we could together go over the recording and develop a content analysis of the interview to see what dimensions we could discover for evaluation. He bought an expensive Stromberg Carlson recorder and started recording his interviews. After several months he again invited me for dinner and at the end, pulled out a cigar, lit it, and puffed on it and then gingerly pushed the button to start the recording. No sooner had the record started when I noticed that Oberndorf grew uneasy and as time went on his face reddened and finally he rose and turned off the sound, saying: "This never happened—it's impossible." That was the end of our attempt at evaluation.

I had better luck in studying the reliability of the ratings on interviews with the aid of videotapes in our U.S.-U.K. project. Instead of having a second interviewer sit with the main interviewer to get reliability ratings, we offered the videotapes as a basis for reliability studies. Furthermore, groups of raters could be obtained either individually by mailing them the videotapes or we could gather raters at a convention and obtain their ratings simultaneously. In one such experiment, which Dr. Katz and I conducted, we found large discrepancies in the judgment of whether the patient was neurotic or psychotic. An analysis of the ratings indicated that the differential was based on the rating of apathy. Those who gave a high rating on apathy judged the patient to be psychotic, while those who rated the patient low in apathy judged him to be neurotic.

### Validity

The history of the search for validity began only when the reliability of our measuring instruments was established. Until the etiology of mental disorders is discovered, our validity estimates will have to depend on such criteria as response to treatment or follow-up outcomes, insofar as diagnostic instruments are concerned. The search for "markers" identifying the individuals who have already developed episodes of illness or who are at high risk of developing such episodes is one hopeful way of tackling the validity problem. Several indicators have now been found that are potential markers for vulnerability to schizophrenia in both probands and their unaffected siblings (Zubin 1985b), and there are also some markers for affective disorders and other disorders. These markers may eventually lead us to the discovery of etiology, which will provide the validity criteria we need.

## Summary

We have traced the development of research instruments for measurement from primitive times to their current status. The progress in measurement in psychopathology has not been as rapid in psychopathology as in the physical sciences, but, nevertheless, considerable advances have been made. The history of the development of the interview technique was traced, and its current advances with regard to reliability but not validity seem promising. The newly developing search for markers may prove to be of help in providing a firmer basis for validity.

## References

Burdock EI, Hardesty AS: The Structured Clinical Interview. New York, Springer-Verlag, 1969

Cooper JE, Kendell RE, Gurland BJ, et al: Psychiatric Diagnosis in New York and London: A Comparative Study of Mental Health Admissions. Maudsley Monograph No. 20. London, Oxford University Press, 1972

Dohrenwend BP, Oksenberg L, Shrout PE, et al: What psychiatric screening scales measure in the general population, Part I: Jerome Frank's concept of demoralization, in Health

Survey Research Methods: Third Biennial Research Conference. Edited by National Center for Health Services Research. Washington, DC, U.S. Department of Health and Human Services, 1979, pp 188–198 (Publication no. 81–3268)

Frank JD: Persuasion and Healing. 2nd ed. Baltimore, Johns Hopkins University Press, 1973

Heymans G, Wiersma E: Beiträge zur speziellen Psychologie auf Grund einer Massenuntersuchung. Zeitschrift f. Psychologie 51:1–72, 1909

The Holy Bible, Judges, chapter 12

Kraepelin D: Der Psychologische Versuch in der Psychiatrie. Psychologische Arbeiten 1:1–91, 1896

Kreisman D: Social interaction and intimacy in preschizophrenic adolescence, in The Psychopathology of Adolescence. Edited by Zubin J, Freedman AM. New York, Grune & Stratton, 1970, pp 229–318

Lea HC: The inquisitorial process, in A History of Inquisition of the Middle Ages, Vol I. New York, Harper, 1888, pp 399–429

Lewinson TS, Zubin J: Handwriting Analysis: A Series of Scales for Evaluating the Dynamic Aspects of Handwriting. New York, Kings Crown Press, 1942

Malamud W, Sands SL: A revision of the psychiatric rating scale. Am J Psychiatry 104:231–237, 1947

Malamud W, Hoagland E, Kaufman IC: A new psychiatric rating scale. Psychosom Med 8:234–245, 1946

Matarazzo JD: The interview, in Handbook of Clinical Psychology. Edited by Wolman BB. New York, McGraw-Hill, 1965, pp 403–450

McReynolds P, Ludwig K: Christian Thomasius and the origin of psychological rating scales. Isis 75:546–553, 1984

McReynolds P, Ludwig K: On the history of rating scales. Personality and Individual Differences 8:281–283, 1987

Shepherd M: The Maudsley Lecture 1987: changing disciplines in psychiatry. Br J Psychiatry 153:493–504, 1988

Spitzer R, Fleiss JL, Burdock EI, et al: The Mental Status Schedule: rationale, reliability, and validity. Compr Psychiatry 5:384–395, 1964

Spitzer R, Endicott J, Fleiss JL, et al: Psychiatric Status Schedule: a technique for evaluating psychopathology and impairment of role functioning. Arch Gen Psychiatry 23:41–55, 1970

Strauss JS, Carpenter WT, Bartko JJ: The diagnosis and understanding of schizophrenia, Part III: speculation on the processes that underlie schizophrenic symptoms and signs. Schizophr Bull 11:61–69, 1974

Wing JK: Clinical concepts of schizophrenia, in Schizophrenia: Towards a New Synthesis. Edited by Wing JK. London, Academic Press, 1978, pp 1–30

Wing JK, Birley JLT, Cooper JE, et al: Reliability of a procedure for measuring and classifying 'present psychiatric state.' Br J Psychiatry 113:499–515, 1967

World Health Organization: Report of the International Pilot Study of Schizophrenia, Vol. I. Geneva, World Health Organization, 1973

Zubin D, Zubin J: From speculation to empiricism in the study of mental disorder: research at the New York Psychiatric Institute in the first half of the twentieth century. Ann NY Acad Sci 291:104–135, 1977

Zilboorg G, Henry GW: A History of Medical Psychology. New York, W.W. Norton, 1941

Zubin J: Recent advances in screening the emotionally maladjusted. J Pers 17:141–145, 1948

Zubin J: Psychopathology and the social sciences, in Perspectives in Social Psychology. Edited by Klineberg O, Christie R. New York, Holt, Rinehart, & Winston, 1965a

Zubin J: The unstructured interview as a clinical tool, in Experimental Approaches to Assessment of Behavior in Psychopathology. Unpublished manuscript edited by Zubin J, Burdock EI, Salzinger K. New York, Columbia University Book Store, 1965b

Zubin J: Biometric assessment of mental patients, in The Role and Methodology of Classification in Psychiatry and Psychopathology. Edited by Katz M, Cole JH, Barton WE. Washington, DC, U.S. Department of Health, Education, and Welfare, 1968, pp 353–376 (PHS publication no. 1584)

Zubin J: Scientific models for psychopathology in the '70s. Seminars in Psychiatry 4:283–296, 1972

Zubin J: Negative symptoms: are they indigenous to schizophrenia? Schizophr Bull 11:461–470, 1985a

Zubin J: Psychobiological markers for schizophrenia: state of the art and future perspectives. Psychopharmacol Bull 21:490–496, 1985b

Zubin J, Thompson WJ: Sorting Tests in Relation to Drug Therapy in Schizophrenia. Ann Arbor, MI, Edwards Bros, 1941

Zubin J, Eron L, Schumer F: An Experimental Approach to Projective Techniques. New York, Wiley, 1965

# Chapter 3

# Use of Structured Interviews for Diagnosis

**EILEEN P. RUBINSON, M.S.W.**
**GREGORY M. ASNIS, M.D.**

# Chapter 3

# Use of Structured Interviews for Diagnosis

*T*he psychiatric literature of the 1950s and 1960s reported that clinicians, both internationally and locally, failed to agree when diagnosing patients. What was schizophrenia to the American psychiatrist was affective disorder to the British clinician (Kendell et al. 1971). In order for meaningful research to proceed, relatively homogeneous patient groups that could be compared and contrasted had to be reliably discriminated. When large, multicenter studies proposed to pool patient data, the importance of standardizing diagnostic technique became all the more critical. Improvements in the psychiatric nosology together with the creation of interview guides have constituted a major advance in the standardization of diagnosis.

## Problems in Achieving Diagnostic Reliability

An oft-quoted study by Ward et al. (1962) demonstrated that the largest source of diagnostic disagreement between clinicians was due to inadequacies of the nosology. Earlier classification systems provided brief, general descriptions of diagnostic categories, including a list of common features of each disorder, but did not clearly specify which signs and symptoms were required for a particular diagnosis. For example, was a formal thought disorder necessary, let alone sufficient, for a diagnosis of schizophrenia?

Efforts to improve the classification system have centered on the specification of clear-cut inclusion and exclusion criteria for disorders so that clinicians would be using the same

45

guidelines when summarizing data into diagnostic conclusions. Further, dictionary-style glossaries have been developed to assure that therapists mean the same thing when referring to various criterion signs and symptoms. Thus, when provided with a definition, it is less likely that two interviewers will disagree on what constitutes a nonaffective hallucination or flight of ideas. A crucial source of disagreement, "criterion variance," has been addressed (Spitzer et al. 1975).

A second important source of disagreement, "information variance," occurs when clinicians obtain different data about patients (Spitzer et al. 1975). This can result from disparate interviewing styles, varying coverage of topics, as well as different sources of information about subjects. Not only will clinicians differ one from the other in interviewing style, but they may alter their own method of interviewing from patient to patient. The development of structured interviews (SIs) was sparked by the need to standardize interviewing technique and reduce information variance.

## History of Recent Advances in Diagnosis

Since some structured interviews are tied to particular diagnostic schemas, it is important to become familiar with the most recent ones. All emphasize a descriptive, syndromal rather atheoretical approach to diagnosis. The descriptive approach attempts to bypass controversies among clinicians from different schools of thought about the cause of many functional disorders.

The first effort to delineate clear-cut criteria was the Feighner criteria (1972), named for the first author of the paper in which criteria for 14 disorders were presented. Next came the Research Diagnostic Criteria (RDC) (Spitzer et al. 1978), an expansion and modification of the Feighner criteria. These were developed in conjunction with the structured interview—the Schedule for Affective Disorders and Schizophrenia (SADS) for use in the National Institute of Mental Health (NIMH) Multicenter Collaborative Study on the Psychobiology of Depression (Katz et al. 1979). Created for use with or without the SADS, the RDC provide a glossary of psychiatric definitions plus criteria for 24 diagnostic categories. The RDC yield information on current (within the past 2 months), past, and lifetime disorders. It emphasizes the differential diagnosis of the affective disorders and schizophrenia and defines subtypes of these disorders for further specification. For example, in order to isolate concepts and test particular hypotheses about major depression, 10 non-mutually-exclusive subtypes were identified.

While the RDC were initially spurred by the exigencies of research, they have impacted significantly on clinicians as well, since many of the categories, concepts and principles of the RDC were incorporated into the Diagnostic and Statistical Manual of Mental Disorders, Third Edition (DSM-III) (American Psychiatric Association 1980). The current (1987) official American Psychiatric Association diagnostic manual, DSM-III-Revised (DSM-III-R), follows most of the principles laid down in DSM-III. However, reflecting knowledge from recent research, it permits the codiagnosis of categories that were formerly considered mutually exclusive for the same period of illness, and significantly alters some of the symptom, duration, and exclusion criteria for certain disorders. Thus, while some of the categories in the RDC, DSM-III, and DSM-III-R have the same names, they may not be strictly comparable in terms of criteria and rules of preemptive hierarchy. The three diagnostic schemes have significant differences, and those wishing to make corresponding diagnoses across classification systems should be thoroughly familiar with each manual to avoid error and should not necessarily generalize conclusions based on different systems. The interviewer's knowledge of inclusion and exclusion criteria for a particular diagnostic system is an important first step toward improving reliability.

Studies of diagnostic reliability involve demonstration of the reproducibility and consistency of diagnostic discriminations. It is generally accepted that with or without the use of SIs, diagnostic reliability is higher with the newer classification systems. According to Spitzer et al. (1978) the $\kappa$ coefficients of reliability for diagnostic categories using RDC are good, ranging from .68 to .98, but somewhat lower for the depressive subtypes. The DSM-III field trials also reported good reliability for such major diagnostic categories as schizophrenia ($\kappa=.82$) and the major affective disorders ($\kappa=.70$). The overall $\kappa$ for major classes on Axis I was .78 for joint interviews. However, more disagreements were found in the diagnosis of schizoaffective disorder (for which there were no specified criteria), chronic minor affective disorder, and the personality disorders (Spitzer et al. 1979).

There is some controversy about the methods used to arrive at the sanguine estimates of diagnostic reliability based on the more recent nosologies. Some of the studies on which such data are based have used clinicians with a particular interest or expertise in diagnosis. For example, in the DSM-III field trials, participating clinicians were self-selected and perhaps, therefore, more tuned in to phenomenologic issues. The situation may be somewhat different in routine clinical practice. A recent study of the knowledge of diagnostic criteria for major depression demonstrated that clinicians of varied disciplines and levels of experience harbored significant misconceptions about the diagnostic criteria. Thus, the mere existence of such criteria does not ensure that they are applied correctly (Rubinson et al. 1988). Structured interviewing would be expected to improve this problem.

## Introduction to Structured Interviews for Diagnosis

According to Zubin (Chapter 2) the first structured interviews were used during the Inquisition to systematically assess heretics and witches. Some clinicians continue to regard structured interviews with the distrust appropriate to such infamous ancestry. Criticisms of structured interviews for diagnostic assessment of patients can be summarized by the following three statements: 1) they are countertherapeutic; 2) they devalue the expertise of the clinician; 3) they are unnecessary and uneconomical. The purpose of the remainder of this chapter is to address these concerns, elucidate the rationale for the use of structured diagnostic interviews, and describe the three most commonly used interviews: the SADS, the NIMH Diagnostic Interview Schedule (DIS), and the Structured Clinical Interview for DSM-III (SCID).

### Objections to the Use of Structured Interviews

Clinicians sometimes complain that structured interviews depart too drastically from basic psychotherapeutic principles. Won't rigidity of format and the emphasis on manifest psychopathology inherent in such approaches result in a choppy, artificial style; prevent the development of a therapeutic alliance as well as the exploration of unconscious conflicts; and prevent the assessment of a patient's suitability for psychotherapy?

It is important to recognize what SIs were designed to do. Their chief purpose was to provide some uniformity in the comprehensive collection of psychopathological data. Some of these interviews provide information on various dimensions of illness and functioning in addition to providing criteria for making differential diagnostic distinctions. However, such interviews were not meant to be used to explore dynamic issues per se, or to provide an opportunity for interpretations, although an astute clinician will be able to make insightful observations about dyadic interactions, defense mechanisms, etc., which can be useful later, particularly if a course of psychotherapy is to be embarked on.

Although SIs have been used chiefly by researchers, that has not been exclusively the case. Helzer (1981) studied the use of an SI by psychiatric residents consulting on a medical service. Residents found it to be an excellent training experience, and while they complained that it was time consuming, they frequently felt satisfied that their interviews were more complete and therefore presumably in the patient's best interests. Rarely did patients object to use of the SI.

Saghir (1971) compared the use of structured and unstructured interviews and found no difference in the number
of empathic statements or interruptions in the interview flow
between the two. The chief differences were the frequency of
interpretations used by the unstructured interviewers due to
a shift from a diagnostic to a psychotherapeutic focus, and
the finding that the SIs were more comprehensive in their
coverage of psychopathology.

While clinicians often associate an SI with short-changing
the patient, it is important to recognize that some patients
find a structured or semistructured interview to be a more
comfortable way to discuss their difficulties initially, and feel
gratified that such considerable detail is requested. From the
authors' experience, it is quite possible to shift to an insight-
oriented psychotherapy following the use of a structured interview with a patient. On the other hand, it may be somewhat
awkward to interrupt an ongoing psychotherapy to administer
such an interview.

What does the use of an SI mean to the clinician? After
years of study and patient contact, the experienced clinician
is bound to feel an assault on his/her competence when faced
with relegating second place to clinical judgment in favor of
a structured question-and-answer methodology. It is sometimes
more difficult for experienced clinicians to accept the use of
such interviews and they at times can be less careful in their
administration while a less confident, inexperienced interviewer
may follow the interview guide too rigidly. However, contrary
to popular belief, clinical judgment does play a critical role
in the proper use of two of the three structured diagnostic
interviews to be discussed. At this point it is unlikely that
technicians or computers can replace the skilled clinician.

The final objection to the use of SIs is that they are overly
detailed and time consuming compared to a freestyle interview. Are such techniques necessary? A considerable portion
of diagnostic disagreement is due to information variance. The
SI reduces examiner bias in the collection and interpretation
of data about a patient and ensures uniform coverage of psy-

chopathology. For example, Spitzer and colleagues (1982) showed that even with the use of DSM-III criteria, but without the benefit of SI, psychiatric residents failed to recognize affective disorder in cases in which the experts did. According to Lipton and Simon (1985), clinicians in a state hospital continued to overdiagnose schizophrenia relative to affective disorder even after the dissemination of DSM-III, thus demonstrating that the existence of diagnostic criteria alone may be insufficient to overcome this persistent trend. It is likely that an SI would counteract this tendency to bypass mood syndromes by forcing careful attention to such symptomatology.

Just as the existence of explicit criteria does not ensure their correct application, the SI does not ensure that without training it will be used correctly, or that correct diagnostic conclusions will be drawn from it. Helzer's (1981) study of the use of SIs by residents showed that they occasionally made diagnoses not warranted by the data coded on the interview guide and therefore may have failed to count symptoms correctly.

## Available Structured Interviews for Diagnosis

Since 1978, two diagnostic interviews have been developed and widely used in the United States, and a third has more recently been created. They are the SADS, the NIMH DIS, and the SCID. Their properties, characteristics, and the pros and cons of usage will be described and compared.

Before determining which instrument to use, the clinician/researcher must be clear on goals and available resources in terms of time and personnel. The clinician/researcher must ask, "What kinds of subjects will be evaluated, what kind of data do I need, which diagnostic scheme will I wish to use, and to what other studies do I want to compare data?"

### The Schedule for Affective Disorders and Schizophrenia (SADS)

As stated, the SADS (Endicott and Spitzer 1978) was developed in conjunction with the RDC, and together they emphasize the differential diagnosis of the affective disorders and schizophrenia. Some DSM-III diagnoses may be extrapolated from data elicited with the SADS. However, the interview will have to be modified when an investigator has an interest in DSM-III or DSM-III-R categories not addressed by the SADS. The instrument is designed to provide broad coverage of psychopathology as well as to elicit criteria for differential diagnosis.

One of several related inteview guides, the SADS is a semistructured protocol of considerable detail and complexity that requires from 1.5 to 2.5 hours to complete, depending on the skill of the interviewer, the loquacity of the respondent, and the degree of disturbance present. While the main source of information for SADS ratings is the subject, in the interests of validity, all sources of data such as chart notes and relatives' input may be used and the patient can be gently confronted about conflicting observations.

The SADS interview is divided into two parts. Part I provides a picture of a current episode or the past year of an ongoing illness. Part II emphasizes past psychiatric history and treatment but includes chronic or lifetime disorders that may be current as well. Part I begins with an open-ended inquiry to get an overview of the current disturbance including onset, development of symptoms, and treatment as well as a background of the patient's life circumstances. The evaluator will refer back to this information, as the interview should not be a question-and-answer session applied in a meaningless vacuum.

Additionally, SADS Part I covers two time periods within the current episode or past year. First, each symptom is rated for the 1-week period when it was at its worst. Ratings are made on a 0–6 severity scale and are based on the degree of their persistence, intensity, and effect on functioning. Questions are provided for each item in order to assess these dimensions.

The SADS focus on symptoms when they were at their worst attempts to assure that the peak of the episode when a patient is most likely to meet syndromal criteria will be addressed. Since some patients present to clinicians when symptoms are in partial remission, a cross-sectional inquiry at that time may result in a failure to spot a full syndrome that had occurred earlier in the course. The ratings for symptoms at their worst can also be used to yield eight composite summary scores, each based on a group of SADS items that have been delineated based on factor analytic work. Scale scores enable patients to be described or compared on such dimensions as endogeneity, depression, and formal thought disorder.

Second, ratings are also made for symptoms as they existed during the 1-week period prior to the interview. A subset of items rated for the prior week can then be used as a measure of change (SADS-C) for following symptoms over time during treatment or follow-up studies. Endicott et al. (1981) have developed a method for obtaining an extracted Hamilton Depression Rating Score from the SADS-C past week items. The SADS and the SADS-C also include a Global Assessment Score (GAS), which provides a measure of overall severity of psychiatric disturbance (Endicott et al. 1976).

The organization of the SADS interview permits it to flow somewhat like a freestyle interview. In addition to an open-ended prelude to the structured sections, symptom questions are grouped together in a way that makes clinical sense. However, a clinician may be flexible in wording questions so the patient can best understand and respond to them. Unlike other, less flexible interviews, it is possible (although not encouraged in training sessions) for the interviewer to begin "where the patient is at" and alter the order of topics covered. Thus, if a patient is preoccupied with a bizarre delusion, the discussion may begin there.

The importance of the interviewer's skill goes beyond the elicitation and clarification of SADS data and ratings. A computer, for example, could not summarize diagnostic conclusions from the SADS. While a rating of 3 or more on the scale of 0–6 for a symptom or behavior is generally considered significant, it is up to the clinician to determine whether the symptoms occurred together for the required amount of time and severity to constitute a syndrome for diagnosis. Further, if a clinician has some reason to be skeptical about the veracity of a patient's report even in the presence of a sufficient number of symptoms, he/she may make a diagnosis at the "probable" level of confidence—an assessment the computer is incapable of.

Based on the rules and hierarchical principles of the RDC, the clinician enters the diagnoses for past, present, and lifetime disorders on a separate score sheet after the interview. Use of a narrative summary is recommended to describe the patient and the diagnostic conclusions.

Endicott and Spitzer (1978) report that intraclass coefficients of reliability are high for most of the individual SADS items, with 90% of the coefficients exceeding .60 for joint interviews. For the summary scale scores, the intraclass $r$ ranged from .82 to .95. Following a test-retest reliability study, Keller et al. (1981) concluded that diagnostic, summary scale, and item reliability with the SADS is good, and particularly so for affective symptoms and syndromes. For example, intraclass $r$ for major depression and mania were .85 and .72, respectively. For schizophrenia it was only .52, however. Further, disagreements occurred about specific psychotic symptoms, ratings of functional impairment, and characterizations of disorders as episodic or chronic.

The studies cited above were performed predominantly with psychiatric inpatients who had comparatively severe disorders. It is the impression of the authors that mild cases of mental disorders (i.e., outpatients) result in the greatest disagreement between raters for individual SADS items. Helzer and colleagues (1985) have noted that borderline cases with fewer and less intense symptoms cause greater diagnostic confusion than do the more severe, clear-cut cases.

## Additional SADS Instruments and Modifications

The SADS–lifetime version (SADS-L) is roughly equivalent to part II of the SADS and is generally used with nonpatients, i.e., normal control subjects or community respondents in epidemiological studies, when there is no need for a detailed description of the current illness or there is no current illness. Because it omits the detailed part I, the SADS-L requires far less time to complete than the SADS. There are two modified version of the SADS-L, the SADS-LA and the SADS-LB. The SADS-LA has been "designed specifically for studies requiring detailed lifetime information on anxiety disorders, symptoms, and traits" (Mannuzza et al. 1986). The SADS-LB focuses on information relevant to the understanding of the bipolar disorders. In addition to the SADS-C, two other less lengthy versions of the SADS exist for patient follow-up. These are the Comprehensive Follow-Up (Comp-SADS) and the SADS Interval version (SADS-LI).

For family studies, an interview guide can be used to produce diagnoses on relatives that have not been directly interviewed. This method, the Family History–RDC (FH-RDC), is considered to be quite specific, but generally less sensitive in producing diagnoses than the direct interview method. Thus, it results in false negatives (Andreasen et al. 1977; Thompson et al. 1982). In 1985, the Family Informant Schedule and Criteria (FISC), an expansion of the FH-RDC, was developed to address certain limitations of the FH-RDC, including the insufficient number of diagnoses addressed by the former method.

The Kiddie-SADS-P (present episode version), developed for use with children 6–17 years of age, pools responses of patient and parent and has been shown to have somewhat less reliability than the SADS for adults (Chambers et al. 1985). The Kiddie-SADS-E assesses past episodes of child and adolescent psychiatric disorder (Orvaschel et al. 1982).

Ideally, those who administer the SADS should be experienced in the assessment of psychopathology and diagnosis.

Questions require the elicitation of more than a simple yes or no, and ambiguous or contradictory responses that need clarification will require evaluation by a skilled clinician. In addition, rigorous training in the RDC/SADS is recommended and can take a number of weeks. Raters of different backgrounds and levels of experience and those who have had exposure to very different types of patients as a reference point may require more effort to establish reliability. A model training approach including methods of establishing reliability has been described by Gibbon and colleagues (1981). The training for the SADS includes learning of the RDC through written case vignettes, mock interviews, and observation of videotaped SADS interviews conducted by experts. Once trained, raters of different backgrounds have been shown to demonstrate good reliability.

From the research point of view, because of the rigorous training, need for experienced personnel, and the amount of time required to administer the interview, the full-length SADS is not an economical method for large-scale studies. Also, without modification, the SADS cannot produce certain DSM-III or DSM-III-R diagnoses. However, the SADS provides comprehensive and reliable data and has been used in numerous studies. Further, it has been translated into several languages. In order to replicate or compare results to prior research using the SADS/RDC, an investigator may wish to use the same instruments. This is particularly true for research in depression, where according to Rabkin and Klein (1987) the SADS has been the diagnostic interview of choice. For routine clinical diagnostic interviews, the SADS will probably be too time-consuming and overly detailed, although its principles of coverage and assessment can be applied. Information on SADS training and materials may be obtained from the Research Assessment and Training Unit at the New York State Psychiatric Institute.

## The Diagnostic Interview Schedule

The DIS was developed by Robins et al. (1981) at Washington University in St. Louis at the request of the division of biometry and epidemiology of NIMH. The DIS was designed for use in the Epidemiological Catchment Area (ECA) project. A study of 20,000 persons in five United States communities, the ECA strove to collect data about the incidence and prevalence of mental illness and related variables in the general population. Before development of the DIS, many survey instruments located the mentally ill in the community but were unable to make specific diagnoses (Robins and Helzer 1985). While the DIS was developed as a survey technique for case detection, it has also been used as a diagnostic instrument in clinical populations. Since 1978, there have been several versions of the DIS. The most current, version III-A, is in the process of revision.

While the DIS was designed to yield diagnostic data from three classification systems (Feighner, RDC, and DSM-III), the newest revision will focus on DSM-III and DSM-III-R. Forty-three DSM-III diagnoses (including some subtypes) can be made now with the DIS. To have included them all would have made the interview too long. Thus, predominantly Axis I adult diagnoses are covered. Except for antisocial personality, all other personality disorders are excluded as are the adjustment disorders and most of the residual, atypical categories. One category for organic brain syndrome is diagnosable— dementia. The DIS determines recency of disorders, with "current" referring to several different time frames: the past 2 weeks, past 1 month, past 6 months, or past 1 year.

According to the training manual, the DIS is designed to be used with adults over 18 and is administered in a single session lasting from 1 hour (for uncomplicated cases or normal subjects) to a less common maximum of 3 hours. Data are coded and edited, and a computer may be used to make the diagnoses.

57

In contrast to the SADS and SCID, the DIS is a highly structured interview with little or no flexibility. Standard questions must be asked exactly as written, and a yes or no response is coded. There are no open-ended queries about past psychiatric treatment or dysfunctional episodes. Since the interview was designed for use with an extremely large sample, it was desirable for economic reasons that laypersons administer the interview. The rigidity of structure assures that nonclinical personnel will not be called on to use judgment in the elicitation and interpretation of data. Further, since only the index subject provides data, the lay evaluator need not be asked to weigh the merits of conflicting sources of information.

Unlike the SADS or SCID, which permit an interviewer to skip out of some diagnostic categories if basic screening questions are not positive, the DIS limits skip-outs. In addition to providing specified levels of severity for distinguishing a clinically significant symptom from the disturbances of everyday life, the DIS attempts to determine whether symptoms are due to physical illness or to the influence of drugs or alcohol. A coding system of 1–5 is employed to make these assessments. Unlike the SADS, which provides no organic screening device, the DIS incorporates the mini-mental-state exam for this purpose (Folstein et al. 1975).

Either a clinician or layperson may administer the DIS after approximately 1 week of training. A computerized version of the DIS in which subjects interact directly with the computer has been tested. After comparing this version to the interviewer-administered one, Griest et al. (1987) recommended that it be used as an adjunct and not as a substitute for the clinical interview. In addition to training sessions, a training manual and five audiovisual tapes are available for self-instruction or group training through the Veterans Administration Medical Center library.

The DIS was shown to have high interrater reliability when an interviewer-observer design was used ($\kappa = .94$) Further, agreement between clinicians and nonclinicians across diagnostic categories was also high ($\kappa = .95$) (Robins et al. 1981).

Several studies have evaluated the validity of the DIS by comparing it to some external criterion. Each ECA site has produced data about this, and some have assessed the validity of the DIS in clinical populations (Helzer et al. 1985; Anthony et al. 1985; Robins et al. 1982; Hesselbrock et al. 1982). Assessments of the DIS vary depending on the interview with which the DIS is compared, who administers it, and in what population. For example, the DIS has been reported to underdiagnose major depression (Helzer et al. 1985) or overdiagnose it (Folstein et al. 1985). It may overdiagnose schizophrenia (Folstein et al. 1985) or fail to accurately assess lifetime prevalence of psychotic symptoms (Pulver and Carpenter 1983).

Anthony and colleagues (1985) compared the lay-administered DIS to a standardized psychiatric examination and discussed several potential reasons for the discrepant findings. The DIS does not in all cases follow diagnostic criteria exactly, it seems to have overinclusive questions for certain disorders, and it may not discriminate between current and remitted disorders in the same way that the psychiatrist does. Spitzer (1983) suggested that problems could result from the instrument's reliance on unskilled interviewers. He suggests that merely accepting a yes and no response from a patient can result in false positives. As pointed out by Robins et al. (1982), diagnostic accuracy is generally higher when disturbances are current and/or more severe. Population studies produce many borderline or threshold cases in which the failure to agree on one symptom may result in diagnostic disagreement. The reader is referred to Hedlund and Viewig's review article (1981) on the reliability and validity of various scales and interviews for an extended discussion of this topic.

While the DIS is used only with adults over 18, a modification of it, the Diagnostic Interview Schedule for Children (DIS-C) and the parent version (DIS-P) is used to make diagnostic assessments for children and adolescents 6–17 years of age. Older children demonstrate higher reliability and tend to agree more often with their parents. Observable behavior, i.e., conduct disturbance, produces more agreement than such "private" phenomena as affective and neurotic symptoms (Edelbrock et al. 1986).

The main disadvantage of the DIS is its rigid format and its reliance on lay interviewers. This same disadvantage makes it also the only case-finding, diagnostic instrument that is economical.

### The Structured Clinical Interview for DSM-III-R (SCID)

The SCID, developed by Spitzer et al. (1987), is a semistructured interview guide that is designed to yield many DSM-III-R Axis I mental disorders as well as all the official Axis II personality disorders. Three basic versions of the SCID exist for the assessment of Axis I disorders in adults. A fourth covers the personality disorders. The SCID-P (patient version) is for use with psychiatric inpatients or in cases where the differential diagnosis requires a careful evaluation of psychotic symptomatology. The SCID-OP (outpatient version) is designed for use with outpatients or for situations in which there is a need for only a few screening questions for psychotic disorders. When there is no assumption of patienthood, i.e., with normal control subjects or community respondents, the SCID-NP (nonpatient version) is used. Finally, the SCID-II assesses the personality disorders located on Axis II.

Each of the three versions for obtaining an Axis I diagnosis contains eight to nine "modules." Each module consists of questions to elicit criteria for a different class of disorder such as substance abuse, mood syndromes, or the anxiety disorders. Because of the independence of each module, the SCID may be modified for the requirements of specific studies. Disorders are noted for two time periods: lifetime occurrence and current (past month).

The SCID is more similar to the SADS than to the DIS in that it is only administered by a clinically trained interviewer and in that it utilizes all sources of information in making diagnostic judgments. Further, like the SADS, it begins with a semistructured overview to elicit the development and history of the disturbance. Like a routine clinical interview, the overview portion yields a tentative diagnosis which is then systematically assessed through questions tied to the DSM-III-R criteria embedded in the structured portion of the interview. Symptoms are rated ?, 1, 2, or 3. A question mark means that there is inadequate information to code a symptom, 1 indicates a negative rating, 2 means the item is subthreshold in severity or duration, and 3 refers to a symptom or criterion that is clearly present. As is the case with the SADS, time-saving skip-outs are permitted when essential criteria for disorders are not met.

Unlike the DIS, the SCID requires the use of considerable clinical judgment on the part of the interviewer. Not only must conflicting sources of information be evaluated, but questions can be open-ended so that a coding of criteria must be assessed and extrapolated from the subject's responses.

Use of a clinician as opposed to a lay interviewer for diagnostic assessment holds certain advantages. According to Spitzer (1983) these advantages may be particularly apparent when evaluating disorders in a community sample where confusing clinical presentations abound and denial of psychotic symptoms may be more likely. He suggests that a clinician can better probe for clues to the presence of psychiatric disorder.

A 500-subject, multicenter test-retest reliability study of the SCID involving inpatients, outpatients, and nonpatients has been conducted. Results will soon be analyzed and reported (personal communication from M. Gibbon, March 1988). A study examining the interrater reliability in the diagnostic differentiation of major depression and generalized anxiety disorder using the SCID recommends the SCID for use with these disorders (Riskind et al. 1987).

Clinicians can administer the SCID after following a pre-scribed training sequence outlined in the SCID training manual (Spitzer et al. 1987). Videotapes of SCID interviews conducted by experts are available for study, and courses lasting 3 days are conducted at the New York State Psychiatric Institute. Information about the SCID can be obtained from the Biometrics Research Department of that Institute.

Until the DIS revision is complete, the SCID is the only interview guide currently geared specifically for the DSM-III-R. Using the SCID will result in a diagnostic assessment suitable for both research and clinical purposes. Training in the SCID or the other instruments discussed is an excellent way for trainees or even seasoned clinicians to learn or brush up on their knowledge of psychopathology and diagnostic assessment.

## References

American Psychiatric Association: Diagnostic and Statistical Manual of Mental Disorders, Third Edition. Washington, DC, American Psychiatric Association, 1980

American Psychiatric Association: Diagnostic and Statistical Manual of Mental Disorders, Third Edition, Revised. Washington, DC, American Psychiatric Association, 1987

Andreasen NC, Endicott J, Spitzer RL, et al: The family history method using diagnostic criteria: reliability and validity. Arch Gen Psychiatry 34:1229–1235, 1977

Anthony JC, Folstein M, Romanoski AJ, et al: Comparison of the lay Diagnostic Interview Schedule and a standardized psychiatric diagnosis: experience in eastern Baltimore. Arch Gen Psychiatry 42:667–675, 1985

Chambers WJ, Puig-Antich J, Hirsch M, et al: The assessment of affective disorders in children and adolescents by semi-structured interview: test-retest reliability of the Schedule for Affective Disorders and Schizophrenia for school-age children, present episode version. Arch Gen Psychiatry 42:696–702, 1985

Edelbrock C, Costello AJ, Dulcan MK, et al: Parent-child agreement on child psychiatric symptoms assessed via structured interview. J Child Psychol Psychiatry 27:181–190, 1986

Endicott J, Spitzer RL: A diagnostic interview: the Schedule for Affective Disorders and Schizophrenia. Arch Gen Psychiatry 35:837–844, 1978

Endicott J, Spitzer RL, Fleiss JL, et al: The Global Assessment Scale: a procedure for measuring overall severity of psychiatric disturbance. Arch Gen Psychiatry 33:766–771, 1976

Endicott J, Cohen J, Nee J, et al: Hamilton Depression Rating Scale: regular and change versions of the Schedule for Affective Disorders and Schizophrenia. Arch Gen Psychiatry 38:98–103, 1981

Feighner JP, Robins E, Guze SB, et al: Diagnostic criteria for use in psychiatric research. Arch Gen Psychiatry 26:57–62, 1972

Folstein MF, Folstein SC, McHugh PR: 'Mini-Mental State': A practical method for grading the cognitive state of patients for the clinician. J Psychiatr Res 12:189–198, 1975

Folstein MF, Romanoski AJ, Nestadt G, et al: A brief report on the clinical reappraisal of the DIS carried out at the Johns Hopkins site of the ECA Program of the NIMH. Psychol Med 15:809–814, 1985

Gibbon M, McDonald-Scott P, Endicott J: Mastering the art of research interviewing: a model training procedure for diagnostic evaluation. Arch Gen Psychiatry 38:1259–1262, 1981

Griest JH, Klein MH, Erdman HP, et al: Comparison of computer and interviewer-administered versions of the Diagnostic Interview Schedule. Hosp Community Psychiatry 38:1304–1315, 1987

Hedlund JL, Viewig BW: Structured psychiatric interviews: a comparative review. Journal of Operational Psychiatry 12:39–67, 1981

Helzer JE: The use of a structured interview for routine psychiatric evaluations. J Nerv Ment Dis 169:45–49, 1981

Helzer JE, Robins LN, McEvoy LT, et al: A comparison of clinical and Diagnostic Interview Schedule diagnoses: physician reexamination of lay-interviewed cases in the general population. Arch Gen Psychiatry 42:657–666, 1985

Hesselbrock V, Stabenau J, Hesselbrock M, et al: A comparison of two interview schedules: the SADS-L and the NIMH DIS. Arch Gen Psychiatry 39:674–677, 1982

Katz MM, Secunda SK, Hirschfeld RMA, et al: NIMH Clinical Research Branch Collaborative Program on the Psychobiology of Depression. Arch Gen Psychiatry 36:765–771, 1979

Keller MB, Lavori PW, Andreasen NC, et al: Test-retest reliability of assessing psychiatrically ill patients in a multicenter design. J Psychiatr Res 16:213–227, 1981

Kendell RE, Cooper JE, Gourlay AJ, et al: Diagnostic criteria of American and British psychiatrists. Arch Gen Psychiatry 25:123–130, 1971

Lipton AA, Simon FS: Psychiatric diagnosis in a state hospital: Manhattan State revisited. Hosp Community Psychiatry 36:368–373, 1985

Mannuzza S, Fyer AJ, Klein DF, et al: Schedule for Affective Disorders and Schizophrenia-Lifetime Version modified for the study of anxiety disorders (SADS-LA): rationale and conceptual development. J Psychiatr Res 20:317–325, 1986

Orvaschel H, Puig-Antich J, Chambers W, et al: Retrospective assessment of prepubertal major depression with the Kiddie-SADS-E. J Am Acad Child Psychiatry 21:392–397, 1982

Pulver AE, Carpenter WT Jr: Lifetime psychotic symptoms assessed with the DIS. Schizophr Bull 9:377–382, 1983

Rabkin JG, Klein DF: The clinical measurement of depressive disorders, in The Measurement of Depression. Edited by Marsella AJ, Hirschfeld RMA, Katz MM. New York, Guilford Press, 1987, pp 30–83

Riskind JH, Beck AT, Berchick RJ, et al: Reliability of DSM-III diagnoses for major depression and generalized anxiety disorder using the Structured Clinical Interview for DSM-III. Arch Gen Psychiatry 44:817–820, 1987

Robins LN, Helzer JE: DIS Version III-A Training Manual for Self-Instruction and Group Training. St. Louis, MO, Veterans Administration Medical Center, 1985

Robins LN, Helzer JE, Croughan J, et al: National Institute of Mental Health Diagnostic Interview Schedule: its history, characteristics, and validity. Arch Gen Psychiatry 38:381–389, 1981

Robins LN, Helzer JE, Ratcliff KS, et al: Validity of the Diagnostic Interview Schedule version II: DSM-III diagnoses. Psychol Med 12:855–870, 1982

Rubinson EP, Asnis GM, Harkavy Friedman JM: Knowledge of the criteria for major depression: a survey of mental health professionals. J Nerv Ment Dis 176:480–484, 1988

Saghir MT: A comparison of some aspects of structured and unstructured interviews. Am J Psychiatry 128:180–184, 1971

Spitzer RL: Psychiatric diagnosis: are clinicians still necessary? Compr Psychiatry 24:399–411, 1983

Spitzer RL, Endicott J, Robins E: Clinical criteria for psychiatric diagnosis and DSM-III. Am J Psychiatry 132:1187–1192, 1975

Spitzer RL, Endicott J, Robins E: Research Diagnostic Criteria: rationale and reliability. Arch Gen Psychiatry 35:773–782, 1978

Spitzer RL, Forman JBW, Nee J: DSM-III field trials, I: initial interrater diagnostic reliability. Am J Psychiatry 136:815–817, 1979

Spitzer RL, Skodol AE, Williams JBW, et al: Supervising intake diagnosis: a psychiatric 'Rashomon.' Arch Gen Psychiatry 39:1299–1305, 1982

Spitzer RL, Williams JBW, Gibbon M: Instruction Manual for the Structured Clinical Interview for DSM-III-R (SCID, 4/1/87 revision). New York, Biometrics Research Department, New York State Psychiatric Institute, 1987

Thompson WD, Orvaschel H, Prusoff BA, et al: An evaluation of the family history method for ascertaining psychiatric disorders. Arch Gen Psychiatry 39:53–58, 1982

Ward CH, Beck AT, Mendelson M, et al: The psychiatric nomenclature: reasons for diagnostic disagreement. Arch Gen Psychiatry 7:198–205, 1962

# Assessment of Psychopathological Disorders

# Chapter 4

# Assessment of Depression

**SCOTT WETZLER, Ph.D.**
**HERMAN M. VAN PRAAG, M.D., Ph.D.**

# Chapter 4

# Assessment of Depression

The greatest advances in psychometric assessment have been in the area of depression. Numerous self-report tests, structured diagnostic interviews, and observer rating scales have been developed to measure different components of the depressive state. Table 1 lists a few of the most popular ones. The selection of the appropriate measurement instrument depends on the aim of the assessment. We can delineate two general aims of assessment: the identification of patients with various depressive syndromes, especially major depression, and the measurement of the dimension of depression in major depression as well as in other psychopathological states.

The identification of patients with major depression addresses the problems of diagnosing cases of major depression in the general community and of differentiating patients with major depression from patients with other psychiatric disorders. This determination is a categorical or typological one; that is, the clinician must fit the individual into one or another diagnostic category—categories that are defined by traditional diagnostic nosology. Therefore, diagnostic decision-making depends on the adequacy of the diagnostic system (e.g., DSM-III). While such a nosological approach presents certain obvious advantages, it is a gross oversimplification to think that behavioral disorders actually exist in clearly separable categories (van Praag et al. 1975, 1987).

The dimensional or functional approach analyzes and dissects the complex psychopathological state into its constituent

**Table 1.** Popular Instruments for the Assessment of Depression

| Name | Type | Reference |
|------|------|-----------|
| Symptom Checklist 90 (SCL-90) | SR | Derogatis 1983 |
| Beck Depression Inventory | SR | Beck et al. 1961 |
| Zung Self-Rating Depression Scale | SR | Zung 1965 |
| Center for Epidemiological Studies—Depression Scale (CES-D) | SR | Radloff 1977 |
| Minnesota Multiphasic Personality Inventory (MMPI) | SR | Hathaway and McKinley 1943 |
| Millon Clinical Multiaxial Inventory (MCMI) | SR | Millon 1983 |
| Structured Clinical Interview for DSM-III (SCID) | SI | Spitzer et al. 1986 |
| Schedule for Affective Disorders and Schizophrenia (SADS) | SI | Endicott and Spitzer 1978 |
| Diagnostic Interview Schedule (DIS) | SI | Robins et al. 1981 |
| Hamilton Rating Scale for Depression (HDRS) | OR | Hamilton 1960 |
| Montgomery-Asberg Depression Rating Scale (MADRS) | OR | Montgomery and Asberg 1979 |

*Note.* SR = self-report test; SI = structured interview; OR = observer rating scale.

parts, fully recognizing that these dimensions are actually completely intermingled. Each clinical syndrome can be dissected into certain fundamental psychopathological dimensions. In this sense, depression exists to varying degrees in all psychopathological states (obviously to a greater degree in major depression than in other disorders).

These two general aims of assessment are frequently confused, and measurement instruments are inappropriately applied on the basis of this misunderstanding. In this chapter, we review the most popular assessment methods with regard to these two aims.

# The Diagnosis of Major Depression

## *Structured Interviews*

At present, the structured interview represents the gold standard of psychiatric diagnosis. Insofar as diagnosis is an activity that remains within the purview of clinicians, then by definition a clinician's diagnosis is the gold standard, and all other assessment methods and vantage points must be evaluated against this criterion. Following this line of reasoning, the best clinician's diagnosis is derived from information obtained during the administration of a comprehensive structured interview to a patient (and to other relevant informants) by a trained, reliable clinician. While other assessment methods may approach this standard, the most that can possibly be said is that they are interchangeable with a structured-interview-based diagnosis. If diagnosis is the only aim of assessment and if manpower, training, and professional time are unlimited, then structured interviews are clearly the best assessment instruments.

An earlier chapter reviewed the history, rationale, and main characteristics of the most important structured interviews and consequently these issues are not covered here. The selection of one or another interview depends on which diagnostic system is being used. The Present State Exam, despite widespread use in Europe, is not tied to DSM-III or Research Diagnostic Criteria (RDC) and therefore is rarely used in the United States. Alternatively, the Structured Clinical Interview for DSM-III (SCID) and the Diagnostic Interview Schedule (DIS) were specifically designed to make DSM-III diagnoses, and the Schedule of Affective Disorders and Schizophrenia (SADS) was designed to make RDC diagnoses of major depression and its subtypes. Since the DIS was designed to be administered by lay interviewers (or by a computer), it is actually a variant of self-report assessment rather than a clinician-based method, and it has demonstrated very poor diagnostic efficiency for major depression compared with a clinician's diagnosis (Anthony et al. 1985). In contrast, the SCID and SADS exhibit quite good reliability and validity. The success of these two structured interviews depends on the training of the clinician in the use of the diagnostic system and the administration of the interview. Training includes watching videotapes, reading case vignettes, and administration of live interviews under supervision along with reliability testing by an expert. Training ensures standardization and reproducibility of diagnosis; the interview itself ensures standardization and comprehensiveness of questioning.

In summary, the SADS and SCID are recommended as the best assessment methods for making the diagnosis of major depression. Unfortunately, it may be unwieldy to administer lengthy structured interviews to all patients who need to be assessed. When professional time is scarce, self-report assessment may be indicated.

### Self-Report Tests

Self-report tests are the most cost-efficient method of assessment, and they have therefore proliferated. However, their weaknesses with regard to diagnosing major depression must be understood. As our review indicates, diagnoses based on self-report depression scales should never be used as a substitute for a clinician's diagnosis (i.e., based on a structured interview). Nevertheless, particular self-report scales do approach a clinician's diagnosis and may be used in certain assessment contexts (Plutchik and van Praag 1987). One appropriate clinical context is, for example, a screening clinic where patients are quickly evaluated and later receive further assessment. Another clinical context might be in an epidemiological study to determine individuals who are likely to have major depression, or more importantly, to rule out with certainty those subjects who do not have major depression.

Our own data on the Symptom Checklist 90 (SCL-90), the Minnesota Multiphasic Personality Inventory (MMPI), and the Millon Clinical Multiaxial Inventory (MCMI) as well as published data on the Center for Epidemiological Studies–Depression Scale (CES-D) will illustrate and support this conclusion. A review of the extensive literature on the use of the MMPI and the few papers on the use of the SCL-90 indicate the state of the art of self-report tests for the diagnosis of major depression (although pre-DSM-III criteria were frequently used). The literature examines common profiles and group mean profiles of patients with major depression on these tests (e.g., Marks et al. 1974). Each test is multidimensional, and the profiles may be characterized by their high point codes.

The traditional MMPI profiles characteristic of depressed patients according to DSM-II may apply even better to the more clearly defined DSM-III depressed patient. One study showed that the five code types of depression defined by Marks et al. (1974) applied to 71% of DSM-II cases of major depression and to 84% of DSM-III cases (Winters et al. 1981). Two subsequent studies indicated that similar code types characterized at least 79% of patients with either bipolar or unipolar depression[1] (Silver et al. 1981; Winters et al. 1985). The problem with lists of frequent code types is that they may not be diagnostically useful. It appears that many psychiatric patients without major depression have MMPI code types similar to those with major depression (Vincent et al. 1983; Wetzler et al., in press). In our own study, patients with major depression had qualitatively different MMPI profiles than other psychiatric patients according to multivariate analyses, but the high point code types were similar.

The same conclusion may be reached on the basis of the few studies using the SCL-90 in depressed patients. Certain SCL-90 profiles characterize patients with major depression (Derogatis 1983); however, these same profiles also character-

---

[1]Bipolar depressed patients exhibit more denial and have generally lower scores on all MMPI scales than do unipolar depressed patients (Donnelly et al. 1980). By recovery, there are no differences between these patients (Donnelly et al. 1976).

ize psychiatric patients without major depression (i.e., schizophrenia, generalized anxiety disorder) (Clark and Friedman 1983; Cyr et al. 1985; Wetzler et al., in press). Considerable research has been conducted with the SCL-90 to investigate one of the most difficult differential diagnostic problems—anxiety disorders versus major depression. Whereas the initial work indicated a clear discrimination of anxiety patients from depressed patients on the SCL-90 (Derogatis et al. 1972; Prusoff and Klerman 1974), subsequent studies have failed to corroborate this finding (Angst and Dobler-Mikola 1985; Clark and Friedman 1983; Cyr et al. 1985; Dinning and Evans 1977).

Our own study on self-report testing in major depression represents the only study of the MCMI. We again found that the clinical scale profiles of patients with major depression and those without major depression were qualitatively different; however, the code types were similar (Wetzler et al., in press).

In addition to examining the diagnostic value of the entire multidimensional profile of these tests, one may base diagnostic decisions solely on the tests' depression scales. Is it possible to accurately and efficiently diagnose major depression by comparing depression scale scores with commonly used cut-off scores? This review will consider findings using the MMPI depression scale (T score $\geq$ 70) and Mezzich index (score $\geq$ 190) (Mezzich et al. 1974), the SCL-90 depression scale (T score $\geq$ 70), the MCMI dysthymia and psychotic depression scales (base rate scores $\geq$ 85), and the CES-D scale (score > 16).

Initially, Post and Lobitz (1980), using the MMPI to diagnose major depression, found that the false positive rate for the Mezzich index (12%) was lower than for the depression scale alone (22%). In a later study using the MMPI to discriminate patients with major depression from depressed patients without major depression, Post et al. (1985) found that both the Mezzich index and the depression scale had a 73% hit rate with a high percentage of false positives in this population (73% and 55%, respectively).

Table 2 displays the diagnostic efficiency statistics of these scales for diagnosing major depression in a heterogeneous psychiatric inpatient and outpatient sample ($n$ = 116) at Montefiore Medical Center (Wetzler et al., in press). By comparing the classification rate to the negative base rate (predicting that all patients do not have major depression), one can determine whether or not these scales perform better than chance alone. The MMPI depression, MCMI dysthymia, and SCL-90 depression scales all performed better than chance. The MMPI Mezzich index offered no improvement over the MMPI depression scale, and the MCMI psychotic depression scale was insensitive to the diagnosis of major depression.

**Table 2.** The Diagnostic Efficiency of Self-Report Depression Scales

| Scale | Sen. | Spec. | NPP | PPP | Class. | Base rate |
|---|---|---|---|---|---|---|
| MMPI Depression [a] | .92 | .50 | .90 | .59 | .66 | .37 |
| MMPI Mezzich [a] | .77 | .53 | .75 | .56 | .61 | .37 |
| MCMI Dysthymia [a] | .71 | .70 | .77 | .63 | .69 | .41 |
| MCMI Psychotic Depression [a] | .04 | .97 | .59 | .50 | .58 | .41 |
| SCL-90 Depression [a] | .67 | .72 | .75 | .63 | .70 | .41 |
| CES-D (inpatient) [b] | .96 | .66 | .93 | .77 | .82 | .53 |
| CES-D (community) [c] | .64 | .94 | .98 | .33 | .93 | .05 |
| CES-D (community) [d] | .60 | .83 | .99 | .07 | .83 | .02 |

*Note.* Sen. = sensitivity: The percentage of patients with major depression who were correctly diagnosed by the test. Spec. = specificity: The percentage of patients without major depression who were correctly not diagnosed by the test. NPP = negative predictive power: The percentage of patients not diagnosed by the test who do not have major depression. PPP = positive predictive power: The percentage of patients diagnosed by the test who have major depression. Class. = classification rate: The percentage of patients correctly classified by the test. Base rate = base rate of major depression.

[a] From Wetzler et al., in press.
[b] From Weissman et al. 1977.
[c] From Myers and Weissman 1980.
[d] From Roberts and Vernon 1983.

Considering its good sensitivity and negative predictive power, the MMPI depression scale seems to be a useful instrument for screening major depression; its mediocre specificity necessitates following up patients who score above the threshold with another type of assessment. The MCMI dysthymia and SCL-90 depression scales offer better overall diagnostic accuracy, but they are by no means 100% accurate. As Goldberg et al. (1987) have recently concluded, the MCMI psychotic depression scale appears to have significant limitations as a predictor of major depression.

Table 2 also displays the diagnostic efficiency statistics for the CES-D in three different samples. In an inpatient psychiatric setting ($n = 406$) comparable to our sample, the CES-D was able to diagnose depression at 82% accuracy (Weissman et al. 1977). While this figure may be somewhat artificially inflated by the looseness of the criterion diagnosis (Raskin score $> 7$), the results in general corroborate our findings in a different psychiatric sample. In two community samples ($n = 482$ and $n = 511$), however, the CES-D exhibited quite poor positive-predictive power (Myers and Weissman 1980; Roberts and Vernon 1983). It is unlikely that any psychological test could predict major depression at adequate rates in the community at large because the disorder has very low prevalence. In such settings, psychological tests may be expected to function as screening instruments detecting all cases of the disorder even at the expense of many false positives. For such a purpose, the CES-D did fairly well.

Based on this research, we may conclude that depressed patients exhibit different psychological test characteristics than other psychiatric patients, but that there are not specific high point codes that are pathognomonic for major depression. We recommend, however, that the depression scales of various self-report tests may be used for the diagnosis of major depression (at clearly defined cut-off scores). They may be used effectively as initial screening instruments for diagnosing major depression, i.e., identifying patients likely to have major depression and screening out those unlikely to have it. But they will not be 100% accurate, and therefore for optimal results they should not be used as the sole assessment method. The diagnostic precision of self-report depression scales depends on the particular differential diagnostic decision. If the differential diagnosis is simple (e.g., major depression vs. no psychopathology), then self-report scales will be adequate. However, as the differential diagnosis becomes more difficult (e.g., major depression vs. anxiety disorders, or major vs. minor depression, or major vs. atypical depression), any instrument would be expected to perform poorly. For overall accuracy in a psychiatric setting, the SCL-90 depression and MCMI dysthymia scales are best; for ruling out major depression in a psychiatric setting, the MMPI depression scale is best; for identifying cases of major depression in a community sample, the CES-D appears to be effective.

## The Assessment of Depression as a Dimension

The dimensional or functional approach is fundamentally denosological. Important dimensions or constructs are defined because they have psychopathological significance, and each disorder is dissected into these dimensions. Representative dimensions include, for example, lowered mood, anxiety/agitation, hostility, psychoticism, and extraversion (van Praag et al. 1975, 1987). Others may be defined as well. For a dimension to be meaningful it must be specific, that is, independent of other dimensions. Such dissection or analysis is an artificial psychometric feat, not a fact of nature, because psychopathology rarely exists in these pure dimensional forms. Rather, all dimensions of psychopathology are intermingled and must therefore be disentangled by the scientist. Measurement instruments that assist the clinician in the difficult process of disentangling are much needed. The ideal dimensional analysis is one that identifies multiple psychopathological dimensions that are defined as specifically as possible.

While many psychopathological dimensions may be defined, the one that is of greatest interest in this context is the dimension of depression. How can one define a dimension of depression that is independent of other important dimensions? What does this dimension consist of? In our opinion, most studies indicate that the dimension of depression is characterized by a lowering of mood, a decrease in initiative, and an impaired hedonic capacity. These depressive features cohere and define a specific and independent dimension of depression. Based on this conceptualization, one may ask which assessment instruments have the capacity to measure a dimension of depression defined as such.

### Observer Rating Scales

By far the most well known and frequently used observer rating scale of depression is the Hamilton Rating Scale of Depression (HRSD). It was developed in order to measure the severity of major depression once the disorder has been diagnosed by a clinician. The HRSD was not intended to be a diagnostic instrument itself; patients with other disorders (i.e., medical patients) may have very high HRSD scores without being at all depressed.

The HRSD was also not intended to be used as a dimensional instrument, although it is frequently used as such in treatment studies. It is commonly viewed as an indicator of the antidepressant qualities of a particular drug. This application and interpretation of the HRSD is misguided because it appears to be sensitive to many facets of psychopathology that are not specifically depressive. For example, the HRSD contains many items that are related to anxiety and agitation, and the HRSD does not seem to differentiate between depression and anxiety as dimensions of psychopathology (see Wetzler 1986).

One observer rating scale that shows promise as an instrument for measuring depression is the Montgomery-Asberg Depression Rating Scale. This scale was derived from the HRSD with the aim of eliminating all items related to anxiety. It appears to be a reliable and valid measure of depression and is quite sensitive to differences in severity (Kearns et al. 1982; Maier and Philipp 1985).

## Self-Report Tests

Whereas earlier we had discussed the use of self-report scales for the diagnosis of major depression, they may be even more useful as instruments that measure the dimension of depression from the patient's perspective. The patient has a unique vantage point from which to observe his or her internal experience. When a self-report scale is well-constructed, it may give access to this experience, and for outpatient depressives self-report scales may be the earliest indicators of change (Hollon and Mandell 1979; Lambert et al. 1986; McNair 1973; Raskin and Crook 1976).

Self-report rating scales of depression are basically very much alike. This conclusion may be surprising because there are differences in item content. For example, 64% of the Beck Depression Inventory items are verbal/cognitive features, and 9% are affective features; whereas the CES-D has 40% verbal/cognitive features and 32% affective features. Also, the time frame of the rating varies from the past week for the SCL-90 depression scale to a lifetime rating for the MMPI depression scale. Despite these variations, all self-report depression scales are highly correlated with one another across a wide range of psychiatric populations (Schaefer et al. 1985; Wetzler 1986). In general, the choice of a particular depression rating scale may not matter; apparently, they are all equally good at measuring the dimension of depression.

In order to determine the construct validity of these depression rating scales we need to examine the correlations between them and self-report scales that measure other constructs (e.g., anxiety) as well as the correlations between them and observer rating scales of depression. Unfortunately, as Table 3 indicates, self-report depression scales are as highly correlated with self-report anxiety scales as they are among themselves (Wetzler 1986). This suggests poor discriminant validity. A self-report depression scale may be measuring anxiety as much as it is measuring depression. Dysphoria or generalized distress may best characterize what is being measured by these scales. Second, correlations between self-report and observer rating scales of depression are less strong than those between different self-report scales (e.g., $r = .33–.56$ vs. $r = .60–.69$, respectively) (Glazer et al. 1981; Hughes et al. 1982; Schaefer et al. 1985). This suggests only mediocre convergent validity. Method variance seems to overwhelm construct variance.

For a self-report depression scale to be psychometrically sound it must exhibit good internal consistency; that is, it should measure a single, consistent dimension. One recent review of self-report depression scales criticized the internal consistency of these scales for being too redundant, too narrow, and too heterogeneous (Boyle 1985). In fact, Harris and Lingoes (1955) have demonstrated that the MMPI depression scale is composed of multiple factors. As a result, it would be a mistake to interpret elevations on these scales as indicative of a single, unidimensional depressive construct. Rather, there are multiple determinants for scale elevation that make interpretation of results difficult.

In summary, self-report depression scales appear to be fairly interchangeable. They correlate at high levels with each other and at moderate levels with observer rating scales of

**Table 3.** Intercorrelations of Self-Report Anxiety and Depression Scales

|  | Depression with depression | Depression with anxiety |
|---|---|---|
| Mendels et al. 1972 | .69 | .60 |
| Dobson 1985 | .69 | .61 |
| Meites et al. 1980 | .60 | .61 |
| Tanaka-Matsumi and Kameoka 1986 | .61 | .68 |
| Claghorn 1970 |  | .70 |
| Schaefer et al. 1985 | .68 |  |

depression. Their discriminant validity, however, is limited; they seem to tap anxiety as much as depression. Keeping these strengths and weaknesses in mind, self-report tests may be useful for assessing depression. In particular, in certain settings they may be the earliest indicators of therapeutic improvement.

## Conclusion

Contemporary assessment research has made significant strides in the measurement of depression. There are a plethora of new scales and psychological testing instruments designed specifically with depression in mind. Two separate assessment aims have been defined (the diagnosis of major depression and the measurement of the dimension of depression), and different types of assessment instruments have been discussed (self-report tests, structured interviews, observer rating scales). For the diagnosis of major depression, a structured interview such as the SCID is highly recommended. When time constraints prohibit a lengthy interview, then self-report tests such as the MCMI or SCL-90 may offer adequate diagnostic accuracy and may function well as screening instruments. A patient can easily complete a self-report test while sitting in a waiting room. For the measurement of the dimension of depression, self-report depression scales are again indicated. They offer a quick and simple way to quantify the level of the patient's dysphoria and are quite sensitive to changes in the patient's mood. We do not recommend any particular depression scale over the others because they are fairly comparable. For those clinicians who are interested in measuring changes in the severity of the depressed state during treatment with antidepressants, we recommend the use of the Montgomery-Asberg Depression Rating Scale, an observer-rated scale.

Although the state of the art is by no means perfect, it seems reasonable to conclude that we can now quantify many aspects of depression.

# References

Angst J, Dobler-Mikola A: The Zurich study, VI: a continuum from depression to anxiety disorders? Eur Arch Psychiatry Neurol Sci 235:179–186, 1985

Anthony JC, Folstein M, Romanoski A, et al: Comparison of the lay Diagnostic Interview Schedule and a standardized psychiatric diagnosis. Arch Gen Psychiatry 42:667–675, 1985

Beck AT, Ward CH, Mendelson M, et al: An inventory for measuring depression. Arch Gen Psychiatry 4:561–571, 1961

Boyle GJ: Self-report measures of depression: some psychometric considerations. Br J Clin Psychol 24:45–59, 1985

Claghorn J: The anxiety-depression syndrome. Psychosomatics 11:438–441, 1970

Clark A, Friedman MJ: Factor structure and discriminant validity of the SCL-90 in a veteran psychiatric population. J Pers Assess 47:396–404, 1983

Cyr JJ, McKenna-Foley JM, Peacock E: Factor structure of the SCL-90-R: is there one? J Pers Assess 49:571–577, 1985

Derogatis LR: The Symptom Checklist–90 Manual II. Towson, MD, Clinical Psychometric Research, 1983

Derogatis LR, Lipman RS, Covi L, et al: Factorial invariance of symptom dimensions in anxious and depressive neuroses. Arch Gen Psychiatry 27:659–665, 1972

Dinning WD, Evans RG: Discriminant and convergent validity of the SCL-90 in psychiatric inpatients. J Pers Assess 41:304–309, 1977

Dobson KS: An analysis of anxiety and depression scales. J Pers Assess 49:522–527, 1985

Donnelly EF, Murphy DL, Goodwin FK: Cross-sectional and longitudinal comparisons of bipolar and unipolar depressed groups on the MMPI. J Consult Clin Psychol 44:233–237, 1976

Donnelly EF, Murphy DL, Waldman IN: Denial and somatization as characteristics of bipolar depressed groups. J Clin Psychol 36:159–162, 1980

Endicott J, Spitzer RL: A diagnostic interview: the Schedule for Affective Disorders and Schizophrenia. Arch Gen Psychiatry 35:837–844, 1978

Glazer HI, Clarkin JF, Hunt HF: Assessment of depression, in Depression: Behavioral and Directive Intervention Strategies. Edited by Clarkin J, Glazer H. New York, Garland, 1981, pp 3–30

Goldberg JO, Shaw BF, Segal ZV: Concurrent validity of the Millon Clinical Multiaxial Inventory Depression scales. J Consult Clin Psychol 55:785–787, 1987

Hamilton M: Rating depressive patients. J Clin Psychiatry 41:21–24, 1960

Harris RE, Lingoes JC: Subscales for the MMPI: an aid to profile interpretation. 1955 (unpublished manuscript)

Hathaway SR, McKinley JC: Minnesota Multiphasic Personality Inventory (MMPI). Minneapolis, University of Minnesota Press, 1943

Hollon S, Mandell M: Use of the MMPI in the evaluation of treatment effects, in New Developments in the Use of the MMPI. Edited by Butcher J. Minneapolis, University of Minnesota Press, 1979

Hughes JR, O'Hara MW, Rehm LP: Measurement of depression in clinical trials: an overview. J Clin Psychiatry 43:85–88, 1982

Kearns NP, Cruickshank CA, McGuigan KJ, et al: A comparison of depression rating scales. Br J Psychiatry 141:45–49, 1982

Lambert MJ, Hatch DR, Kingston MD, et al: Zung, Beck, and Hamilton rating scales as measures of treatment outcome: a meta-analytic comparison. J Consult Clin Psychol 54:54–59, 1986

Maier W, Philipp M: Comparative analysis of observer depression scales. Acta Psychiatr Scand 72:239–245, 1985

Marks P, Seeman W, Haller D: The Actuarial Use of the MMPI with Adolescents and Adults. New York, Oxford University Press, 1974

McNair DM: Self-evaluations of antidepressants. Psychopharmacologia 37:281–302, 1973

Meites K, Lovallo W, Pishkin V: A comparison of four scales for anxiety, depression and neuroticism. J Clin Psychol 36:427–432, 1980

Mendels J, Weinstein N, Cochrane C: The relationship between depression and anxiety. Arch Gen Psychiatry 27:649–653, 1972

Mezzich JE, Damarin FL, Erickson JR: Comparative validity of strategies and indices for differential diagnosis of depressive states from other psychiatric conditions using the MMPI. J Consult Clin Psychol 42:691–698, 1974

Millon T: Millon Clinical Multiaxial Inventory Manual, 3rd ed. Minneapolis, National Computer Systems, 1983

Montgomery SA, Asberg M: A new depression scale designed to be sensitive to change. Br J Psychiatry 134:382–389, 1979

Myers J, Weissman M: Use of a self-report symptom scale to detect depression in a community sample. Am J Psychiatry 137:1081–1084, 1980

Plutchik R, van Praag HM: On measuring depression. Psychiatry Res 22:243–256, 1987

Post RD, Lobitz WC: The utility of Mezzich's MMPI regression formula as a diagnostic criterion in depression research. J Consult Clin Psychol 48:673–674, 1980

Post RD, Petersen JL, Jackson AM, et al: The Mezzich regression formula revisited. J Pers Assess 49:258–259, 1985

Prusoff B, Klerman GL: Differentiating depressed from anxious neurotic outpatients: use of discriminant function analysis for separation of neurotic affective states. Arch Gen Psychiatry 30:302–309, 1974

Radloff LS: The Center for Epidemiological Studies-Depression Scale: a self-report scale for research in the general population. Applied Psychological Measurement 1:385–401, 1977

Raskin A, Crook TH: Sensitivity of rating scales completed by psychiatrists, nurses and patients to antidepressant drug effects. J Psychiatr Res 13:31–41, 1976

Roberts RE, Vernon SW: The CES-D: its use in a community sample. Am J Psychiatry 140:41–46, 1983

Robins LN, Helzer JE, Croughan J, et al: National Institute of Mental Health Diagnostic Interview Schedule. Arch Gen Psychiatry 38:381–389, 1981

Schaefer A, Brown J, Watson CG, et al: Comparison of the validities of the Beck, Zung, and MMPI depression scales. J Consult Clin Psychol 53:415–418, 1985

Silver RJ, Isaacs K, Mansky P: MMPI correlates of affective disorders. J Clin Psychol 37:836–839, 1981

Spitzer RL, Williams JB, Gibbon M: Structured Clinical Interview for DSM-III-R (SCID). New York State Psychiatric Institute, 1986

Tanaka-Matsumi J, Kameoka V: Reliabilities and concurrent validities of popular self-report measures of depression, anxiety, and social desirability. J Consult Clin Psychol 54:328–333, 1986

van Praag HM, Korf J, Kakke JP, et al: Dopamine metabolism in depression, psychoses and Parkinson's disease: the problem of the specificity of biological variables in behavior disorders. Psychol Med 5:138–146, 1975

van Praag HM, Kahn RS, Asnis GR, et al: Denosologization of biological psychiatry or the specificity of 5HT disturbances. J Affective Disord 13:1–8, 1987

Vincent KR, Castillo I, Hauser RI, et al: MMPI code types and DSM-III diagnoses. J Clin Psychol 39:829–842, 1983

Weissman M, Sholomskas D, Potenger M: Assessing depressive symptoms in 5 psychiatric populations: a validation study. Am J Epidemiol 106:203–214, 1977

Wetzler S: Methodological issues for the differentiation of anxiety and depression. Clin Neuropsychopharm 9(Suppl 4):248–250, 1986

Wetzler S, Kahn R, Strauman TJ, et al: The diagnosis of major depression by self-report. J Pers Assess 53:22–30, 1989

Winters KC, Newmark CS, Lumry AE, et al: MMPI codetypes characteristic of DSM-III schizophrenics, depressives, and bipolars. J Clin Psychol 41:382–386, 1985

Winters KC, Weintraub S, Neale JM: Validity of MMPI codetypes in identifying DSM-III schizophrenics, unipolars and bipolars. J Consult Clin Psychol 49:486–487, 1981

Zung, W: A self-rating depression scale. Arch Gen Psychiatry 12:63–70, 1965

# Chapter 5

# Clinical Assessment in Schizophrenia

**JOHN A. SWEENEY, Ph.D.**
**GRETCHEN L. HAAS, Ph.D.**
**PETER J. WEIDEN, M.D.**

# Chapter 5

# Clinical Assessment in Schizophrenia

*T*he diverse clinical manifestations of schizophrenia create many difficult assessment problems for clinicians. First, the differential diagnosis of schizophrenia can be difficult—particularly early in the course of illness. Diagnostic dilemmas often result from the clinical heterogeneity of the disorder, controversy over the definition of the syndrome and its boundaries with other psychotic disorders (Andreasen 1987), problems assessing prodromal characteristics and deterioration in functioning, and the lack of confirmatory laboratory tests. Examples of typical diagnostic challenges include cases in which psychotic beliefs are held but with less than certain conviction, paranoid patients deny psychotic symptoms, historical information is lacking, or substance abuse is prominent.

Second, major clinical decisions such as hospitalization and initiating antipsychotic medication need to be based on a comprehensive assessment—not just of psychotic symptoms but also of other factors including, for example, treatment compliance and suicidality. Many of these features may be inaccurately assessed given the poor reliability of psychotic patients. In this context, it is all too easy to neglect an important aspect of the diagnostic assessment, or to be surprised by the severity of an ignored symptom in a chronic patient. Third, the planning of treatment programs for chronic, relatively stable patients requires the assessment of such features as interpersonal skills, social supports, and stressors. The assessment of social factors is vital in planning treatment programs most likely to prevent relapse (Falloon et al. 1985; Hogarty et al. 1986).

## A Role for Clinical Rating Scales

The vast majority of clinical rating instruments were originally developed for research purposes. However, the quality of care of schizophrenic patients can be greatly enhanced by the use of clinical rating scales, because such scales can increase the breadth and value of assessments. First, structured interviews can guide comprehensive diagnostic evaluations and are likely to increase the reliability and validity of clinical assessments. Standardized assessments can be invaluable in transmitting clinical information about symptoms, treatment response, and side effects that would otherwise be lost, especially for schizophrenic patients who all too often receive fragmented care with frequent changes of doctors and hospitals. What is recorded on rating forms speaks for itself and can serve as a common clinical "language." Second, the use of rating scales can serve an important educational function. In academic settings, such scales can provide a structure for teaching trainees. For nursing and paraprofessional staffs, they can provide a formal procedure for regular evaluation and patient reports.

Rating scales should be selected on the basis of their relevance to immediate diagnostic and treatment decisions. For example, decisions about hospitalization or initiating neuroleptic treatment are typically based on a patient's clinical presentation of positive symptoms. In contrast, clinical decisions about stabilized schizophrenic patients often require more attention to the assessment of patients' psychosocial skills and supportive social resources, their level of treatment compliance, and their functional capacities. Rating scales are available that focus assessment on each of these independent areas, and the choice of scales can be guided by relevant clinical goals.

Finally, structured quantitative assessments can prove useful in monitoring change in the clinical presentation and response to treatments. Quantifying the severity of symptoms can be useful for quality assurance programs (e.g., ratings for monitoring tardive dyskinesia) to document the comprehensiveness of assessments and to monitor treatment response over time for purposes such as justifying continued hospitalization (Table 1).

## Use of Standard Assessment Instruments in Clinical Practice

**Diagnostic evaluation.** Several diagnostic tasks confront the clinician assessing psychotic patients. One task is to determine whether medical disease or substance abuse is contributing to or causing psychiatric symptoms. It is crucial to undertake rigorous and systematic assessments of the symptom profile, recent history, and prodromal course of psychotic patients, particularly for first episode cases or when major changes in symptoms occur. A second goal is to determine whether the patient has met criteria for an affective syndrome during a period of psychosis. If so, a differential diagnosis of schizophrenia versus diagnoses of mania, psychotic depression, and schizoaffective disorder needs to be considered.

Third, in milder cases, decisions about whether symptoms are truly psychotic (e.g., illusions vs. hallucinations; overvalued ideas vs. delusions) are necessary to warrant the diagnosis of schizophrenia. Fourth, the duration of illness may be difficult to ascertain in cases of gradual onset. Fifth, the assessment of "prodromal" and "residual" features of illness is important, but often difficult because these symptoms have not been well studied and often merge with personality characteristics.

The shift to a criterion-based diagnostic system requires the presence of specific signs and symptoms for assigning clinical diagnoses. A major advantage of criterion-based diagnoses, such as those used in the Diagnostic and Statistical Manual of Mental Disorders, Third Edition, Revised (DSM-III-R; American Psychiatric Association 1987), is an increased reliability of diagnoses and homogeneity of diagnostic groups. Criterion symptoms serve to define the boundaries of psychiatric disor-

**Table 1.** Instruments Useful for Increasing the Reliability and Systematic Nature of Clinical Assessments of Schizophrenic Patients

| Assessment domain | Instrument | Application |
|---|---|---|
| 1. Diagnosis | SCID<br>SADS | Hospitalization<br>New symptoms<br>Pharmacotherapy decisions |
| 2. Positive symptoms | BPRS<br>SAPS | Hospitalization<br>Monitor treatment response |
| 3. Negative symptoms | SANS | Stabilization |
| 4. Depression Suicide | HAM-D<br>Beck Hopelessness Scale | Hospitalization<br>Dysphoria<br>Suicidal ideation |
| 5. Extrapyramidal symptoms | ESRS<br>Simpson-Angus | Baseline<br>Behavioral deterioration<br>After neuroleptic increase |
| 6. Tardive dyskinesia | AIMS<br>Rockland<br>ADS | Baseline<br>Every 6 months |
| 7. Neuropsychology | WAIS-R<br>Wisconsin Card Sort | Stabilization |
| 8. Social functioning | SAS-II | Stabilization |
| 9. Life events | SRRS | Stabilization |

*Note.* SCID = Structured Clinical Interview for DSM-III Diagnoses. SADS = Schedule for Affective Disorders and Schizophrenia. BPRS = Brief Psychiatric Rating Scale. SAPS = Scale for the Assessment of Positive Symptoms. SANS = Scale for the Assessment of Negative Symptoms. HAM-D = Hamilton Scale for Rating Depression. ESRS =Extrapyramidal Symptom Rating Scale. ADS = Abbreviated Dyskinesia Scale. WAIS-R = Wechsler Adult Intelligence Scale, Revised. SAS-II = Social Adjustment Scale II. SRRS = Social Readjustment Rating Scale.

ders. The change from DSM-II to DSM-III significantly narrowed the definition of schizophrenia to include only cases with more chronic and/or severe symptoms (Andreasen 1987). It seems likely that diagnostic boundaries and treatment guidelines will continue to evolve through ongoing research efforts, making it even more important to conduct detailed (and recorded) symptom assessments for making both current and future diagnoses. Monitoring acute psychotic symptoms and affective features is particularly important as diagnostic and treatment decisions for schizophrenic patients with affective features are lacking definitive clinical guidelines.

To standardize case evaluation and reduce unreliability of diagnoses, researchers developed structured clinical interviews. These elicit information required for assigning diagnoses in terms of the criterion-based diagnostic schemes. Use of diagnostic interviews, such as the Schedule for Affective Disorders and Schizophrenia (SADS) (Endicott and Spitzer 1978), designed for assigning Research Diagnostic Criteria (RDC) diagnoses (Spitzer et al. 1978), and the Structured Clinical Interview for DSM-III Diagnoses (SCID), for DSM-III-R diagnoses (Spitzer et al. 1988), provide a structure for clinical evaluation that can reduce common diagnostic errors and ensure a common nosology in keeping with currently accepted diagnostic criteria. Structured diagnostic interviews assess not only criteria for what the clinician considers the likely diagnosis, but also criteria relevant to ruling out alternate possible diagnoses. In this way, errors such as a failure to rule out affective disorders in patients who meet symptom criteria for schizophrenia become less frequent.

Clinical use of structured interviews reduces any tendency to overemphasize the diagnostic significance of certain features of an illness. For example, when making a DSM-III diagnosis of schizophrenia, structured interviews may prevent overemphasis on such clinical features as longstanding deterioration in occupational and/or social functioning, a quality of detachment or "oddness" in clinical interviews, formal thought disorder, neuroleptic response, family psychiatric history, and the presence of specific psychotic features (e.g., first rank symptoms). While many of these factors may affect confidence in a diagnosis, limiting overemphasis of such factors preserves the communication value and validity of diagnoses. Also, clinical decisions to deviate from DSM-III criteria in special situations are brought to the fore, and so can be more readily identified and documented. Sections of the SCID can be administered to address specific diagnostic concerns. Thus, if there is concern about affective symptoms or substance abuse history, the relevant section from the SCID can be administered as is clinically indicated.

**Symptom assessment.** The clinical heterogeneity of schizophrenia was well known to Kraepelin (1919) and Bleuler (1950). This heterogeneity requires not only broad-based symptom assessments for diagnostic purposes, but also flexibility in assessing patient characteristics depending on the current state of illness. Clinical rating instruments for assessing global symptom severity are particularly useful for repeated evaluations of a patient over time. Scales such as the Brief Psychiatric Rating Scale (BPRS) (Overall and Gorham 1962) yield a global score based on the aggregate total of individual symptom ratings, whereas the Global Assessment Scale (GAS) (Endicott et al. 1976) provides a single rating of global functioning. In acute care settings, these scales can provide an efficient and reliable mechanism for monitoring treatment response. Regular use of these scales in stabilized outpatients can provide a clear quantitative baseline against which any early signs of relapse can be quickly identified.

Two major foci of assessment of schizophrenic patients are 1) acute psychotic features (commonly referred to as "positive" symptoms), and 2) pervasive deficits in cognitive, emotional, and psychosocial functioning (the so-called "negative" or "deficit" syndrome) (Andreasen 1982b; Lewine et al. 1983). While the concepts of positive and negative symptoms are still being developed and refined, the distinction is of clinical value in describing distinct categories of symptoms that appear to have different treatment and prognostic implications. Positive symptoms, usually variable over the course of illness, may reflect dopaminergic overactivity and are relatively neuroleptic responsive. In contrast, negative symptoms are more chronic features of maladjustment. Negative symptoms may be related to structural brain atrophy. While their manifestation may vary over the course of an acute episode (Goldberg 1985), negative symptoms are generally considered less treatment responsive and more stable over time.

Clinical ratings of positive and negative symptoms are most commonly conducted using two scales developed by Nancy Andreasen: the Scale for the Assessment of Positive Symptoms (SAPS; Andreasen 1984) and the Scale for the Assessment of Negative Symptoms (SANS; Andreasen 1983). These scales represent a major step forward in the clinical assessment of schizophrenic patients because they define, organize, and quantitatively assess distinct clinical manifestations of acute versus deficit symptoms. Both scales have a high degree of face validity, in that they require the clinician/rater to assign severity ratings to well-defined features of the disorder. The positive symptom scale assesses four clusters: hallucinations, delusions, bizarre behavior, and positive formal thought disorder. The negative symptom scale assesses five clusters: affective blunting, alogia (impoverished thinking), avolition/apathy, anhedonia/asociality, and attention disturbance. Confidence in the assessment of negative symptoms should be greater when ratings are performed on stabilized patients. In acutely psychotic patients, co-existing depression, paranoia, and drug-induced akinesia can cause secondary negative symptoms. However, assessing these features independently can help tease out which factors are causing negative-like symptoms to guide decisions about differential therapeutics (Carpenter et al. 1985).

The precise definition of terms and the comprehensiveness of coverage of clinical features are among the best characteristics of Andreasen's scales, yet there remains a need for more explicit behavior anchors for quantitative ratings of positive and negative symptoms. In our experience, interrater reliabilities have been lower for negative than for positive symptoms. This may be fairly common as ratings of positive symptoms require a lower level of clinical inference. These scales are very useful clinically because they help monitor fluctuations in psychotic symptoms and any improvement or deterioration in social and emotional deficits. Assessment of negative symptoms in stable outpatients can help clinicians make appropriate interventions pertaining to work and social problems.

**Self-report of psychiatric symptoms.** There is a long tradition of using self-report instruments for assessing psychiatric symptoms, as they provide a quantitative and reliable assessment requiring minimal professional time. Certain potential problems must be considered in using self-report measures with psychotic patients. For example, some acutely disturbed patients are disorganized or uncooperative to the point of being unable or unwilling to complete forms. However, in our experience, over 70–80% of schizophrenic patients have been able to complete even a long scale such as the Minnesota Multiphasic Personality Inventory (MMPI; 1943) within a week after hospitalization. A scale such as the MMPI has the advantages of being particularly well standardized, having "validity" scales that help assess the degree to which patients minimize or exaggerate symptoms, and broad validation for use with a wide variety of clinical disorders. Other widely used but briefer scales such as the Symptom Checklist 90 (SCL-90) (Derogatis et al. 1973) can provide a somewhat less reliable but broad quantitative assessment of patient functioning. These self-report scales permit ready documentation of clinical change, allow comparison to test norms, and provide a good screening of any changes in depression, anxiety, and psychotic symptoms.

Loren Chapman and colleagues developed scales for the dimensional assessment of psychosis proneness, including the Magical Ideation Scale, the Perceptual Aberration Scale, and the Physical Anhedonia Scale (Chapman and Chapman 1980) to identify individuals at risk for psychosis. While these scales are not in wide clinical use, they have been reasonably well validated, and might prove useful in assessing patients when there is concern about prodromal features of schizophrenia, or in assessing the presence of near-psychotic experiences in recovered patients.

**Suicide risk.** The markedly increased risk for suicide in schizophrenia is often underestimated. Miles (1977) estimated that one of every 10 schizophrenic patients commits suicide, and many others make serious attempts. The suicide rate among patients with schizophrenia may have even increased in recent years under the stress of briefer hospitalizations, living in the community, and the limited supportive care available (Drake et al. 1984). That suicide risk in this population is difficult to assess is demonstrated by the fact that suicides often occur in recently discharged patients shortly after clinical contact.

Demoralization, secondary to chronic symptoms and role functioning impairment, may be a major risk factor in schizophrenia. Also, acute psychosis can increase suicide risk by causing 1) intense distress that patients may try to escape through suicide, 2) psychotic ideas such as persecutory delusions causing behavior that results in self-harm or death, and 3) command hallucinations to suicide. Dysphoria and hopelessness about the future, with or without a full depressive syndrome, are associated with risk for suicide in schizophrenia. Thus, the Beck Depression Inventory (Beck et al. 1961), the Hamilton Scale for Rating Depression (Hamilton 1967), and particularly the Beck Hopelessness Scale (Beck et al. 1974) may be useful for assessing depression and suicide risk in this population.

**Assessment of thinking and cognition.** There is a long tradition of assessing formal thought disorder in schizophrenia (Chapman and Chapman 1973). Attempts to identify *the* critical distinguishing form of thought disorder in schizophrenia were a major focus of theoretical and research investigations of schizophrenia for several decades. The growing recognition that thought disorder has only limited diagnostic specificity for schizophrenia (Andreasen 1979; Harrow and Quinlan 1977) and the difficulty defining and reliably assessing "thought disorder" contributed to a de-emphasis of thought disorder in the diagnosis of schizophrenia.

However, there has been renewed interest in the use of psychological tests for assessing thought disorder. Harrow and Quinlan (1985) and Holzman (Solovay et al. 1987) have conducted investigations to assess the diagnostic specificity of different features of thought disorder to schizophrenia. Harrow and Quinlan rated thought disorder in a longitudinal study of a large cohort of patients with schizophrenia or affective disorders and reported that the continued presence of thought disorder outside acute episodes was most common in schizophrenia. Holzman's group rated different forms of thought disorder in Rorschach responses and found that flippant, playful over-elaborations were more common in bipolar patients while deteriorated responses were relatively specific to schizophrenia. Thus, the assessment of thought disorder using refined measures of different aspects of thought disorder and when patients are relatively recovered may have some diagnostic value. Further, assessing the organization of thinking can help guide suggestions to patients and families about work capacity and potential interpersonal difficulties.

Neuropsychological assessment in schizophrenia continues to have important research and clinical applications. Cognitive assessments have been useful in identifying a subgroup of patients with more prominent negative symptoms, neuroanatomic abnormalities, and poor course of illness (Andreasen 1982a; Keilp et al. 1988; Shelton and Weinberger 1986). Neuropsychological assessments can be useful in assessing deterioration in intellectual resources and in identifying patients likely to have impaired role functioning.

**Extrapyramidal rating scales.** Since extrapyramidal symptoms (EPS) are a major source of morbidity in schizophrenia, it is both clinically sound and ethically necessary (Wettstein

1985) to include regular and ongoing EPS assessments in the clinical management of schizophrenia. Unfortunately, current clinical practice may be seriously inadequate, as underrecognition of clinically significant EPS ranges from 50 to 90% (Weiden et al. 1987). This problem arises partly because clinicians usually do not use standardized EPS ratings. It seems reasonable to assume that the routine clinical implementation of EPS scales would improve diagnostic rates.

EPS can be subdivided into acute dystonic reactions, akathisia, akinesia, parkinsonism, and tardive dyskinesia. Acute dystonic reactions can be rated by a section of the Extrapyramidal Symptom Rating Scale (ESRS) (Chouinard et al. 1979). The acute and focal nature of these events makes them easy to quantify, with the important caveat that a historical rating from patient and nursing staff is essential due to the intermittent nature of dystonic reactions, which often are not observable on physical examination.

Akathisia is included as a component of most EPS rating scales such as the ESRS and the Simpson-Angus Parkinsonism Scale (Simpson and Angus 1970). However, these scales tend to "bury" akathisia among other parkinsonian symptoms and minimize the serious behavioral toxicity associated with this side effect. Therefore, use of an independent akathisia scale is recommended, such as the Van Putten and May scale (1978). Furthermore, akathisia has both motoric and subjective components which do not always coexist for any patient. Therefore, akathisia ratings should always include subjective and objective (motoric) components.

Akinesia can either be scored as a subcomponent of any standard parkinsonism scale, or separately from parkinsonism signs such as bradykinesia, masked facies, and decreased gestures on the ESRS. If the Simpson-Angus scale is used, akinesia is not heavily emphasized, so akinesia should be rated separately on an akinesia scale (e.g., Rifkin et al. 1975) or a parkinsonism scale weighted towards akinesia. The ESRS and Webster's scale (Webster 1968) have several akinesia subcomponents. Other parkinsonism signs of tremor, rigidity, and motor weakness need to be rated separately from akinesia and are included in the ESRS and Simpson-Angus.

Tardive dyskinesia (TD) is a movement disorder that can be quantified by major body area components, type of dyskinetic movement, and global severity (which can either be frequency or amplitude). A general rule of thumb for TD is that the more detailed and specific the movements measured, the less reliable their ratings will be (Gardos et al. 1977). However, global TD scores are often sufficiently reliable across raters. Therefore, for routine clinical follow-up, the AIMS scale (AIMS 1976)—a widely accepted 5-point measure of global body area dyskinesia—is an adequate and widely used measure. For research purposes and for more complicated cases, TD is best assessed with more detailed scales like the Rockland Scale (Simpson et al. 1979) or the ESRS. A brief TD scale that is a compromise between global and detailed assessments that emphasize type of dyskinesia is the Abbreviated Dyskinesia Scale (ADS) derived from the Rockland Scale. Most scales (with the exception of AIMS and ESRS) do not include subjective distress ratings and lack historical ratings or disability assessments. In these crucial areas, the clinician is left to his or her own devices pending improved rating scale development, although behavioral toxicity ratings are available (Campbell and Palij 1985; Van Putten 1974).

Clinical ratings for EPS need to be supplemented with physician/staff training and knowledge of the differential diagnosis of EPS. While the accuracy of EPS rating scales is limited to the rater's diagnostic abilities, mandatory EPS ratings serve to call clinical attention to EPS syndromes as well as create a standardized EPS record. If a patient has never received neuroleptics, all pertinent EPS scales should be completed to create a baseline quantitative record and to help rule out neurologic or psychiatric diagnoses that present with movement disorders (e.g., Huntington's chorea, cocaine abuse). On hospital admission, we recommend incorporating EPS assessment and a TD examination into the routine medical history and physical examination form. Such documentation will help alert clinicians to the past EPS history (e.g., dystonia) and/or the need for anticholinergic therapy. If an acutely ill patient recently received neuroleptics, it is vitally important to rule out worsening EPS (i.e., akathisia or neuroleptic malignant syndrome) as the cause of psychiatric symptoms. During acute hospitalization, the dystonia, akathisia, and akinesia assessments should be performed at least every other week. Ratings of TD do not need to be done as frequently; a baseline and discharge AIMS is adequate for routine cases. Outpatients need periodic TD examinations (e.g., every 6 months).

**Social and occupational functioning.** One of the hallmarks of schizophrenia is the debilitating effect of the illness on the day-to-day functioning of the individual in the community. While psychotic symptoms may be adequately controlled with pharmacological agents, chronic social and occupational deficits are less likely to be resolved by such treatments. Such deficits reduce the quality of life and cause problems in social, family, leisure time, and occupational role functioning.

The earliest measures of social adjustment were designed to evaluate posthospital adjustment of patients discharged from the hospital to treatment programs in the community (Weissman et al. 1981). With enhanced community-based treatment modalities and a growing emphasis on involvement of family in outpatient treatment programs for schizophrenia, it has become commonly recognized that the patient's social skills, social support system, and the frequency and quality of the patient's relationships with others constitute important dimensions of outcome.

Measures of premorbid social adjustment may be the most powerful tools in predicting long-term treatment outcome and course of illness (Strauss and Carpenter 1977). It appears that good premorbid social skills may insulate against deterioration of functioning. A thorough evaluation of patients' social and occupational functioning before onset of illness (and between episodes) is prerequisite to good clinical treatment planning and preparation for the patient's return to the community. It provides important information for discussing prognosis with the patient and family, and can guide decisions about rehabilitation treatment (e.g., low level day hospital vs. more aggressive resocialization).

Information regarding the patient's past and current role functioning is generally obtained from five sources—patient, significant other, clinician, other professionals in the community, and medical records. The Social Adjustment Scale-II (SAS-II), based on the Social Adjustment Interview (Schooler et al. 1979), has been adapted for assessment of social, occupational, and family functioning with a schizophrenic population. The SAS-II includes scales that permit assessment of functioning over 4 weeks before interview in the work role, household role, parental role, extended family role, conjugal and nonconjugal sexual role, romantic involvement, social and leisure activities, and assessment of the patient's personal wellbeing. Questions are designed for assessment of instrumental and affective components of functioning in each domain. One particularly desirable feature is the structuring of questions to take into account the particular living situation and needs of the schizophrenic patient.

Self-report instruments for assessment of level of functioning in schizophrenic patients include the Community Adaptation Schedule (CAS; Burnes and Roen 1967), the Social Stress and Functioning Inventory for Psychotic Disorders (SSFIPD, Patient and Informant Versions; Serban 1978), and the Denver Community Mental Health Questionnaire (Ciarlo and Reihman 1977). Family informant measures include the Katz Adjustment Scales (KAS-R; Katz and Lyerly 1963), the Personal and Role Adjustment Scale (PARS; Ellsworth et al. 1968), and the Social Behavior Assessment Schedule (SBAS; Platt et al. 1980). The Role Activity Performance Scale (RAPS; Good-Ellis et al. 1987) is a semistructured interview schedule that permits assessment of variable time frames (from 1 to 18 months) on each of several roles. It is designed to make use of information gathered from patient, family, and other sources, permitting the clinician to plot the longitudinal course of deterioration or improvement. Completing these scales based on the patient and family informants early in the course of treatment can help guide prognostic judgments, and help tailor discharge planning of hospitalized patients to the expected intermorbid functioning. Assessing stable patients early in treatment can similarly help guide the development of realistic treatment aims.

**Life events and social environment.** Research findings indicate that reducing social stressors can be as effective as neuroleptic treatment in preventing relapse (Vaughn and Leff 1976). This underscores the need to consider social and environmental factors as well as pharmacological treatments in the clinical management of schizophrenia. Two major lines of investigation have yielded important information concerning the influence of social environment on schizophrenia: 1) "life-events" research has directed attention to the impact of traumatic life events on the vulnerable individual; and 2) research on family interaction has shown that modification of the social environment can reduce relapse rates.

A sizable literature documents the association between life events and the onset and exacerbation of schizophrenia (Brown and Birley 1968; Lukoff et al. 1984). Moreover, life events appear to be most strongly associated with relapse in patients who are compliant with their maintenance medication regimen (Leff et al. 1973). Clinicians need to be alert to impending and recent stressors, and methods for systematic assessment of life changes are now available. For example, standard life-events interview procedures (e.g., the Social Readjustment Rating Scale developed by Holmes and Rahe in 1967) offer an assessment of common stressors, and also the potential for increased stress—a factor associated with onset of psychotic symptoms (Uhlenhuth and Paykel 1973).

Assessment of chronic stressors (e.g., expressed emotion) can be of greatest utility in the prophylactic treatment of nonpsychotic symptoms such as anxiety and depression (Harder et al. 1980; Uhlenhuth and Paykel 1973). Also relevant in assessing chronic stressors and the individual's capacity for coping with stressful life events is the assessment of available social supports and the social network with which the patient has contact (Sarason et al. 1983). Careful clinical assessment of the availability of social supports and the density of the social network can give some indication of what to expect in terms of need for a structured treatment setting or adjunct support services.

**Longitudinal clinical assessment.** Regular quantitative monitoring of symptoms may also ensure more reliable objective evaluations than open-ended, impressionistic clinical assessments. The linear graphing of patient response over time (using quantitative ratings on standard clinical measures) can provide excellent visual documentation of the effectiveness of treatment plans, and can play a major role in discharge and disposition planning. Accurately determining a patient's expected level of functioning and need for supportive care can often make the difference between a revolving door of rehospitalizations and a progressive return to a higher level of functioning. Longitudinal data that can be reviewed together with the patients and their families can facilitate acceptance of outpatient programs.

**Training for standardized assessments.** For clinicians in a clinic or group-practice setting, regular meetings for the purpose of discussing clinical ratings improves the reliability (and probably the validity) of ratings. Such meetings for training (preferably including a clinician with training in the use of scales) are particularly useful for teaching clinicians to use terms in similar ways. If several different clinicians together interview a patient and then independently complete a rating scale, the discussion of rating disagreements in staff meetings can be particularly informative. Such discussions are an informative way to learn about the idiosyncrasies of how different clinicians (including oneself!) interpret clinical phenomena. In hospital or clinic settings, staff meetings to practice the use of rating scales can desensitize staff to quantitative rating scales, making their use a more natural part of clinical routine.

## Summary

Patients with schizophrenia present several unique challenges with respect to diagnostic evaluation and clinical assessment. The clinical use of rating instruments developed for research purposes can add to the comprehensiveness and reliability of assessments. Such procedures can help clinicians conduct more systematic longitudinal assessments, focus attention on both positive and deficit features of the illness, and direct attention to the less obvious or underemphasized features of a patient's clinical presentation. Much as the quantitative assessment of biological abnormalities advanced the understanding and treatment of medical disorders, the use of quantitative behavioral rating instruments can significantly enhance the quality of psychiatric care. These instruments can also play a major role in training individuals how to systematically and comprehensively assess patients. Although contemporary assessment strategies are far from the final stage of refinement, they are a major supplement to but not a substitute for sound clinical judgment.

## References

AIMS, in ECDEU Assessment Manual. Edited by Guy W. Rockville, MD, U.S. Department of Health, Education, and Welfare, 1976, pp 534–537

American Psychiatric Association: Diagnostic and Statistical Manual of Mental Disorders, Third Edition, Revised. Washington, DC, American Psychiatric Association, 1987

Andreasen N: The clinical assessment of thought, language, and communication, II: diagnostic significance. Arch Gen Psychiatry 36:1325–1330, 1979

Andreasen N: Negative symptoms in schizophrenia: definition and reliability. Arch Gen Psychiatry 39:784–788, 1982a

Andreasen N: Negative vs. positive schizophrenia: definition and validity. Arch Gen Psychiatry 39:789–794, 1982b

Andreasen N: The scale for the assessment of negative symptoms (SANS). Iowa City, The University of Iowa, 1983

Andreasen N: The scale for the assessment of positive symptoms (SAPS). Iowa City, The University of Iowa, 1984

Andreasen N: The diagnosis of schizophrenia. Schizophr Bull 13:9–22, 1987

Beck A, Ward H, Mendelson M, et al: An inventory for measuring depression. Arch Gen Psychiatry 4:561–571, 1961

Beck A, Weissman A, Lester D, et al: Measurement of pessimism: the Beck Hopelessness Scale. J Consult Clin Psychol 42:861–865, 1974

Bleuler E: Dementia Praecox or the Group of Schizophrenias. Translated by Zinkin J. New York, International Universities Press, 1950

Brown G, Birley J: Crises and life changes and the onset of schizophrenia. J Health Soc Behav 9:203, 1968

Burnes A, Roen S: Social roles and adaptation to the community. Community Ment Health J 3:153–158, 1967

Campbell M, Palij J: Measurement of side effects including tardive dyskinesia. Psychopharmacol Bull 21:1063–1080, 1985

Carpenter W, Douglas W, Alphs L: Treatment of negative symptoms. Schizophr Bull 3:440–452, 1985

Chapman L, Chapman J: Disordered thought in schizophrenia. New Jersey, Prentice-Hall, 1973

Chapman L, Chapman J: Scales for rating psychotic and psychoticlike experiences as continua. Schizophr Bull 6:476–489, 1980

Chouinard G, Annabele C, Ross-Chouinard A, et al: Ethopropazine and benztropine in neuroleptic-induced parkinsonism. J Clin Psychiatry 40:73–81, 1979

Ciarlo J, Reihman J: The Denver Community Mental Health Questionnaire: development of a multidimensional program evaluation, in Program Evaluation for Mental Health: Methods, Strategies, and Participants. Edited by Coursey RD, Specter GA, Murrell SA, et al. New York, Grune & Stratton, 1977

Derogatis L, Lipman R, Covi L: SCL-90: an outpatient psychiatric rating scale: preliminary report. Psychopharmacol Bull 9:13–27, 1973

Drake R, Gates C, Cotton P, et al: Suicide among schizophrenics: who is at risk? J Nerv Ment Dis 172:613–619, 1984

Endicott J, Spitzer R: A diagnostic interview: schedule for affective disorders and schizophrenia. Arch Gen Psychiatry 35:837–844, 1978

Endicott J, Spitzer R, Fleiss J, et al: The global assessment scale. Arch Gen Psychiatry 33:766–771, 1976

Ellsworth R, Foster L, Childers B, et al: Hospital and community adjustment as perceived by psychiatric patients, their families and staff. J Consult Clin Psychol Monograph 32(5, Pt. 2), 1968

Falloon I, Boyd J, McGill C, et al: Family management in the prevention of morbidity of schizophrenia. Arch Gen Psychiatry 42:887–896, 1985

Gardos G, Cole JO, La Brie R: The assessment of tardive dyskinesia. Arch Gen Psychiatry 34:1206–1212, 1977

Goldberg S: Negative and deficit symptoms in schizophrenia do respond to neuroleptics. Schizophr Bull 11:453–460, 1985

Good-Ellis M, Fine S, Spencer J, et al: Development of a role activity performance scale. Am J Occup Ther 41:232–241, 1987

Hamilton M: Development of a rating scale for primary depressive illness. British Journal of Social and Clinical Psychology 6:278–296, 1967

Harder D, Strauss J, Kokes R, et al: Life events and psychopathology severity among first psychiatric admissions. J Abnorm Psychol 89:165–180, 1980

Harrow M, Quinlan D: Is disordered thinking unique to schizophrenia? Arch Gen Psychiatry 34:15–21, 1977

Harrow M, Quinlan D: Disordered thinking and schizophrenic psychopathology. New York, Gardner Press, 1985

Hogarty G, Anderson C, Reiss D, et al: Family psychoeducation, social skills training and maintenance chemotherapy in the aftercare treatment of schizophrenia. Arch Gen Psychiatry 43:633–642, 1986

Holmes TH, Rahe R: The social readjustment rating scale. J Psychosom Res 11:213–218, 1967

Katz MM, Lyerly S: Methods for measuring adjustment and social behavior in the community, I: rationale, description, discriminative validity and scale development. Psychol Rep 13:503–535, 1963

Keilp J, Sweeney J, Jacobsen P, et al: Cognitive impairment in schizophrenia: specific relations to ventricular size and negative symptomatology. Biol Psychiatry 24:47–55, 1988

Kraepelin E: Dementia Praecox and Paraphrenia. Translated by Barclay RM. Edinburgh, E. and S. Livingstone, 1919

Leff J, Hirsch S, Rhode P, et al: Life events and maintenance therapy in schizophrenic relapse. Br J Psychiatry 136:659–660, 1973

Lewine R, Fogg L, Meltzer H: Assessment of negative and positive symptoms in schizophrenia. Schizophr Bull 9:368–376, 1983

Lukoff D, Snyder K, Ventura J, et al: Life events, familial stress, and coping in the developmental course of schizophrenia. Schizophr Bull 10:258–292, 1984

Miles C: Conditions predisposing to suicide: a review. J Nerv Ment Dis 164:231–246, 1977

Minnesota Multiphasic Personality Inventory. Minneapolis, University of Minnesota Press, 1943

Overall J, Gorham D: The brief psychiatric rating scale. Psychol Rep 10:799–812, 1960

Platt S, Weyman A, Hirsch S, et al: The Social Behaviour Assessment Schedule (SBAS): rationale, contents, scoring and reliability of a new interview schedule. Soc Psychiatry 15:43–55, 1980

Rifkin A, Quitkin F, Klein D: Akinesia. Arch Gen Psychiatry 32:672–674, 1975

Sarason I, Levine H, Basham R, et al: Assessing social support: the social support questionnaire. J Pers Soc Psychol 44:127–139, 1983

Schooler N, Hogarty G, Weissman M: Social Adjustment Scale II (SAS II), in Materials for Community Mental Health Program Evaluators. Edited by Hargreaves WA, Attkisson CC, Sorenson JE. (Publ. No. 79-328.) Washington, DC, U.S. Department of Health and Human Services, 1979

Serban G: Social Stress and Functioning Inventory for Psychotic Disorders (SSFIPD): measurement and prediction of schizophrenics' community adjustment. Compr Psychiatry 19:337–347, 1978

Shelton R, Weinberger D: X-ray computerized tomography studies in schizophrenia: a review and synthesis, in Handbook of Schizophrenia, Vol 1: The Neurology of Schizophrenia. Edited by Nasrallah H, Weinberger D. New York, Elsevier, 1986

Simpson G, Angus J: Drug induced extrapyramidal disorders. Acta Psychiatr Scand 45 (Suppl 212):11–19, 1970

Simpson GM, Lee JH, Zoubok B, et al: A rating scale for tardive dyskinesia. Psychopharmacology 64:171–179, 1979

Solovay M, Shenton M, Holzman P: Comparative studies of thought disorders, I: mania and schizophrenia. Arch Gen Psychiatry 44:13–20, 1987

Spitzer R, Endicott J, Robins E: Research Diagnostic Criteria: rationale and reliability. Arch Gen Psychiatry 35:773–782, 1978

Spitzer R, Williams J, Gibbon M, et al: Structured Clinical Interview for DSM-III-R–Patient Version. New York, Biometrics Research Department, New York State Psychiatric Institute, 1988

Strauss JS, Carpenter WT: Prediction of outcome in schizophrenia, III: two-year outcome and its predictors. Arch Gen Psychiatry 34:159–163, 1977

Uhlenhuth E, Paykel E: Symptom configuration and life events. Arch Gen Psychiatry 28:744–748, 1973

Van Putten T: Why do schizophrenic patients refuse to take their drugs? Arch Gen Psychiatry 31:67–72, 1974

Van Putten T, May P: Subjective response as a predictor of outcome in pharmacotherapy: the consumer has a point. Arch Gen Psychiatry 35:477–480, 1978

Vaughn C, Leff J: The measurement of expressed emotion in the families of psychiatric patients. British Journal of Social and Clinical Psychology 15:157–165, 1976

Webster D: Critical analysis of the disability in Parkinson's disease. Modern Treatments 5:257–282, 1968

Weiden PJ, Mann J, Haas G, et al: Clinical nonrecognition of neuroleptic-induced movement disorders: a cautionary study. Am J Psychiatry 144:1148–1153, 1987

Weissman M, Sholomskas M, John K: The assessment of social adjustment: an update. Arch Gen Psychiatry 38:1250–1258, 1981

Wettstein R: Legal aspects of neuroleptic-induced movement disorders, in Legal Medicine. Edited by Wecht C. New York, Praeger Scientific, 1985

# Chapter 6

# *Assessment of Anxiety Disorders*

**M. KATHERINE SHEAR, M.D.**
**JANET KLOSKO, Ph.D.**
**MINNA R. FYER, M.D.**

# Chapter 6
# *Assessment of Anxiety Disorders*

**I**n the last few decades there have been major advances in the treatment of anxiety disorder patients. The practicing clinician has a range of highly effective and focused treatment modalities available for use. These include medication, cognitive behavioral treatment, and a combination of the two. In order to provide patients with the optimum available treatment, practitioners need to be able to diagnose and assess symptomatology accurately and to follow target symptoms through treatment. Structured assessment measures are available that can assist the clinician in this task. Structured assessment can also be useful in conducting consultations or rethinking treatment plans of refractory patients. In addition, research to elucidate pathophysiology and psychopathologic features of anxiety disorders is ongoing, and new treatment strategies are being developed. It is important that clinicians be familiar with diagnostic and symptom rating scales in order to be able to read research reports critically and make decisions about using new treatment modalities.

Structured assessment methods are central to research work, but such measures are less widely used by practitioners in the field. The purpose of this chapter is to provide the clinician with an overview of the kinds of assessment measures that have been developed for patients with anxiety disorders and to suggest ways they may be incorporated usefully into clinical practice. Scales include diagnostic instruments, symptom scales, functional impairment measures, treatment side-effect ratings, self-monitoring diaries, and structured behavioral testing pro-

115

cedures. We have organized the chapter to include 1) a description of instruments that might be useful to clinicians, 2) clinical guidelines for using structured assessments in patients with anxiety disorders, and 3) assessment issues in research studies.

## Description of Instruments

Most clinical psychometric assessment is done with structured interviews and/or self-report questionnaires. Self-monitoring with diaries and in vivo behavioral testing are specialized techniques that we will also explain.

Structured diagnostic interviews formalize the process through which the clinician and patient discuss the patient's presenting problem. They replace an open-ended, freely exploratory interview with one that is framed and directed by a series of predetermined questions. This mode of interviewing has the advantage of ensuring that the clinician will obtain information directly about all relevant symptoms and will not be led away from important clinical data by the patient's avoidance. In our experience, patients with anxiety disorders are particularly prone to avoid discussing their symptoms. Phobic patients typically avoid detailed discussion of phobic avoidance because even thinking about phobic stimuli raises anxiety. Patients with obsessive-compulsive disorder avoid discussing their symptoms because of triggering anxiety and compulsive urges, because of shame about behaviors they consider "crazy," and because of magical ideas that talking about specific symptoms may have negative consequences. Anxiety patients often feel themselves to be abnormal and strange because they are aware of the irrational nature of their symptoms. Because of this, they usually find structured interviews reassuring. The questions demonstrate an understanding of the patient's syndrome, communicate to the patient that other people experience these symptoms, and help organize symptoms in a coherent way. The disadvantage of structured interviewing is that it interferes with the patient's opportunity to tell his or her own story. Important connections in the patient's mind between symptoms and life events and/or interpersonal relationships may be obscured.

Clinical symptom rating scales, self-report questionnaires, and self-monitoring diaries are structured formats for symptom assessment. Each has advantages and disadvantages. Because the scales are standardized and norms have been developed for many of them, they provide more objective information than an open-ended clinical interview. Because they involve subjective patient reporting, they are less objective than behavioral observation or physiologic measurements. The section that follows describes the available assessment tools. We discuss ways of integrating unstructured with structured interviewing techniques.

## Diagnostic Instruments

**Anxiety Disorders Interview Schedule–Revised (ADIS-R).** The ADIS-R scale was developed over a period of years by staff of the Phobia and Anxiety Disorders Clinic, Albany, New York, a clinic funded by the National Institute of Mental Health (NIMH) to study classification and treatment of anxiety disorders (DiNardo et al. 1985). It is a structured interview designed to provide differential diagnosis among anxiety disorders according to the Diagnostic and Statistical Manual of Mental Disorders (Third Edition, Revised; DSM-III-R) criteria, and to diagnose or rule out psychosis, substance abuse, major affective disorders, and somatoform disorders. It assesses comorbidity of anxiety disorders with one another and with other mental disorders; it allows the interviewer to arrive at primary and additional diagnoses and to rate severity of all diagnoses.

The ADIS-R combines detailed symptom ratings of panic, generalized anxiety, and phobic avoidance with global ratings of interference in functioning, psychiatric history, medical history, and drug and alcohol use. In addition to diagnoses, the ADIS-R provides information for functional behavioral analyses of anxiety disorders. It assesses situational and cognitive factors that influence anxiety. It includes the Hamilton Anxiety Scale (Hamilton 1959) and the Hamilton Depression Scale (Hamilton 1960), both of which may be omitted at the interviewer's discretion.

The organization of the ADIS-R permits interviewing to proceed in an integrated and smooth fashion. Suggested phrasing of questions appears in bold italic print. Because most questions require the patient to elaborate, the interviewer uses clinical judgment to evaluate responses and to determine the flow of subsequent questions. To assist in this process, the ADIS-R provides brief descriptions of DSM-III-R criteria. The content, wording, and arrangement of questions evolved through years of experience interviewing clinic patients and diagnosing them with DSM-III, and more recently DSM-III-R, criteria. Several sections begin with a yes-or-no question. A negative response permits the interviewer to skip the section dealing with that disorder. Rows of stars set apart skip instructions from the text of the interview.

Because the interview is complex, the clinician must become familiar with the text and its accompanying manual before using it. Skilled evaluators take about 2 hours to complete the interview, excluding Hamilton Scales. Clinically, patients generally find the ADIS-R helpful; it organizes their experience and gives them a sense of being understood.

Researchers at the Albany Anxiety Disorders Clinic currently are collecting norms on the ADIS-R across a number of populations, including populations of subjects who fall within various anxiety, depression, and normal categories. Data generally have indicated good reliability for DSM-III diagnoses with the ADIS-R (DiNardo et al. 1983; Barlow, in press).

**The Structured Clinical Interview for DSM-III (SCID).** The SCID was developed as a research and teaching instrument to focus attention of evaluators on establishing DSM-III diagnoses (Spitzer and Williams 1987). The process begins with a semistructured overview of current symptoms and past psychiatric history. Significant life events and functional impairment due to psychiatric disorder are noted. The interviewer then proceeds to a series of highly structured questions that determine the presence or absence of diagnosable DSM-III Axis I disorders. Each symptom is rated as absent, possible, or definite. Diagnoses are made based on definite positive-symptom ratings. A category of subthreshold diagnoses is also available.

The Axis I SCID has been customized for different research teams and is available in a number of forms. For example, a major pharmaceutical company has been involved in multinational studies of panic disorder, and SCIDs have been developed for use in these studies. Accurate use of the SCID requires some training. Depending on the version used, time to administer varies from 1 to 2 hours.

**The Schedule for Affective Disorders and Schizophrenia–Lifetime Anxiety Version (SADS-LA).** The SADS-LA, a modified version of the SADS-L, is a semistructured, clinician-administered interview that requires approximately 1½ to 3 hours to complete (Mannuzza et al. 1985). It was developed primarily for use in situations that require a detailed picture of both anxiety symptoms and other diagnoses over the patient's lifetime. The SADS-LA provides a thorough general psychiatric assessment, but the anxiety section may be used independently as an adjunct to a clinical interview or along with another semistructured diagnostic schedule.

The SADS-LA is unique in that it yields DSM-III, DSM-III-R, and RDC anxiety diagnoses. It also focuses on anxiety symptoms that do not quite meet diagnostic criteria, such as avoidant tendencies or near panics. The interview includes an extensive survey of fears (e.g., of heights, needles, performance), a section that assesses demoralization secondary to anxiety disorders, and a life chart that provides a longitudinal, visual presentation of the patient's psychiatric symptoms, diagnoses, and life events.

Initial test-retest reliability $\kappa$ for DSM-III panic disorder, agoraphobia with panic attacks, social phobia, obsessive-compulsive disorder, and separation anxiety disorder are good and are comparable to those obtained with the ADIS-R (Barlow, in press). As with the ADIS-R, reliability for simple phobia is not good, due to disagreement about the degree of impairment required to meet case threshold.

### Symptom Rating Scales

Various standardized questionnaires measure anxiety, panic, phobic avoidance, social anxiety, and obsessive-compulsive symptomatology. They may be administered pre- and posttreatment and/or at intervals throughout treatment to assess treatment progress. The scales reviewed here include clinician-rated and patient self-report types. The list we present is not exhaustive but includes some of the older, widely used instruments and some that are newer and incorporate more recent conceptualizations of the syndromes.

**General anxiety symptomatology.** Perhaps the most well-known and widely used measure of anxiety is the Hamilton Anxiety Scale (Hamilton 1959). Its use allows comparison with other populations of anxiety patients in the research literature. The scale is completed with a clinical interview that assesses intensity of cognitive and somatic anxiety symptoms on a 0 to 5 scale, from "none" to "severe, grossly disabling." Symptoms rated include such items as muscle tension, phobic symptoms, degree of worry, cardiovascular and respiratory symptoms, and appearance at the interview. Ratings are subtyped into psychic and somatic groups. There are several limitations of this measure. The scale mixes symptoms from all anxiety disorders, and scores are not useful in discriminating one anxiety disorder from another. Questions relevant to depression are included with the anxiety questions so the scale does not clearly distinguish anxiety from depression.

Another widely used questionnaire measure of general anxiety symptomatology is the State-Trait Anxiety Inventory (STAI;

Spielberger et al. 1970; revised by Spielberger et al. 1980). This very brief self-report questionnaire generates separate state (situation specific) and trait (general) anxiety ratings. Although the trait scale originally was designed to measure a stable personality dimension, it has been found to change in a consistent and meaningful way after psychological treatment (Mathews 1984). The scale is not specific for anxiety, but correlates well with a personality dimension of neuroticism on the Maudsley (Eysenck) Personality Inventory (Eysenck and Eysenck 1968). Items include anxiety symptoms (i.e., "some unimportant thought runs through my mind and bothers me," "I get in a state of tension or turmoil as I think over my recent concerns and interests") and depressive symptoms (i.e., "I feel like crying," "I wish I could be as happy as others seem to be"). Patients rate symptoms on 1 to 4 scales that, for trait anxiety, range from "almost never" to "almost always," and for state anxiety from "not at all" to "very much so." Good concurrent validity and test-retest reliability (for the trait scale) have been demonstrated for use of the measure (Spielberger et al. 1970). The state scale, designed to measure feelings occurring at the time of completing the questionnaire, is more focused on anxiety symptoms. However, the stability of the scale is problematic because it may change based on immediate situational factors.

A relatively new self-report questionnaire that measures general anxiety symptomatology is the Anxiety Sensitivity Index (Reiss et al. 1986). It measures sensitivity to, and distress about, various physical sensations associated with anxiety. It seems to have good reliability and validity (Maller and Reiss, in press). Another scale, the Cognitive-Somatic Anxiety Questionnaire (Schwartz et al. 1978) supplies separate scores for cognitive and somatic components. It contains 14 items, one-half cognitive and one-half somatic, in random order. Subjects are instructed to rate the degree to which they generally experience each symptom on a 1 to 5 scale. Sums of ratings are computed separately and together to yield cognitive, somatic, and total scores. There is evidence the scale is valid (Schwartz et al. 1978). A third measure, the Sheehan Patient Rated Anxiety Scale (SPRAS; Sheehan 1983b), has been used in a number of medication treatment studies. It assesses severity of individual anxiety symptoms in the past week. Subjects rate severity on 0 to 4 scales in terms of how much symptoms bothered or distressed them. Items include ratings of physiological, cognitive, and behavioral anxiety symptoms, and global ratings of anxiety and depression. In addition, subjects rate severity of subtypes of anxiety and panic: major or minor spontaneous panic attacks, anticipatory anxiety episodes, and situational panic attacks.

Likert-type scales are used for global self-ratings of interference in functioning produced by anxiety problems. An example is a scale that asks patients to rate the extent to which symptoms interfere in work, social life/leisure activities, and family life/home responsibilities. Severity of impairment is rated on 0 to 10 scales that range from "not at all" to "very severe."

**Measures of panic.** The Sheehan Panic and Anxiety Attack Scales (Sheehan 1983a) measure frequency, intensity, and duration of episodes of panic and anxiety, both in the past month and in the past week. Like the SPRAS, the scales measure major spontaneous and situational panic attacks, spontaneous and situational limited-symptom episodes ("minor" panic attacks with 1 or 2 symptoms), and anticipatory anxiety episodes. Also like the SPRAS, these scales have been used widely in medication studies.

The Agoraphobia Cognitions Questionnaire and the Body Sensations Questionnaire (Chambless et al. 1984) are two questionnaires that assess cognitive and physiological symptoms of panic, respectively. They are suitable for assessment of treatment progress, particularly for interventions that are primarily cognitive or psychophysiological, and for patients who exhibit panic with little agoraphobic avoidance. Both questionnaires appear to have adequate psychometric properties (Chambless et al. 1984).

**Measures of agoraphobic avoidance.** The Fear Questionnaire (Marks and Mathews 1979) is primarily a phobia rating scale. The first part consists of a fear survey schedule on which subjects rate degree of avoidance of 12 objects or situations. The schedule provides a subscale score of the subject's main phobia, described in the subject's own words, and subscale scores for agoraphobia, social phobia, and blood and injury phobias. The second part consists of Likert-type scales of anxiety and depression and a global rating scale of severity of overall phobia symptomatology. The questionnaire is completed by the patient and usually takes only a short time. A recent NIMH conference on anxiety disorders recommended the Fear Questionnaire as a standard measure for all research studies on phobia (National Institute of Mental Health 1980). The agoraphobia subscale is used widely, and thus permits comparison of patients to numerous anxiety research populations. Mavissakalian (1986a, 1986b) suggests that scores greater than 30 represent cases of severe agoraphobia and that scores less than 10 represent cases of good clinical response to treatment.

The Mobility Inventory for Agoraphobia (Chambless et al. 1985) is a relatively new questionnaire that measures primarily agoraphobic avoidance behavior, although it also measures some social and simple phobic avoidance. It presents 30 phobic situations, which patients rate on a 0 to 5 scale, from "never avoid" to "always avoid." Examples of the situations include theaters, supermarkets, staying at home alone, being far away from home, and meeting strangers. Patients rate severity of avoidance both when accompanied and when alone. The authors report good reliability and validity data for the inventory.

**Measures of social anxiety.** One of the most widely used instruments for assessment of social anxiety is the Social Avoidance and Distress Scale (Watson and Friend 1969). The scale has 28 items, presented in true-or-false format. Examples of the various items include "It is easy for me to relax when I

123

am with strangers," "I would avoid walking up and joining a large group of people," and "I often want to get away from people." The authors present evidence that the scale is psychometrically valid for a subclinically social phobic sample.

The Fear of Negative Evaluation Scale (Watson and Friend 1969) measures disturbing thoughts about social disapproval common to socially anxious individuals. It contains 30 items in true-or-false format. Sample items include, "I rarely worry about seeming foolish to others," "When I am talking to someone, I worry about what they may be thinking about me," and "I am usually worried about what kind of impression I make." The authors present evidence that the scale is able to discriminate between groups of anxious and nonanxious subjects and that it demonstrates adequate reliability and validity.

The Irrational Beliefs Test (Jones 1969) assesses the irrational thinking styles that Albert Ellis (1962) suggests form the core of neurotic disorders. Research supports a relationship between scores on this questionnaire and anxiety (Goldfried and Sobocinski 1975), and it has been used as an assessment measure in studies of cognitive treatment of public speaking anxiety (Trexler and Karst 1972). Several questionnaires are available that measure social anxiety in specific situations. One questionnaire that has been used to measure public speaking anxiety is the Personal Report of Confidence as a Speaker (Paul 1966). A second example is the Social Interaction Self-Statement Test (Glass et al. 1982), which measures frequency of various cognitions in heterosexual social interactions. It has two subscales: the first measures frequency of positive cognitions, and the second measures frequency of negative cognitions. Patients rate items on a 1 to 5 scale, from "hardly ever had the thought," to "very often had the thought." Sample items include, "I hope I don't make a fool of myself," and "This is an awkward situation but I can handle it." There is evidence that the questionnaire has good reliability and that it is able to discriminate between socially competent and incompetent college students (Glass et al. 1982).

**Measures of obsessions and compulsions.** The most widely used measure of obsessive-compulsive disorder is the Maudsley Obsessional Compulsive Inventory (MOCI; Hodgson and Rachman 1977). The MOCI is a symptom checklist with 30 items, which patients rate for presence or absence. It yields a total score and four subscale scores for each of four common types of obsessive-compulsive behavior: checking, washing, doubting, and slowness. It seems to demonstrate good reliability (Sanavio and Vidotto 1985). The MOCI is completed by the patient. A similar self-report questionnaire that also is used widely is the Compulsive Activity Checklist (CAC; Philpott 1975). The CAC has a four-point scale, and items focus exclusively on specific compulsive behaviors. Adequate reliability has been demonstrated for a modified version of the CAC (Freund et al. 1987).

The Leyton Obsessional Inventory (Cooper 1970) is a measure of obsessions that contains 69 items, most of which measure obsessional symptoms; remaining items assess obsessive-compulsive personality traits. In addition, there is a short version of the Leyton Inventory (Allen and Tune 1975); in this version about one-half of the items measure obsessional symptoms and one-half measure personality traits. This measure has generally been found to be less useful than the MOCI.

**Likert-type rating scales.** Rating scales of anxiety, such as those introduced by Hafner and Marks (1976) and by Mathews et al. (1976), have been used widely in the literature to provide ratings of symptoms such as panic, general anxiety, phobic avoidance, and global interference in social and occupational functioning. The clinician constructs Likert-type scales, generally ranging from 0 to 8 or from 0 to 10, that assess severity of anxiety symptoms. Such scales can be administered to patients before and after treatment, or periodically throughout treatment, to track progress in symptom reduction. They can be administered by the clinician or completed by the patient. Scales might represent hierarchies of fearful symptoms, activities, or situations for the patient. When the scales are constructed on the basis of the patient's specific presenting picture, i.e., when they reflect the patient's specific pattern of phobic avoidance, they can be used to structure focused treatment strategies such as exposure practices. When scales are constructed for this use, it is important to include items that vary in difficulty from low to high, in order to help the patient gradually develop a sense of mastery and success and to help the patient test the limits of what he or she is capable of accomplishing.

### Self-Monitoring Diaries

The self-monitoring diary is a specialized form of self-reporting that involves continuous observation and recording of aspects of the patient's daily life. Diaries can be used to monitor frequency, intensity, and duration of symptoms; to elucidate the relationship of symptom episodes to triggering events; to identify cognitive, behavioral, and somatic aspects of symptomatology; and to track treatment effects and side effects. Structured diaries are available, but none has yet been subjected to psychometric testing. Research has demonstrated that self-monitoring of behavior is superior to retrospective recall in both accuracy and reliability. In addition, self-monitoring is a very helpful treatment device that helps to focus the patient's interest and attention on therapeutic work between treatment sessions. Self-monitoring requires the patient to put forth sustained effort and to focus on anxiety-provoking material. Researchers have developed procedures to improve accuracy and compliance with self-monitoring (Barlow et al. 1984). Such procedures include the therapist placing great emphasis on the importance of recording to the patient, particularly early in treatment; inclusion of verbal and written instructions on accurate self-monitoring, with frequent opportunities for practice both within and between treatment sessions; and careful review of returned records, with encouragement and feedback given to the patient. Careful attention to self-monitoring rewards both the clinician and patient with fruitful material for treatment sessions, in addition to tracking changes in anxiety symptomatology.

Self-monitoring diaries can also be used with phobic patients as a format for patients to record daily exposure to phobic situations. For example, one might instruct the patient to record amount of time away from home, the number and nature of exposure practices, duration of each practice, whether the patient was alone or accompanied, maximum anxiety, and anxiety on completion of the activity. Particularly for agoraphobia, research shows that amount of exposure practice predicts treatment outcome (Michelson et al. 1986).

Self-monitoring is particularly useful in treatment of panic attacks. Research indicates that retrospective self-reports of panic are subject to distortion and exaggeration (Turner et al., in press). In construction of a self-monitoring record for panic attacks, the clinician might instruct patients to record each panic attack that reaches a set criterion of severity, such as 4 or higher on a 0 to 8 scale (Barlow, in press). The patient might record the times at which the attack began and ended, maximum level of anxiety during the attack, the symptoms experienced during the attack (the clinician might provide the patient with a list the patient merely has to check off), and whether the subject considered the attack cued (situational) or spontaneous. The clinician might wish to instruct the patient to record a measure of anticipatory anxiety, such as average fear of having a panic attack that day, and daily medication use. We have used diaries to record the situation(s) in which panic occurred, associated behavior and cognitions, and the response (cognitive and behavioral) to the panic episode. An example of such a diary is included in the Appendix. A diary enables the clinician to track progress and to work in a cognitive behavioral mode to help the patient identify environmental, physiological, and/or cognitive cues that reliably precede and accompany panic attacks. These cues can then be used to design exposure experiences.

For social anxiety, a record of frequency, intensity, and duration of episodes of social anxiety is used. Avoidance of social situations, ratings of quality of behavioral performance during exposure practices, and relevant cognitions should be included. For general anxiety, we instruct the patient to record levels of anxiety using a time-sampling technique, such as recording of levels of anxiety at regular intervals throughout the day.

The usefulness of a diary in obsessive-compulsive patients is more variable. Some patients use it productively, while others develop compulsive rituals around completion of the diary. If a diary is used, the patient should record frequency, intensity, and duration of obsessive or compulsive episodes, with associated situational and internal cues. For obsessions, it is useful to obtain self-ratings of distress produced by the thoughts. If obsessive thoughts occur very often, overall duration of obsessive preoccupation rated at the end of each day can be used. For compulsions, patients record urges to perform rituals, as well as the rituals themselves. As treatment progresses, recording of urges may replace reporting of rituals.

### Direct Behavioral Observation

Behavioral observation refers to assessment by trained observers or significant others in the patient's environment of samples of behaviors that are a focus of treatment. Direct observation of overt behavior is helpful because ratings require a minimal level of inference. Thus, most researchers consider behavioral observation a form of measurement less subject to distortion than self-report measures. Analogue behavioral assessment involves observing the patient in a specific predesigned situation rather than simply observing the patient "free running" in his or her own environment.

The best known analogue form of behavioral observation of anxiety is the Behavioral Avoidance Test (BAT). Originally the BAT was used for assessment of simple phobia: subjects were presented with a phobic object, such as a snake, and instructed to approach it. Extent of avoidance behavior and self-reports of anxiety were recorded. Anxiety, usually recorded on a scale of 1–10 or 1–100, has been given the acronym SUDs (subjective units of distress). BATs have been extended to measurement of other anxiety disorders, such as agoraphobia and obsessive-compulsive disorder; for example, a patient with contamination fears might be instructed to approach and touch items that provoke obsessional fears, while reporting anxiety levels. For agoraphobic or social phobic patients, the clinician might accompany the patient into phobic situations, such as subways, buses, or supermarkets. In using a BAT with an agoraphobic patient, it is necessary to keep in mind that the presence of the therapist may markedly lower avoidance and anxiety ratings. Nevertheless, we have found this method useful for patients having problems with exposure treatment. The BAT can help identify triggers and responses to anxiety that the patient has not reported.

For social anxiety, role-play of relevant social phobic situations can provide the clinician with excellent measures of anxiety generated from social interactions. Role-play might include the clinician and, if possible, other confederates, such as therapy group members. Examples of social phobic situations suitable for role-play assessments are presentation of a speech before an audience, starting a conversation with a member of the opposite sex, and initiating discussion with an authority figure. The clinician can select situations for role-play on the basis of information gathered from interviews and from diary recordings. The Timed Behavioral Checklist (TBCL; Paul 1966) is a widely used observational measure of performance anxiety. It involves a 3-minute behavioral test divided into six 30-second observation intervals. In each interval, trained observers rate the subject for presence or absence of 20 anxiety signs. Occurrences of each behavior are summed across intervals and represented as an index of anxiety. TBCL scores thus range from 0 (no anxiety signs) to 120 (all 20 anxiety signs present in each of the six intervals). Sample signs of anxiety include pacing, swaying, shuffling of feet, hand tremors, clearing of the throat, quivering of the voice, perspiration, and blushing. The author reports high interrater reliability for the measure.

Behavioral observation does raise the problem of inference due to reactivity to the clinician. Particularly under mild or moderate degrees of anxiety, demand characteristics come into play and may exert large changes on performance (Paul and Bernstein 1973). Moreover, the presence of the clinician may add an element of reassurance (e.g., with agoraphobic subjects) or a further stressor (e.g., a performance anxious subject). To decrease the likelihood of reactivity, Williams (1985) suggests that behavioral tests include high anxiety items. Such items are less likely to be subject to demand characteristics and are more sensitive to changes that occur as a result of treatment. Williams notes further that it is important to eliminate active treatment ingredients, such as modeling and distraction, from behavioral tests as much as possible in order to produce more accurate reflections of natural behavior. Unobtrusive assessment is preferable, because obtrusive assessment procedures may influence the subject's performance. This effect applies particularly in cases of agoraphobia, where it is probable that the therapist functions as a safe person for the patient.

Behavioral tests may be standardized or individualized. Individualized tests typically are more relevant to clinicians; standardized testing conditions are more suitable to research, in which comparisons must be made among groups of individuals. However, clinicians who want to explore the magnitude of treatment effects by comparing a patient to research groups might find standardized tests useful. An example of a standardized test for agoraphobia is the behavioral "walk" (Barlow, in press), in which patients are instructed to walk the length of a 1-mile course that is divided into 20 equidistant stations, each marked with a natural landmark. Patients are instructed to return when they are finished or are unable to proceed further. The walk produces such measures as number of situations completed and anxiety ratings at each station.

If ambulatory monitoring equipment is available, continuous recording of heart rate can be added.

Individualized behavioral tests involve assessment of behaviors that are personally relevant to the patient through such procedures as imagery, the use of contrived situations, or experiments in the natural environment. Individualized tests are preferable to standardized tests in terms of sensitivity to treatment changes and generalization to other situations in the patient's life.

## Clinical Guidelines for Use of Structured Assessment

### Diagnosis and Treatment Planning

Patients who meet DSM-III-R criteria for anxiety disorders are seen commonly in practitioners' offices, but their presenting complaint is not always an anxiety-related symptom. A structured diagnostic assessment will help to identify the anxiety diagnosis and the target treatment symptoms. For example, a patient may present with marital problems or hypochondriacal symptoms that are not identifiable immediately as anxiety-related complaints. On closer questioning, the marital problems may be secondary to a social phobia. Hypochondriacal concerns may be related to a panic disorder or obsessive somatic preoccupations. A patient may not spontaneously elaborate anxiety-related symptoms. As mentioned above, phobic patients are often fearful that talking about their symptoms will raise their anxiety. Such patients have usually been told repeatedly by friends and family that their fears are groundless, and they feel ashamed that they are still afraid. Discussion of a phobic symptom focuses attention on the symptom and raises the possibility that the patient may have to face his or her fear. The use of a structured diagnostic instrument ensures that the clinician will not collude with the patient to avoid discussion of anxiety-provoking phobic symptoms.

The high prevalence of comorbidity is another reason why systematic diagnostic interviews are useful. The treating clinician needs a complete diagnostic picture of the patient. We now know that identification of one anxiety syndrome raises the likelihood that another anxiety diagnosis or affective illness is present as well. Each syndrome needs to be identified, and a decision about treatment approach needs to be made. It may be possible to plan a strategy focused on the primary symptoms that will also be effective in ameliorating the secondary diagnosis. Responsiveness of depression in the treatment of panic is an example. Associated diagnoses may also be important in predicting treatment outcome. For example, it has been shown that patients with panic disorder who have prominent obsessive-compulsive symptomatology respond poorly to medication treatment (Mellman and Uhde 1987). Patients with obsessive-compulsive disorder who have associated depression respond poorly to behavioral interventions (Barlow, in press).

### Conducting and Monitoring the Treatment

After the diagnosis is confirmed and symptoms are identified, it is useful to assess symptom severity and associated functional impairment. This can be accomplished using a group of the standard scales described above. Global illness severity and global improvement are also useful to track at intervals throughout the treatment. Global measures can be constructed using a Likert scale as described above. Symptom status and impairment should be followed during the course of treatment. Scores on symptom rating scales can be compared at intervals through the treatment. Likert scales of symptom intensity can be tracked. This facilitates targeting specific goals and identifying problem areas in the treatment. Diary keeping is an important adjunct to most anxiety disorder treatments. The diary varies in complexity depending on the type of treatment being conducted. For example, in a medication treatment of panic, diaries need only document number, intensity, and duration of panic episodes. In a cognitive-behavioral approach, diaries would include the elaborated stimulus-response information described above. Structured rating scales and behavioral observation techniques can be especially useful in identifying problem areas in a treatment. A patient who is not progressing as expected may have an unrecognized associated disorder. For example, an agoraphobic patient who was not responding well to a cognitive behavioral treatment was reassessed using a structured diagnostic interview. A previously unrecognized obsessive-compulsive disorder was identified and rated as moderately severe. The patient tearfully explained he had been too embarrassed to reveal to the clinician his obsessional thoughts. The treatment plan was reformulated to address the obsessive symptoms and the treatment began to progress.

A behavioral avoidance test may also be particularly useful in situations where exposure exercises are not reducing phobic anxiety and avoidance. For example, a patient with a subway phobia was observed after several months of ineffective treatment. The clinician was able to identify a series of avoidance behaviors that the patient neglected to report. The patient typically waited at the top of the stairs until he heard the subway coming. He then dashed through the turnstile, took the subway one stop, and left the station quickly. Another patient crept along the side of the station holding herself up by placing her hand against the wall. Once these behaviors were identified, the treatment incorporated direct questioning about them and instructions for modifying them.

### Treatment Termination and Follow-Up

The termination process is crucial in solidifying treatment gains and enhancing the likelihood of maintenance of the gains. A clear picture of the changes that have occurred in the treatment, as well as any problems that remain, is essential to this process. The therapist can use structured measures to assist in the process. The patient and therapist can review together the progress of treatment using diaries and/or sequential symptom ratings. A termination diagnostic instrument can be administered to clearly establish which aspects of the presenting syndrome have been alleviated, partially treated, or untreated. For example, a patient with panic disorder with severe agoraphobia may begin treatment with multiple, widespread phobias and an inability to leave his or her home unaccompanied. At termination, the patient may be moving freely within a certain boundary, but may still be unable to travel comfortably on an airplane or to drive over suspension bridges. The patient may feel that these are unimportant obstacles that he or she does not wish to confront. However, the clinician is wise to both underscore the treatment gains and identify remaining phobic avoidance that may, in fact, become a problem in the future. This approach may help prevent demoralization and relapse if the patient does find himself or herself confronted with the remaining phobias in the future.

## Summary and Conclusions

We live in an era when focused, time-limited, effective treatments are increasingly available and funding sources are supporting preferentially short-term interventions. Structured psychometric assessments can be used to support the organization and documentation of treatment programs. Structured diagnostic assessment is useful in characterizing and documenting the patient's symptom patterns. Specific symptom assessment measures and simple Likert-scale ratings can be used to focus and track effectiveness of treatment interventions. Structured assessments at termination can assist in clear communication to the patient of treatment gains. The use of rating scales represents an innovative approach to clinical treatment. We have reviewed the potential uses of structured assessment measures in clinical treatment of patients who meet diagnostic criteria for anxiety disorders or who have prominent anxiety symptoms. Each practitioner will need to explore and develop his or her own way of optimally using these tools.

# References

Allen JJ, Tune GS: The Lynfield obsessional/compulsive questionnaire. Scott Med J 201:21–26, 1975

Barlow DH: The dimensions of anxiety disorders, in Anxiety and the Anxiety Disorders. Edited by Tuma AH, Maser JD. Hillsdale, NJ, Lawrence Erlbaum Associates, 1984

Barlow DH: Anxiety and Its Disorders: The Nature and Treatment of Anxiety and Panic. New York, Guilford Press (in press)

Barlow DH, Hayes SC, Nelson RO: The Scientist-Practitioner: Research and Accountability in Clinical and Educational Settings. New York, Pergamon Press, 1984

Chambless DL, Caputo GC, Bright R, et al: Assessment of fear in agoraphobic cognitions questionnaire. J Consult Clin Psychol 52:1090–1097, 1984

Chambless DL, Caputo GC, Jasin SE, et al: The mobility inventory for agoraphobia. Behav Res Ther 23:35–44, 1985

Cooper J: The Leyton Obsessional Inventory. Psychol Med 1:48–64, 1970

DiNardo PA, O'Brien GT, Barlow DH, et al: Reliability of DSM-III anxiety disorder categories using a new structured interview. Arch Gen Psychiatry 40:1070–1074, 1983

DiNardo PA, Barlow DH, Cerny JA, et al: Anxiety Disorders Interview Schedule–Revised (ADIS-R). Albany, NY, Center for Stress and Anxiety Disorders, 1985

Ellis A: Reason and Emotion in Psychotherapy. New York, Lyle Stuart Press, 1962

Eysenck HA, Eysenck SBG: Manual for the Eysenck Personality Inventory. San Diego, CA, Educational and Industrial Testing Service, 1968

Freund B, Steketee GS, Foa EB: Compulsive activity checklist (CAC): psychometric analysis with obsessive-compulsive disorder. Behavioral Assessment 9:67–79, 1987

Glass CR, Merluzzi TV, Biever JL, et al: Cognitive assessment of social anxiety: development and validation of a self-statement questionnaire. Cognitive Therapy and Research 6:37–55, 1982

Goldfried MR, Sobocinski D: Effects of irrational beliefs on emotional arousal. J Consult Clin Psychol 43:504–510, 1975

Hafner RJ, Marks IM: Exposure in vivo of agoraphobics: contributions of diazepam, group exposure and anxiety evocation. Psychol Med 6:71–78, 1976

Hamilton M: The assessment of anxiety states by rating. Br J Med Psychol 32:50–55, 1959

Hamilton M: A rating scale for depression. J Neurol Neurosurg Psychiatry 23:56–62, 1960

Hodgon RJ, Rachman S: Obsessional-compulsive complaints. Behav Res Ther 15:389–395, 1977

Jones RG: A factored measure of Ellis' Irrational Belief System. (Doctoral dissertation, Texas Technical College, 1968.) Dissertation Abstracts International 29:4379B–4380B, University Microfilms No. 69–6443, 1969

Maller RG, Reiss S: A behavioral validation of the Anxiety Sensitivity Index. Journal of Anxiety Disorders (in press)

Mannuzza S, Fyer AJ, Klein DF: Schedule for Affective Disorders and Schizophrenia–Lifetime Version (modified for the study of anxiety disorders). New York, New York State Psychiatric Institute, 1985

Marks IM, Mathews AM: Brief standard self-rating for phobic patients. Behav Res Ther 17:263–267, 1979

Mathews AM: Anxiety and its management, in Current Themes in Psychiatry, Vol 3. Edited by Gaind R, Hudson B. New York, Spectrum Publications, 1984

Mathews AM, Johnston DW, Lancashire M, et al: Imaginal flooding and exposure to real phobic situations: treatment outcome with agoraphobics. Br J Psychiatry 129:362–371, 1976

Mavissakalian M: The fear questionnaire: a validity study. Behav Res Ther 24:83–85, 1986a

Mavissakalian M: Clinically significant improvement in agoraphobia research. Behav Res Ther 24:369–370, 1986b

Mellman TA, Uhde TW: Obsessive-compulsive symptoms in panic disorder. Am J Psychiatry 144:1573–1576, 1987

Michelson L, Mavissakalian M, Marchione K, et al: The role of self-directed in vivo exposure practice in cognitive, behavioral, and psychophysiological treatments of agoraphobia. Behavior Therapy 17:287–304, 1986

National Institute of Mental Health: Final Report of NIMH Conference #ER-79-003: Behavior Therapies in the Treatment of Anxiety Disorders. Recommendations for Strategies in Treatment Assessment Research. Bethesda, MD, National Institute of Mental Health, 1980

Paul GL: Insights vs. Desensitization in Psychotherapy. Stanford, CA, Stanford University Press, 1966

Paul GL, Bernstein DA: Anxiety and Clinical Problems: Systematic Desentization and Related Techniques. New York, General Learning Press, 1973

Philpott R: Recent advances in the behavioral measurement of obsessional illness: difficulties common to these and other instruments. Scott Med J 201:33–40, 1975

Reiss S, Peterson RA, Gursky DM, et al: Anxiety sensitivity, anxiety frequency, and the prediction of fearfulness. Behav Res Ther 24:1–8, 1986

Sanavio E, Vidotto G: The components of the Maudsley obsessional compulsive questionnaire. Behav Res Ther 23:659–662, 1985

Schwartz GE, Davidson RJ, Goleman DJ: Patterning of cognitive and somatic processes in the self-regulation of anxiety: effects of meditation versus exercise. Psychosom Med 40:321–328, 1978

Sheehan DV: Sheehan Anxiety and Panic Attack Scales. Kalamazoo, MI, Upjohn, 1983a

Sheehan DV: The Sheehan Patient Rated Anxiety Scale. Kalamazoo, MI, Upjohn, 1983b

Spielberger CD, Gorsuch RL, Lushene RE: Manual for the State-Trait Anxiety Inventory. Palo Alto, CA, Consulting Psychological Press, 1970

Spielberger CD, Vagg PR, Barker LR, et al: The factor structure of the State-Trait Anxiety Inventory, in Stress and Anxiety, Vol 7. Edited by Sarason IG, Spielberger CD. New York, Hemisphere, 1980

Spitzer RL, Williams JBM: Structured Clinical Interview for DSM-III. New York, New York State Psychiatric Institute, 1987

Trexler LD, Karst TO: Rational-emotive therapy, placebo, and no-treatment effects on public speaking anxiety. J Abnorm Psychol 79:60–67

Turner SM, Beidel DC, Jacob RG: Assessment of panic, in Panic: Cognitive Views. Edited by Rachman S, Maser JD. Hillsdale, NJ, Erlbaum (in press)

Watson D, Friend R: Measurement of social-evaluative anxiety. J Consult Clin Psychol 33:448–457, 1969

Williams SL: On the nature and measurement of agoraphobia. Prog Behav Modif 19:109–144, 1985

# Chapter 7

# Assessment of DSM-III Personality Disorders

**LAWRENCE B. JACOBSBERG, M.D.**
**SCOTT GOLDSMITH, M.D.**
**THOMAS WIDIGER, Ph.D.**
**ALLEN J. FRANCES, M.D.**

# Chapter 7

# Assessment of DSM-III Personality Disorders

**P**ersonality disorders are patterns of inflexible and maladaptive personality traits that result in significant impairment in social or occupational functioning and/or subjective distress (American Psychiatric Association 1987; Millon 1981). They are chronic behavior patterns with an early and insidious onset that are evident by late adolescence or early adulthood. Persons with a personality disorder are unable to respond flexibly or adaptively to the changes and demands of life. Instead they create and exacerbate stress by provoking aversive reactions in others; by failing to make optimal social, occupational, or other life decisions; and by creating situations that are problematic and pathogenic.

The diagnosis of personality disorders is very important in clinical assessment because many patients will display some degree of an inflexible and maladaptive behavior pattern that has characterized their functioning throughout most of their adult life. This behavior pattern may be the primary concern and the principal focus of treatment or it may contribute to the development of anxiety disorder, sexual dysfunction, depression, or other Axis I syndrome. It will often affect the presentation, course, and the treatment of these disorders (Docherty et al. 1986).

The assessment and diagnosis of personality disorders has been receiving increasing attention (Frances and Widiger 1986; Liebowitz et al. 1986; Siever and Klar 1986). Formerly personality disorders were often overlooked in the presence of a conspicuous or prominent clinical syndrome (Frances 1980). However, the third edition of the Diagnostic and Statistical Manual of Mental Disorders (DSM-III; American Psychiatric Association 1980) included a separate axis for personality disorders and provided relatively explicit criteria for their diagnosis.

The assessment of personality disorders remains problematic, however (Frances 1980; Widiger and Frances 1987). Personality disorder diagnosis has tended to be relatively unreliable in clinical practice, even with the development of the DSM-III criteria (Mellsop et al. 1982). In this chapter we review some of the instruments used to assess DSM-III-Revised (DSM-III-R; American Psychiatric Association 1987) personality disorder diagnosis with special attention to those issues that impair reliable and valid personality disorder assessment. The failure to assess criteria sets systematically is understandable because of the extensive amount of time such a procedure involves. Indeed, other diagnostic schemes utilizing prototypical examples have been proposed (Livesley et al. 1987). However, the DSM-III-R system of personality diagnosis by specific and explicit criteria sets can be implemented only if all the criteria are systematically assessed. Each clinician making diagnoses without reference to the criteria sets may believe that he or she is providing a valid diagnosis of say, borderline personality disorder, but if agreement is no better than a $\kappa$ of .29 (Mellsop et al. 1982), then many of them must be wrong. The only way to ensure that diagnoses are reproducible is to systematically follow a standard set of criteria.

One solution to the problem of reliable DSM-III-R assessment has been the creation of assessment instruments, self-report questionnaires that assess all the diagnostic criteria and structured interviews that force an interviewer to probe the domain of each criterion. Reliability has been obtained when such semistructured interviews have been used (Widiger and Frances 1987). Such instruments are not without problems, however.

It is somewhat ironic that the recognition of low reliability in clinical judgments has resulted to some extent in greater reliance on patients' judgments regarding their own maladaptive personality traits (Widiger and Frances 1987). In the process, the data from clinical interviews come to resemble more closely the data gathered in self-report questionnaires, and there is less emphasis on clinician judgment. Because the individual personality disorder criteria are relatively explicit and specific (e.g., has no close friends or confidants), it is tempting to simply ask patients directly whether the trait applies to them. Reliability appears to be improved because patients are likely to maintain their opinion across time (e.g., whether they have any close friends), and clinicians can agree regarding whether the patient provided an affirmative or a negative opinion. However, this reliability can be somewhat deceiving and may occur at the expense of accuracy. If patients are relied on to tell the clinician whether they have close friends (avoidant, schizotypal, and schizoid), are indecisive (obsessive-compulsive), or have difficulty initiating projects (dependent), then the validity issue is the extent to which different patients are accurate and are using the same criteria when they are describing themselves. Would patients agree regarding what is a close friend, or what constitutes difficulty initiating projects? Even if the patients were to agree among themselves, would a clinician agree with their ratings?

Patients will probably vary considerably in their understanding of what is meant by the various trait terms and the threshold for their attribution. An antisocial patient will probably have a much higher threshold for the attribution of recklessness (antisocial) than an obsessive-compulsive patient. It is therefore not realistic to simply ask patients if they are reckless.

One can at times rectify this by providing examples of what is meant by the various trait terms. Examples are provided in DSM-III-R for many of the items (e.g., recurrent speeding and driving while intoxicated are examples of recklessness). But an additional, more intractable problem is that at least some of the personality disorder items concern socially undesirable traits of which the patient may be unaware or may simply deny. It is questionable whether the average person is aware, informed, and open with respect to his or her socially undesirable traits. It is particularly problematic for persons who have a characteristic tendency to distort self-description and self-presentation. Narcissistic persons tend to deny negative features of their personalities, and it is not realistic to ask them whether they have a sense of entitlement, require constant attention and admiration, and lack empathy. Borderline and dependent persons tend to exaggerate their symptomatology and may then overestimate the extent to which they are indecisive, have difficulty initiating projects, and are reticent in social situations.

In spite of these shortcomings, there has been a major attempt to assess personality disorder using self-report inventories. The Personality Diagnostic Questionnaire inquires directly as to the presence of the DSM-III-R personality disorder criteria. In contrast, the venerable Minnesota Multiphasic Personality Inventory assesses scores on 10 scales: hypochondriasis, depression, hysteria, psychopathy, masculinity-femininity, paranoia, psychasthenia, schizophrenia, hypomania, and social introversion. The Millon Clinical Multiaxial Inventory strikes a middle ground by combining reported symptoms into combinations that produce 9 scales clinically associated with the DSM-III personality diagnoses.

A curious finding, however, is that such self-report inventories tend to report more personality disorder pathology than are reported by clinical interviews (Hurt et al. 1984; Edell 1984). Their simplicity of administration makes them very practical for epidemiologic research.

In contrast, interviews administered by a clinician have the potential to avoid some of the pitfalls inherent in patient self-report. Some of the most popular of these are described below.

The Structured Clinical Interview for DSM-III-R (SCID-II) (Spitzer and Williams 1985a) begins with a written self-report of screening questions to all the DSM-III-R personality disorder criteria. The interviewer then systematically probes each of the items endorsed. The advantages of the SCID-II are its speed of delivery and its incorporation into an assessment of Axis I illness (the SCID-I).

The Personality Disorder Examination (PDE; Loranger et al. 1987, 1985) is a 1- to 2-hour interview involving 328 items. Each section begins with a broad, open-ended question and is followed up by more specific trait questions. The PDE provides a balance of structured and open-ended assessment of DSM criteria by reorganizing these into issues surrounding work, self, interpersonal relations, affect, reality testing, and impulse control. Validity data have not been collected, but the PDE is being translated into several languages for its upcoming use in the World Health Organization/Alcohol, Drug Abuse, and Mental Health Administration (WHO/ADAMHA) International Pilot Study of Personality Disorders.

The Structured Interview of DSM-III Personality Disorders (SIDP; Pfohl et al. 1983, 1984) consists of 160 questions that assess 16 areas of functioning rather than diagnoses per se. The results translate into the DSM-III personality disorder criteria. Reports in the literature attest to the fact that this interview can be done in 90 minutes.

The Personality Interview Questions (PIQ) examination was developed by Widiger (1985) and consists of 81 individual items that together assess the covariation and internal consistency of the diagnostic criteria for the DSM-III personality disorders. Each criterion is rated on a 9-point severity scale. This interview takes between 1 and 2 hours and is unique in that it can employ lay interviewers trained and supervised in the interview. Like the PDE, ratings are not conducted for each diagnosis in turn.

The Personality Assessment Schedule (PAS), developed by Tyrer and Alexander (1979), was perhaps the first published semistructured interview devoted to the assessment of personality. Again using a 9-point severity scale, 24 personality traits are assessed. Unfortunately, the PAS has not been used widely in the United States perhaps because its assessing criteria are more in keeping with the International Classification of Diseases than the DSM system.

These clinician-administered interviews are advantageous over self-report instruments in that they allow the clinician to ask the patient for examples.

## Issues In Clinical Assessment

It is important to base one's assessments on behavioral examples or incidents in addition to the patient's opinion of whether he or she meets a criterion. It is always useful to ask patients to give examples of what they mean by a particular trait or symptom and to then base the assessment on these incidents rather than just the opinions. For example, the schizoid, avoidant, and schizotypal personality disorders include the item of having none or only one close friend or confidant (other than first-degree relatives). Subjects will vary in what they mean by a "close friend," and may say that they have two or three close friends but they never confide in them, never visit them at their homes, never invite them over to visit, and never call them up to talk. Having associates with whom one goes to bars, business meetings, or formal events does not qualify as having close friends.

A further advantage of an administered interview is the ability to use more indirect and subtle inquiries. All things being equal, simple, direct questions are often better than subtle, indirect questions (Holden and Jackson 1985; Wrobel and Lachar 1982). If a person is aware of his or her traits and is motivated to provide an honest and open self-description, then direct questions are preferable to indirect. However, this cannot always be assumed when interviewing persons with personality disorders. It is not realistic to ask an antisocial person whether he or she has repeatedly lied, has no regard for the truth, or lacks remorse. If a person is characteristically dishonest, then it is unrealistic to expect him or her to be honest during the interview, especially with respect to questions concerning social responsibility and trust.

Similarly, it may be unrealistic to ask a narcissistic person whether he or she requires constant attention or admiration, lacks empathy, is interpersonally exploitative, or has a grandiose sense of self-importance. Narcissistic persons have fragile self-esteem (Kohut 1971) and are often preoccupied with how they are regarded by others (Kernberg 1984). It may be expecting too much to ask them to openly acknowledge their faults and shortcomings in a personal interview, particularly those that concern their conflicts with respect to self-esteem.

Many of the personality disorder items must then be assessed with less reliable direct observation and indirect questions. Direct observation is necessary for some of the DSM-III-R items (e.g., odd speech) and is helpful to others. For example, there will be times when patients fish for compliments during an interview, wearing their achievements (whether minor or major) on their sleeve for the interviewer to notice and acknowledge. Because of this direct observation, there is little need to inquire about the patient's view of this item.

The full range of personality disorder pathology is rarely evident during one interview, and subtle, indirect inquiry is then helpful and even necessary. For example, a grandiose sense of self-importance can be assessed by asking patients to describe their special talents or abilities, to describe their future ambitions or goals, and to indicate how they plan to reach these goals. An inflated self-evaluation, exaggeration of talents and achievements, and an expectation to be noticed as special without appropriate achievement will often be evident in response to these questions. Lack of remorse can be assessed by asking patients to indicate why they did some harmful, exploitative, or criminal act. Justifying the act through some form of rationalization without any expression of guilt would indicate lack of remorse. Expressions of guilt might not qualify as actual remorse if the person attempted any reparations, penance, or direct apologies.

Identity disturbance is one of the most difficult items to assess. One approach is to ask patients to describe themselves, with no guidelines or cues as to how to do so. An identity disturbance is indicated by the inability to provide a vivid or clear description that indicates what is unique about themselves (Kernberg 1984). Generalities or concrete statements, such as "patient," "friendly," or "nervous," are insufficient. The patients should be asked to explain further what they mean by general trait terms to determine if they can provide more specific or unique information. If still unsuccessful, useful follow-up questions are "What is distinct or unique about you" and "What are your goals or values in life." Inability to provide anything but concrete statements or generalities in response to these questions (e.g., "to get out of the hospital," "to get well," or "to get my wife back") would suggest an identity disturbance.

Lack of empathy can be assessed in a similar fashion. The DSM-III-R provides two examples [i.e., being unable to understand why a friend whose father has just died does not want to go to a party, and annoyance or surprise when a friend who is seriously ill cancels a date (American Psychiatric Association 1987)] and while these are good illustrations of a failure to understand how others feel, they are likely to be too infrequent to be of much help in assessment. Another approach is to ask the patient to describe or explain the feelings of another person, particularly someone with whom he or she is in conflict. One then observes whether the patient is able to "stand in the shoes" of another person and understand and appreciate this person's feelings and perspective. It is important though to distinguish here a personal and sincere appreciation from simply an intellectual, cognitive description of a contrary, opposing position.

In general, the interviewer should not rely on only one example of a particular item. One example of deliberately working slowly to do a bad job (passive-aggressive), questioning the loyalty of a spouse (paranoid), or engaging in excessive, unsolicited self-sacrifice (self-defeating) is not enough to score the item as present. One should ask for additional examples in other relationships, situations, and time periods. It should be a standard practice to ask "Can you give me any other examples?"; "Did anything like this occur earlier in your life?"; "Was that at all unusual, or was it typical?"; "Has this been a recent change for you or were there similar experiences before?"; "How often did this happen?"; or "Did anything like this happen with your (first wife, other job, or when you lived alone)?"

## Traits Versus States

A personality disorder involves a long-standing tendency (trait) rather than a temporary condition (state). However, personality disorders are easily confused with a temporally circumscribed Axis I condition (Widiger and Frances 1987) on evaluation at a given point in time. Patients who present with an atypical depression will appear borderline, and patients with a social phobia may appear avoidant. Perhaps the two most difficult and controversial distinctions are between borderline personality and affective disorder (Gunderson and Elliot 1985) and between self-defeating personality and depression (Akiskal 1983).

Differentiating borderline personality and affective disorder is particularly difficult because many of the borderline items directly or at least indirectly tap affective symptomatology (e.g., affective instability and inappropriate or intense anger). Most borderline patients, by definition, display affective instability. Borderline personality may in fact represent a disposition to affective dyscontrol. The distinction between states and traits is to some extent arbitrary because traits may include the disposition to experience or display particular states. Depression then neither necessarily suggests nor necessarily excludes the diagnosis of a borderline personality disorder.

Gunderson and Elliot (1985) suggested that a "borderline depression" may be characterized by loneliness, emptiness, and boredom, whereas a purely "affective depression" may be characterized more by guilt, remorse, and low self-esteem. These clinical distinctions might be useful at times, but they might also be difficult to make reliably. Diagnosing borderline personality in a depressed patient requires the further identification of the presence of borderline features that are relatively inde-

149

pendent of depression (e.g., identity disturbance) and a history of a stable pattern of interpersonal and affective instability.

The differentiation of self-defeating personality disorder from dysthymia is similarly problematic. Many depressed persons will appear to be self-defeating, and most self-defeating persons are likely to be depressed. Self-defeating persons tend to choose people and situations that lead to disappointment, reject opportunities for pleasure, and even respond to positive events with depression (American Psychiatric Association 1987). The DSM-III-R self-defeating personality disorder diagnosis is based in part on the psychoanalytic and psychiatric concept of a "depressive character," that describes a person who is chronically self-deprecating, pessimistic, and self-blaming and is therefore likely to be depressed much of the time.

Akiskal (1983) suggests that a characterological depression can be distinguished from a subaffective dysthymia by the presence of dependent, histrionic, or sociopathic traits; a history of parental separation or divorce; a family history of parent assortative mating; normal REM latency; and a lack of response to thymoleptic drugs. However, these indicators may be more useful in identifying a drug-responsive and/or biogenetic depression than in ruling out a characterological depression (Widiger and Frances 1987).

The DSM-III-R suggests that self-defeating personality disorder be distinguished from depression by the presence of the self-defeating behaviors when the person is not depressed. This will at times require a retrospective assessment of the patient's personality before or independent of a current depression. Retrospective reporting is necessary in the assessment of all the personality disorders, but it may be especially problematic when the patient is depressed. Depressed persons are likely to provide an overly pessimistic and critical description of their past, future, and self. Interviews may be less susceptible than self-report inventories to such state factors (Reich et al. 1987; Widiger and Frances 1987), but they are certainly not immune to them.

Interviewers may therefore wish to supplement their patient interviews with interviews with a close relative, friend, or associate of the patient (Widiger and Frances 1987; Zimmerman et al. 1986). These informants can be particularly helpful in personality disorder assessment because they will have observed the patient over a much broader span of time than is available to the interviewer, and they will not be viewing this history through the distorting lens of a depression, anxiety, or psychosis. In addition, they will be particularly familiar with the interpersonal style of the patient, which can be of central importance in the assessment of personality disorders (Kiesler 1986; Widiger and Frances 1985; Wiggins 1982). Informants are certainly not infallible or objective. They may not have observed some aspects of some personality disorders (e.g., schizoid persons may not have any useful informants), and they may have their own ax to grind, but they can offer a useful and informative perspective.

### Traits Versus Situations

The differentiation of traits and situations has been controversial for some time. It should be less of an issue in personality disorder assessment than for Axis I disorder, because personality disorders are by definition consistent behaviors across situations to the point that they are maladaptive (Millon 1981). Persons with personality disorders are unable to respond flexibly to the demands of varying situations. Nevertheless, personality disorders may often be confused with situational reactions. The two most controversial examples are the passive-aggressive and the self-defeating personality disorders.

The passive-aggressive personality disorder was almost excluded from DSM-III because some considered it to be a reaction to being in a powerless, subordinate position (Gunderson 1983). Passive-aggressive behavior may at times be in response to being an inpatient who has lost the control, authority, and freedom experienced before hospitalization and who must follow the dictates and rules of a hospital staff. Similarly, self-defeating behavior in the absence of character pathology may be seen in female victims of abusive relationships. Persons with true self-defeating personality disorder are more likely than others to place themselves within and fail to leave an abusive relationship. However, the apparently self-defeating behavior of an abused woman may at times reflect her spouse's ability to keep her involved through promises to reform, guilt-inducing pleas not to be abandoned, and threats of violence. Furthermore, she may lack real alternatives for action because of limited options for housing, child care, money, and social support.

Complicating the distinction is that traits are at times not evident outside of particular situations. A trait is the disposition to respond in a particular manner within certain situations. If the relevant situations do not occur, then the trait will not be evident. Passive-aggressive behavior that is confined to the hospital or work setting is not necessarily simply a situational reaction. The passive-aggressive trait may be the disposition to respond to hospitalization (and comparable situations) with negativistic resistance, and the self-defeating trait may be the tendency to respond to victimization (and comparable situations) with self-blame and helplessness. The behavior would be solely situational if all persons responded in the same manner to these situations.

One is more confident that the behavior is a reflection of a trait if the behavior is observed across a variety of situations. Interviewers should determine, for example, if patients also display passive-aggressive behavior outside of the hospital in such situations as work, leisure, or family. For example, do they sulk and complain when their friends do something they don't want to do and then spoil the evening for everyone, including themselves? Do they often complain that their friends, as well as their therapists and employers, make unreasonable demands? Similarly, one should assess whether the self-defeating behavior has occurred before and in between abusive relationships.

## Traits Versus Roles

Traits may also be confused with roles (Frances 1980). Persons will choose roles, positions, and jobs because they complement and support their personality, but a person's behavior will also at times reflect the demands or pressures of a social role (aggressive behavior in a soldier is less indicative of a sadistic personality than aggressive behavior in a professor). A role maintained over an extended period may have a substantial effect on personality, but at what point this occurs is difficult to determine.

Social-cultural expectations and biases with respect to certain roles can further handicap the assessment of personality disorders. The most controversial examples concern possible sex-role biases with respect to the dependent, histrionic, and self-defeating personality disorders. These disorders to some extent involve exaggerated or extreme variants of stereotypically feminine behavior (Kaplan 1983; Williams and Spitzer 1983). Clinicians, whether male or female, may possess masculine biases regarding what is socially desirable behavior and thereby pathologize feminine behavior. Emotionality in a woman may be too readily diagnosed as histrionic, devotion as dependency, and sacrifice as self-defeating. On the other hand, feminist political convictions can also hinder a clinician from recognizing such traits in female patients.

The extent to which the dependent, histrionic, and self-defeating personality disorders involve sex biases is unclear. It is important for clinicians to be aware of the controversy and their own assumptions, expectations, and/or biases with respect to their female (and male) patients. There are no persons without biases, and it is likely that sex-role biases do impact on the clinical diagnosis of personality disorders.

## Assess for Functional Impairment

The DSM-III provides rules for determining when a person has each of the personality disorders. A person is not considered to have a borderline personality disorder until he or she displays at least five of the eight criteria. This cutoff point is to some extent arbitrary and debatable, but it is the accepted convention.

However, the threshold for each of the items is not at all clear. There is no absolute, qualitative distinction between a normal, adaptive personality trait and an abnormal, maladaptive one (Cloninger 1987; Frances 1982; Widiger and Frances 1985). At what point impulsivity, unstable and intense relationships, and feelings of emptiness and boredom are above the threshold for clinical significance is not clear and is to some extent arbitrary.

One guiding principle is that an item or symptom is above clinical threshold if it results in significant impairment in social or occupational functioning (American Psychiatric Association 1987). Has the passive-aggressive, indecisive, or impulsive behavior resulted in a loss of a job, promotion, or raise? Has it resulted in loss of or rejection by friends, inability to get along with others, failure to develop friendships, or misperceptions and misunderstandings in relationships?

Subjective distress is another potential indicator (American Psychiatric Association 1987). Complaints by patients that they are troubled by their preoccupation with feelings of envy will suggest the presence of this narcissistic trait. But subjective distress is often less useful than functional impairment. Some patients will be overly distressed by and critical of minor flaws, peccadilloes, and mistakes. Their exaggerated self-deprecation can result in an overestimation of personality disorder pathology. On the other hand, some subjects will not be distressed at all, will be unaware that the traits are detrimental to functioning, and may even value their presence. Lack of empathy (narcissistic) and lack of remorse (antisocial) may be considered by some narcissistic and antisocial patients as a sign of a tough-minded resilience.

Magical thinking, from the schizotypal criteria set, is a good example. A belief in clairvoyance and telepathy is an example of magical thinking but it is not considered to be above clinical threshold until it is inconsistent with subcultural norms and influences behavior in some personally relevant manner (American Psychiatric Association 1987). Many persons will believe in such phenomena as part of an open-minded, scientific interest. It is clinically relevant if they have altered their life or acted on the belief in some personally relevant manner. Did they cancel a trip due to a precognition, attempt to communicate with a dead relative, or join some occult group to further explore the phenomena?

Obsessive-compulsive indecisiveness is another example. It is within normal limits to at times avoid, postpone, or protract decisions. Clinically significant indecisiveness results in a repeated failure to complete assignments on time (due to continual revisions), to ask someone out on a date (worrying about where to go, when to go, how to ask, and whether to ask), or to make necessary purchases for a house (ruminating over various possible complications, details, and uncertainties).

Any single behavior can reflect a variety of traits, and any trait can be associated with a variety of behaviors. Accusing a husband of having an affair after he came home late from work may reflect an unjustified concern with fidelity of the spouse (paranoid), suspicious or paranoid ideation (schizotypal), demand for reassurance (histrionic), or a preoccupation with the fear of being abandoned (dependent). It is unlikely that personality disorder assessment can be done without some degree of clinical judgment.

## Conclusion

It is clear that a degree of subjective (expert) judgment is necessary even though the explicit criteria provided in DSM-III-R are helpful in improving communication and agreement among clinicians (Spitzer and Williams 1985b). Validity does assume reliability, and the latter requires adherence to the diagnostic criteria. Nevertheless, clinical judgments are still necessary with respect to particular traits and are best made on the basis of fully informed assessment. Structured interviews like the PDE, SIDP, and SCID-II combine the diagnostic judgment of a clinician with the careful and systematic evaluation of the diagnostic criteria.

## References

Akiskal HS: Subaffective disorders: dysthymic, cyclothymic and bipolar-II disorders in the "borderline" realm. Psychiatr Clin North Am 4:25–46, 1983

American Psychiatric Association: Diagnostic and Statistical Manual of Mental Disorders, Third Edition. Washington, DC, American Psychiatric Association, 1980

American Psychiatric Association: Diagnostic and Statistical Manual of Mental Disorders, Third Edition, Revised. Washington, DC, American Psychiatric Association, 1987

Cloninger CR: A systematic method for clinical description and classification of personality variants: a proposal. Arch Gen Psychiatry 44:573–588, 1987

Docherty JP, Fiester SJ, Shea T: Syndrome diagnosis and personality disorder, in Psychiatry Update. American Psychiatric Association Annual Review, Vol 5. Edited by Hales R, Frances A. Washington, DC, American Psychiatric Press, 1986, pp 315–355

Edell W: The borderline syndrome index: clinical validity and utility. J Nerv Ment Dis 172:254–263, 1984

Frances A: The DSM-III personality disorders: a commentary. Am J Psychiatry 137:1050–1054, 1980

Frances A: Categorical and dimensional systems of personality diagnosis: a comparison. Compr Psychiatry 23:516–527, 1982

Frances A, Widiger T: Methodological issues in personality disorder diagnosis, in Contemporary Issues in Psychopathology. Edited by Millon T, Klerman G. New York, Guilford Press, 1986

Gunderson J: DSM-III diagnosis of personality disorders, in Current Perspectives on Personality Disorders. Edited by

Frosch J. Washington, DC, American Psychiatric Press, 1983

Gunderson JG, Elliot GR: The interface between borderline personality disorder and affective disorder. Am J Psychiatry 142:277–288, 1985

Holden R, Jackson D: Disguise and the structured self-report assessment of psychopathology, I: an analogue investigation. J Consult Clin Psychol 53:211–222, 1985

Hurt S, Frances A, Clarkin J, et al: Assessing borderline personality disorder with self-report, clinical interview, or structured interview. Am J Psychiatry 141:1288–1231, 1984

Kaplan M: A woman's view of DSM-III. Am J Psychol 38:786–792, 1983

Kernberg O: Severe Personality Disorders. New Haven, Yale University Press, 1984

Kiesler D: The 1982 interpersonal circle: an analysis of DSM-III personality disorders, in Contemporary Issues in Psychopathology. Edited by Millon T, Klerman G. New York, Guilford Press, 1986

Kohut H: The Analysis of the Self. New York, International Universities Press, 1971

Liebowitz MR, Stone MH, Turkat ID: Treatment of personality disorders, in Psychiatry Update: American Psychiatric Association Annual Review, Vol 5. Edited by Hales R, Frances A. Washington, DC, American Psychiatric Press, 1986, pp 356–393

Livesley WJ, Reiffer LI, Sheldon AE, et al: Prototypicality ratings of DSM-III criteria for personality disorders. J Nerv Ment Dis 175:395–401, 1987

Loranger AW, Susman VL, Oldham JM, et al: Personality disorder examination: a structured interview for DSM-III Axis II diagnoses (PDE). White Plains, NY, The New York Hospital-Cornell Medical Center, Westchester Division, 1985

Loranger AW, Susman VL, Oldham JM, et al: The personality disorder examination: a preliminary report. Journal of Personality Disorders 1:1–13, 1987

Mellsop G, Varghese F, Joshua S, et al: Reliability of Axis II of DSM-III. Am J Psychiatry 139:1360–1361, 1982

Millon T: Disorders of Personality. DSM-III: Axis II. New York, Wiley, 1981

Pfohl B, Stangl D, Zimmerman M: Structured Interview for DSM-III Personality Disorders, SIDP, 2nd Ed. Unpublished manual. Iowa City, University of Iowa College of Medicine, 1983

Pfohl B, Stangl D, Zimmerman M: The implications of DSM-III personality disorders for patients with major depression. J Affective Disord 7:309–318, 1984

Reich J, Noyes R, Hirschfeld R, et al: State and personality in depressed and panic patients. Am J Psychiatry 144:181–187, 1987

Siever LJ, Klar H: A review of DSM-III criteria for the personality disorders, in Psychiatry Update: American Psychiatric Association Annual Review, Vol 5. Edited by Hales R, Frances A. Washington, DC, American Psychiatric Press, 1986, pp 279–317

Spitzer R, Williams J: Structured Clinical Interview for DSM-III-R Personality Disorders (SCID-II, 7/1/85). New York, Biometrics Research Department, New York State Psychiatric Institute, 1985a

Spitzer R, Williams J: Classification of mental disorders, in Comprehensive Textbook of Psychiatry/IV, 4th Ed. Edited by Kaplan H, Sadock B. Baltimore, Williams & Wilkins, 1985b, pp 592–613

Tyrer P, Alexander J: Classification of personality disorder. Br J Psychiatry 135:163–167, 1979

Widiger T: Personality interview questions. Unpublished manuscript, Lexington, University of Kentucky, 1985

Widiger TA, Frances A: The DSM-III personality disorders: perspectives from psychology. Arch Gen Psychiatry 42:615–623, 1985

Widiger TA, Frances A: Interviews and inventories for the measurement of personality disorders. Clinical Psychology Review 7:49–75, 1987

Wiggins J: Circumplex models of interpersonal behavior in clinical psychology, in Handbook of Research Methods in Clinical Psychology. Edited by Kendall P, Butchers J. New York, John Wiley, 1982, pp 183–221

Williams J, Spitzer R: The issue of sex bias in DSM-III: a critique of "A woman's view of DSM-III" by Marcie Kaplan. Am Psychol 38:793–798, 1983

Wrobel T, Lachar D: Validity of the Weiner subtle and obvious scales for the MMPI: another example of the importance of inventory-item content. J Consult Clin Psychol 50:469–470, 1982

Zimmerman M, Pfohl B, Strangl D, et al: Assessment of DSM-III personality disorders: the importance of interviewing an informant. J Clin Psychiatry 47:261–263, 1986

## Chapter 8

# Assessment of Alcoholism and Substance Abuse

**LESLIE C. MOREY, Ph.D.**
**PETER R. MARTIN, M.D.**

# Chapter 8

# Assessment of Alcoholism and Substance Abuse

**A**lcohol and substance abuse are among the most commonly encountered health care problems, with considerable medical and psychosocial consequences for the individual and great economic cost to society. However, these problems are often difficult to identify, perhaps because of the stigma associated with the disorders as well as the nature of the disorders themselves. The purpose of this chapter is to provide an introduction to some of the more widely used assessment techniques for alcoholism and substance abuse.

The difficulties encountered in the validation of diagnostic tests for alcohol and substance abuse are somewhat unique among psychiatric disorders. For example, it is widely believed that denial is almost universal among substance abusers, leading them to minimize the extent of their difficulties. With illegal substances, diagnosis can be complicated by legal considerations, which may lead patients to further distort their presentation of the clinical picture. Finally, the boundaries between clinical disorder and normality are often vague and elusive; it is often difficult to distinguish between abusive and nonabusive use of substances, or between alcoholism, problem drinking, and social drinking. The complexity of these issues makes it difficult to establish a universally accepted criterion against which to validate diagnostic tests.

Clearly the most frequently used and least expensive means of assessing substance abuse involves a direct questioning of the patient. Consistent with this popularity, most techniques described in this chapter use the direct approach. Although the accuracy of such information is often questioned, most studies indicate that self-report data are reasonably valid. For example, Sobell and Sobell (1975) examined self-reports of alcoholics on 15 questions that were later verified through contact with agencies such as the Federal Bureau of Investigation, the Department of Motor Vehicles, and state and county hospitals. For 86% of all responses, no discrepancies were noted between self-report and verified information. Answers given in response to true/false types of questions were particularly accurate. Of the discrepant responses, overestimates of problems by the patients were more frequent than underestimates. Another study of alcoholic self-reports (Guze et al. 1963) found an 85% agreement between information obtained from patients and collateral reports from family members, with the patient data generally found to be more consistent with the impressions of diagnosing clinicians familiar with these cases. Similar accuracy figures have been reported in work conducted with narcotic addicts (e.g., Bale et al. 1981). In general, research findings suggest that the information obtained from the self-report of substance abusers is useful in identifying problems in this area, although obviously situational factors can influence the accuracy of any patient's description of his or her substance use.

The following sections provide an overview of some of the most commonly used approaches to diagnosing substance abuse. The instruments are presented in order of their complexity; rapidly administered screening measures are described first, with more complex and detailed tests presented later. It is important to emphasize that the utility of these different measures will vary according to the context in which they are used and the purposes for which they are given. For example, a test that is used as a screening measure should ideally be very sensitive; that is, it should accurately identify nearly all true cases of alcoholism or drug abuse. However, the same test may be of limited utility in establishing a definitive diagnosis, since it may misdiagnose too many normal individuals as being substance abusers. Similarly, a test that is useful in a setting where roughly 50% of patients are alcoholic may be of little use in a clinic where alcohol problems are relatively rare. Tests derived from post hoc investigations of previously diagnosed alcoholics need to be validated in diverse samples with variable prevalence rates. In order to use these or any other diagnostic tests appropriately and effectively, the reader should be familiar with basic psychometric principles described in texts such as Anastasi (1988).

## Diagnostic Measures for Substance Abuse

### The CAGE Questionnaire

The CAGE questionnaire (Ewing 1984) has become one of the most widely used screening devices for alcoholism. It derives its name as an acronym for the following four questions that are asked of patients:

1. Have you ever felt you ought to *CUT DOWN* on your drinking?
2. Have people *ANNOYED* you by criticizing your drinking?
3. Have you ever felt bad or *GUILTY* about your drinking?
4. Have you ever had a drink first thing in the morning to steady your nerves or get rid of a hangover *(EYE OPENER)*?

In Ewing's original study with the CAGE, he found that a score of two or more yes answers to these questions was highly efficient in discriminating male alcoholics from male medical control patients. A number of studies have subsequently examined the validity of the CAGE in different populations and settings (Hays and Spickard 1987). Generally, sensitivity and specificity values have been found to be quite high (81–97%) in medical or psychiatric inpatient settings, although in outpatient and community samples these values tend to be lower (66–84% sensitivity). One study of an urban black sample (Robinson et al. 1987) obtained a sensitivity value of 55%, suggesting that the utility of the CAGE may be more limited in this population. The suitability of the test for other specific populations remains to be explored.

Studies of the positive predictive power of the CAGE (King 1986; Bush et al. 1987) have obtained divergent values ranging from 45% to 82%. The lower value suggests that in some settings (particularly outpatient) the test tends to yield a relatively large number of false-positive diagnoses of alcoholism. However, given the brief nature of the instrument and the need for such a device to be highly sensitive, the CAGE should be considered as a useful and efficient screening measure for alcoholism.

### The MAST

The Michigan Alcoholism Screening Test, or MAST (Selzer 1971), is a widely used 25-item, true/false questionnaire that contains questions about alcohol consumption and consequences of alcohol use. The test can be administered either as a self-report questionnaire or as a structured interview. The items are differentially weighted, resulting in a summary score that ranges from 0 to 50. Although different cut-scores for identifying alcoholism have been recommended, these scores generally range between 5 (the original cutoff) and 7, with higher scores reflecting greater impairment and a higher likelihood of significant alcoholism. Internal consistency estimates of reliability of the MAST have generally been found to be between .85 and .95 (Skinner 1979; Zung 1979).

Validation studies of the MAST have generally yielded favorable results. Sensitivity estimates have ranged between 84% and 100%, and specificity values have been comparable (Selzer 1971; Moore 1972). Skinner (1979) found that the MAST was only moderately influenced by response styles such as denial, and was a useful predictor of psychological distress and symptomatology in an alcoholic population.

Two abbreviated versions of the MAST have been proposed, one with 13 items and the other with 10 items (Zung 1979). Each of these brief scales correlates well with the full MAST, and each has demonstrated reasonable validity. For example, one study (Bernadt et al. 1982) found that the 10-item MAST was much more successful at identifying alcoholism than were any of a number of laboratory tests. Given its ease of administration, the MAST represents a useful and powerful screening device for the identification of alcohol-related problems.

### The DAST

The Drug Abuse Screening Test, or DAST (Skinner 1982), is a 28-item, true/false self-administered questionnaire that contains questions about the extent and consequences of substance use. The items were selected to parallel items from the MAST. Unlike the standard scoring of the MAST, each DAST item is equally weighted so that summary scores range from 0 to 28. Skinner (1982) emphasized that the DAST score is best conceptualized as a quantitative index of substance abuse problems. However, he noted that no patients in his sample who sought treatment for drug abuse alone obtained scores below 6, 9% of those who had mixed drug/alcohol problems scored below 6, while 75% of patients seeking treatment for alcoholism alone scored between 0 and 5. Thus, scores above 6 can be considered suggestive of significant drug abuse problems.

Internal consistency reliability for the DAST is estimated at .92, while a shortened 20-item version that correlates nearly perfectly ($r$=.99) with the full version yielded a .86 reliability estimate (Skinner 1982). The DAST was found to be only moderately correlated with response-style biases such as denial or social desirability. Higher scores are related to more frequent use of most major classes of substances, as well as to increased impulsivity, depression, and interpersonal problems. Finally, as described above, the DAST clearly differentiated among individuals seeking treatment for drug abuse versus those who presented with alcohol problems (Skinner 1982).

## Clinical Indicators

A number of potential indicators for alcoholism involve observable clinical signs that may be more objective and less influenced by denial than self-report information. Skinner et al. (1986) created an alcohol clinical index, comprised of a number of clinical signs and information available from the medical history, which yielded a positive predictive power of 97% and a negative predictive power of 92% in distinguishing alcoholic outpatients from family practice patients. Clinical signs involved information on the following: hand tremor, tandem gait, deep knee bend, spider nevi ($>$ 5), collateral circulation, gynecomastia, abdominal tenderness, rhinophyma, facial erythema, coated tongue, edema of soft palate, nicotine stains, palmar erythema, bruises or abrasions, scars secondary to trauma, cigarette burns, and tattoos. Pertinent medical history items included: inability to concentrate; mental confusion; poor memory for recent events; hallucinations; hand shaking in A.M.; nightmares; headache upon awakening; injured in assault or fight; feeling thirsty upon awakening; dry, coated tongue; cough on most days; and bringing up phlegm. These clinical indicators were found to be considerably more accurate in identifying alcoholics than a number of the most promising laboratory markers, suggesting that the indicators may be a useful indirect means of identifying alcoholics when denial is felt to be a problem.

## Alcohol Dependence Scale (ADS)

The ADS (Skinner and Horn 1984; Skinner and Allen 1982) was designed to provide a brief measure of the extent to which alcohol use has progressed from psychological involvement to the point of impaired control over drinking. The scale is patterned after the concept of the alcohol dependence syndrome described in a World Health Organization (WHO) Task Force Report (Edwards et al. 1977), which portrays alcohol dependence as existing in degrees rather than as an all-or-none phenomenon. It is worth noting that a similar measure designed to assess the same construct has been proposed by Stockwell et al. (1979).

The ADS consists of 25 multiple-choice items pertaining directly to alcohol use and its consequences; scores on the scale range between 0 and 47. Reliability data for the scale are impressive, with both internal consistency and test-retest reliability correlations estimated at .92. Initial validity evidence is also promising, as high scores on the scale have been found to be related to a variety of alcohol-related psychosocial and medical impairments, early dropout from treatment, and differential treatment response (Skinner and Horn 1984). Although no strict cutoffs are recommended in the use of the scale, raw scores of 14 and above are suggestive of moderate alcohol dependence, scores of 22 and above represent substantial dependence (i.e., alcoholism), while scores above 30 indicate severe dependence.

### The MMPI

The Minnesota Multiphasic Personality Inventory (MMPI; Hathaway and McKinley 1943) is certainly among the most widely used psychodiagnostic instruments, and it has a long history of use in the diagnosis of alcoholism and/or drug abuse. The test consists of 550 unique items whose content ranges from psychiatric symptoms to political and social attitudes. Since the MMPI has very few questions that pertain directly to alcohol or drug use, it is generally considered to be an indirect diagnostic measure in this area. As such, many researchers have felt that the MMPI can be a particularly useful diagnostic measure in instances where denial of drug or alcohol problems may be an important consideration.

In using the MMPI, researchers have taken one of two approaches to diagnosing alcoholism and/or drug abuse: one directed at identifying a particular personality code type or profile associated with substance abuse and the other focused on the development of specific scales, using MMPI items, with which to identify substance abuse problems.

The MMPI, as it is most commonly used, consists of 13 different scales, 3 (the *validity* scales) that attempt to determine the accuracy of a subject's self-description and 10 (the *clinical* scales) that measure various aspects of personality and psychopathology. There is a long history of research with the MMPI that has attempted to identify a particular pattern of elevations on the clinical scales that might be associated with alcoholism or drug abuse. However, this research has met with only limited success. Although there are certain profiles that occur with relative frequency in alcoholic samples, these profiles are typically found frequently in nonalcoholic psychiatric samples as well (e.g., Rosen 1960). Thus, the search for a single MMPI profile that characterizes alcoholics has essentially been abandoned, although a number of researchers have identified alcoholic MMPI subtypes that may have some utility (Morey and Blashfield 1981). In particular, severely dependent alcoholics often have marked elevations on depression (2), psychopathic deviance (4), psychasthenia (7), and schizophrenia (8) scales (Morey et al. 1987). It must be emphasized that this pattern is by no means specific to alcoholism and thus is of limited utility as a diagnostic sign. However, if found in conjunction with positive results from a brief screening device such as the CAGE, this pattern may indicate the presence of particularly severe alcohol problems.

The second diagnostic strategy using the MMPI involves special scales, created from MMPI items, designed to diagnose alcoholism and/or drug abuse. For example, at least six different scales have been developed for the purpose of diagnosing alcoholism. Of these scales, the MacAndrew (1965) alcoholism scale, or MAC, has generally been found to be the most promising (Preng and Clopton 1986). The MAC consists of 49 items from the MMPI, none of which directly address alcohol use

and few of which concern behaviors that might reflect consequences of alcohol use. Instead, the MAC was designed to
identify stable personality characteristics associated with alcoholism. There are a number of studies that support this claim;
for example, MAC scores do not seem to measure either short-
term or long-term consequences of alcohol use (MacAndrew
1981).

MacAndrew (1965) originally proposed a cutting score of
24 for making a diagnosis; however, the efficiency of this score
varies as a function of setting, age, race, and gender. Cutting
scores between 23 and 28 have been recommended by various
authors. As with most instruments, it is likely that the optimal
cutting score will vary across different applications, and users
should make some effort to establish a cutting score that is
best suited for their purposes and setting. In general, research
results have confirmed the utility of the MAC in making alcoholism diagnoses. For example, Svanum et al. (1982), using
cutting scores of 25 for men and 23 for women, reported sensitivities of 91% and 83% and specificities of 76% and 80%
for men and women, respectively. Their study involved discriminating alcoholics from psychiatric outpatient control subjects.

Because there has been a fair amount of validation research examining the MAC, the shortcomings and limitations
of the test as a screening device for alcoholism tend to be
relatively well understood. For example, there are certain circumstances that limit the specificity of the scale, where it may
identify individuals as having alcohol problems when in fact
they do not. Foremost among these are findings that MAC
scores consistently fail to discriminate alcoholics from other
substance abusers (e.g., Lachar et al. 1976); this result might
be expected from the increasing prevalence of polydrug abuse.
Thus, many authors have suggested that the MAC is most
useful as a general substance dependence scale, rather than
as a marker specific to alcoholism. A second circumstance
limiting specificity involves antisocial behaviors; some research

evidence suggests that nonalcoholic, antisocial individuals obtain MAC scores comparable to alcoholic patients.

A second limitation of the MAC involves sensitivity; some studies have found that the MAC fails to identify certain individuals who have alcohol problems. Cernovsky (1985) has reported that using the MMPI repression (R) research scale in conjunction with the MAC can lead to a reduction of false-negative diagnoses of male alcoholics. Specifically, high repression scores seemed to characterize the MAC false negatives, suggesting that elevated repression scores may serve as a warning sign when screening for addiction using the MMPI.

In summary, the MMPI has utility in the identification of substance abuse, but it is probably best used in conjunction with the more direct measures discussed elsewhere in this chapter. It is interesting to note that the upcoming revision of the MMPI is intended to greatly expand the scope of information pertinent to substance abuse and alcoholism. Such additional questions should greatly enhance the utility of the MMPI in making these diagnostic decisions.

### Biological Detection of Alcohol and Substance Abuse/Dependence

In part because structured clinical interviews and questionnaire-derived data are vulnerable to deliberate falsification and/or denial, there has been a continuing interest in the biological correlates of alcohol and drug abuse or dependence. Adverse psychosocial consequences are considered by many to be the earliest signs of substance abuse and only with chronicity do the biomedical sequelae associated with these disorders appear. However, such biomedical techniques are only well developed for detection of alcoholism, and their utility in other substance use disorders has not been systematically explored.

Every initial study of a new laboratory measure for identification of alcoholism reports being able to differentiate diagnosed alcoholics from nonalcoholics. Excessive alcohol consumption has been associated with elevations of uric acid, mean cell volume, and liver function tests as well as decreases in numbers of red blood cells and phosphorus levels (Eckardt et al. 1986). These observations, coupled with the findings of statistically significant relationships between clinical laboratory tests and amounts of alcohol consumed in alcoholics as well as those presumed not to be alcoholics, provide the basis for suggesting that commonly ordered laboratory tests might be of use in identifying alcohol abusers. However, these tests appear to have relatively limited sensitivity and specificity in identifying alcoholics (Bernadt et al. 1982).

Although the search for a single biological marker for alcoholism has so far proved unsuccessful, several investigators have recently demonstrated that combinations of tests are more likely to identify alcoholics than single tests. For example, quadratic discriminant analysis is a statistical form of pattern recognition that has demonstrated some promise for identifying people with alcohol abuse using a battery of routinely requested clinical laboratory tests. Nonetheless, problems persist with the application of these more sophisticated techniques. The difficulties encountered in attempting to identify biological markers of alcoholism are exemplified by a recent study of the inhibition by ethanol of platelet monoamine oxidase and the response of adenylate cyclase to various forms of physiological stimulation in alcoholics and matched controls (Tabakoff et al. 1988). The inhibition of monoamine oxidase by ethanol was significantly higher in the platelets of alcoholics compared with controls, whereas platelet adenylate cyclase activity after stimulation was significantly lower in alcoholics. A discriminant analysis showed that these findings could be used to correctly classify only 75% of alcoholics and 73% of nonalcoholic controls from the derivation sample (in other words, these functions were not cross-validated). Neither enzyme activity returned to normal levels after 23 days of abstinence, and the abnormality of platelet adenylate cyclase activity persisted in alcoholic subjects who abstained from alcohol for up to 4 years. These results suggest that such markers are of limited utility in assessing recent alcohol consumption.

It is noteworthy that laboratory values are in many cases less sensitive and specific than are the more economical methods involving direct questioning of the patient (Bernadt et al. 1982; Skinner et al. 1986). Nevertheless, biological definition of substance use disorders may provide validation criteria of these disorders that are individually determined and are not dependent on self-report or the report of others.

### The Drinking Profile

Marlatt (1976) designed the Drinking Profile to be used in conjunction with a behavioral treatment program for alcoholics. The profile is a structured interview set up for use by trained interviewers, and it typically requires approximately 45 to 60 minutes to complete. The interview is divided into three primary segments: identification and demographic material, drinking pattern and behavior, and alcohol-related attitudes and preferences. The section on drinking pattern obtains detailed information concerning the onset and development of drinking and typical drinking patterns (e.g., binge or continuous). The section on attitudes and preferences yields specific data concerning amount and frequency of consumption of various alcoholic beverages. It also asks the interviewee about reasons for drinking in terms of both internal (personal feelings) and external (situational or environmental) factors. Finally, this section investigates motivation for past and present treatment and explores expectations relating to treatment outcome.

The Drinking Profile includes both quantitative and open-ended questions about alcohol use. For the open-ended questions, Marlatt (1976) has devised scoring categories for responses given by patients; he reports scorer agreement for these coding categories to be 80% at minimum. Although the validity evidence for this instrument is currently limited, the interview obtains much information that Marlatt (1983) has found to be useful in assessing and predicting relapse phenomena.

## Addiction Severity Index

The Addiction Severity Index (ASI; McLellan et al. 1980) is an instrument designed to assess the multiple problems seen in both drug- and alcohol-dependent individuals. Set up as an interview, it can be administered by a trained technician in less than 1 hour, and it can be readministered as a posttreatment follow-up evaluation. The ASI produces a problem severity profile across six domains of difficulty: substance (drug and alcohol) abuse, medical, psychological, legal, family and social, and employment/support. Data from both objective sources and patient self-report are integrated into six 10-point scales that represent severity of impairment.

The results of reliability testing demonstrate that the scale can be used reliably with trained baccalaureate-level technicians (interrater reliability correlation = .918 across the six areas). Test-retest reliability data indicate excellent consistency across a 3-day time span (coefficient of concordance = .92), even across interviews conducted by different technicians. The convergent validity of the different scales appears to be reasonably good (McLellan et al. 1985), with the strongest concurrent validity for drug use severity (validity correlations about .60) and the weakest in the area of family and social functioning (correlations about .30). In general, these validity results point to the utility of the ASI in diagnosis and treatment planning for substance abusers.

McLellan et al. (1985) note that the ASI has certain limitations that users should recognize. First, the level of detail provided in the medical and psychiatric problem areas tends to be more general than that provided in other areas, although even this general information has been found to serve as a useful predictor in a number of studies. The authors also caution against the use of the ASI with older, cognitively impaired alcoholics; drug abusers with criminal involvement; and adolescents younger than age 16 who are supported by their families. However, the ASI is a detailed interview yielding a wealth of information about substance abuse that can be very useful in both clinical and research contexts.

### The Alcohol Use Inventory

The Alcohol Use Inventory (AUI; Horn et al. 1983; Wanberg et al. 1977) represents an important outcome of an extensive research program directed at identifying major dimensions of variation among the personalities and drinking styles of alcoholics (Wanberg and Horn 1983). Beginning with a compilation of presenting complaints and concerns typically expressed by new admissions to alcohol treatment, the authors eventually developed a hierarchical model of dimensions within the domain of drinking styles through the use of factor analytic techniques. The model originally had 16 primary factors tapping specific stylistic features of alcohol use; 6 second-order factors; and a general factor representing involvement with alcohol in a broad sense. The 6 second-order factors are particularly interesting and include the following:

1. Drinking to enhance perceived functioning;
2. Obsessive, sustained drinking;
3. Overt disruption of life functioning;
4. Subtle disruption of life functioning;
5. Anxiety and concern over drinking;
6. Awareness of problem and receptivity to treatment.

The AUI was developed as an assessment instrument with which to measure these different dimensions of alcohol use. The scales of the AUI are arranged in the hierarchical structure described above, with 17 primary scales, 6 second-order scales, and a general scale tapping broad consequences of alcohol abuse. The original form of the AUI has 147 multiple-choice questions that take 35 to 60 minutes to complete.

Subsequent psychometric evaluation of the AUI has determined that it is internally consistent (median Kuder-

Richardson-20 = .72 for the primary scales, .82 for second-order scales), has good test-retest reliability (median = .82 for primary scales, .83 for second-order scales), is relatively free from response-style biases, and is concurrently valid with respect to other important variables related to alcohol use. For example, a 3-month follow-up study (Rohsenow 1982) demonstrated that the loss of control and sustained drinking primary scales were significantly related to amount of drinking at followup. Jacobsen and Rubin (1981) found that dropouts from treatment were likely to score high on gregarious drinking, while patients completing treatment scored high on obsessive-compulsive drinking. Although high scorers on obsessive-compulsive drinking may not be high risks for treatment dropout, Rohsenow and Smith (1985) have found that they respond poorly to a stress-management-based intervention. These examples illustrate that the AUI represents a promising approach to the development of empirically based treatment assignment decisions based on detailed information concerning features of alcohol use.

## Conclusion

Although there are a number of diverse instruments for the assessment of alcoholism and substance abuse, it is safe to conclude that this area has seen a great deal of progress over the past two decades. However, the researcher and practitioner should be aware that no assessment method is infallible. If possible, a comprehensive assessment should include information gathered across modalities (e.g., questionnaire and interview) as well as across sources (e.g., patient and spouse). Although such multimodal assessments are often not plausible, it is essential that some form of routine inquiry into alcohol and substance abuse be conducted in all health care settings. Given the costs of these disorders to the individual and to society, a failure to do so is unjustifiable.

## References

Anastasi A: Psychological Testing. New York, Macmillan, 1988

Bale RN, Van Stone WW, Engelsing TMJ, et al: The validity of self-reported heroin use. Int J Addict 16:1387–1398, 1981

Bernadt MW, Mumford J, Taylor C, et al: Comparison of questionnaire and laboratory tests in the detection of excessive drinking and alcoholism. Lancet 325–328, 1982

Bush B, Shaw S, Cleary P, et al: Screening for alcohol abuse using the CAGE questionnaire. Am J Med 82:231–235, 1987

Cernovsky ZZ: MacAndrew alcoholism scale and repression: detection of false negatives. Psychol Rep 57:191–194, 1985

Eckardt MJ, Rawlings RR, Martin PR: Biological correlates and detection of alcohol abuse and alcoholism. Prog Neuropsychopharmacol Biol Psychiatry 10:135–144, 1986

Edwards G, Gross MM, Keller J, et al: Alcohol-related disabilities. Offset Publication Number 32, Geneva, World Health Organization, 1977

Ewing JA: Detecting alcoholism, the CAGE questionnaire. JAMA 252:1905–1907, 1984

Guze SB, Tuason VB, Stewart MA, et al: The drinking history: a comparison of reports by subjects and their relatives. Q J Stud Alcohol 33:111–116, 1963

Hathaway SR, McKinley JC: The Minnesota Multiphasic Personality Inventory. Minneapolis, University of Minnesota Press, 1943

Hays JT, Spickard WA: Alcoholism: early diagnosis and intervention. Journal of General Internal Medicine 2:420–427, 1987

Horn JL, Wanberg KW, Foster FM: The Alcohol Use Inventory. Baltimore, Psych Systems, 1983

Jacobson GR, Rubin EM: Premature termination of treatment among alcoholics: predicting outpatient clinic dropouts, in Currents in Alcoholism, Vol VIII. Edited by Galanter M. New York, Grune & Stratton, 1981, pp 162–174

King M: At risk drinking among general practice attenders: validation of the CAGE questionnaire. Psychol Med 16:213–217, 1986

Lachar D, Berman W, Grisell JL, et al: The MacAndrew alcoholism scale as a general measure of substance misuse. J Stud Alcohol 37:1609–1615, 1976

MacAndrew C: The differentiation of male alcoholic outpatients from nonalcoholic psychiatric outpatients by means of the MMPI. Q J Stud Alcohol 26:238–246, 1965

MacAndrew C: What the MAC scale tells us about men alcoholics: an interpretive review. J Stud Alcohol 42:604–625, 1981

Marlatt GA: The Drinking Profile: a questionnaire for the behavioral assessment of alcoholism, in Behavior Therapy Assessment. Edited by Mash EJ, Terdal LG. New York, Springer, 1976

Marlatt GA: Stress as a determinant of excessive drinking and relapse, in Stress and Alcohol Use. Edited by Pohorecky LA, Brick J. New York, Elsevier, 1983

McLellan AT, Luborsky L, O'Brien CP, et al: An improved evaluation instrument for substance abuse patients: the Addiction Severity Index: reliability and validity in three centers. J Nerv Ment Dis 168:26–33, 1980

McLellan AT, Luborsky L, Cacciola J, et al: New data from the Addiction Severity Index: reliability and validity in three centers. J Nerv Ment Dis 173:412–423, 1985

Moore RA: The diagnosis of alcoholism in a psychiatric hospital: a trial of the Michigan Alcoholism Screening Test (MAST). Am J Psychiatry 128:1565–1569, 1972

Morey LC, Blashfield RK: The empirical classification of alcoholism: a review. J Stud Alcohol 42:925–937, 1981

Morey LC, Roberts WR, Penk W: MMPI alcoholic subtypes: replicability and validity of the 2-8-7-4 subtype. J Abnorm Psychol 96:164–166, 1987

Preng KW, Clopton JR: The MacAndrew scale: clinical application and theoretical issues. J Stud Alcohol 47:228–236, 1986

Robinson KS, Burger MC, Spickard WA: Tools for office diagnosis of alcoholism in blacks. Clin Res 35:92A, 1987

Rohsenow DJ: The Alcohol Use Inventory as a predictor of drinking by male heavy social drinkers. Addict Behav 7:387–395, 1982

Rohsenow DJ, Smith RE: Stress management training as a prevention program for heavy social drinkers: cognition, affect drinking, and individual differences. Addict Behav 10:45–54, 1985

Rosen AC: A comparative study of alcoholic and psychiatric patients with the MMPI. Q J Stud Alcohol 21:253–266, 1960

Selzer ML: The Michigan Alcoholism Screening Test: the quest for a new diagnostic instrument. Am J Psychiatry 127:1653–1658, 1971

Skinner HA: A multivariate evaluation of the MAST. J Stud Alcohol 40:831–844, 1979

Skinner HA: The Drug Abuse Screening Test. Addict Behav 7:363–371, 1982

Skinner HA, Allen BA: Alcohol dependence syndrome: measurement and validation. J Abnorm Psychol 91:199–209, 1982

Skinner HA, Horn JL: Alcohol Dependence Scale User's Guide. Toronto, Canada, Addiction Research Foundation, 1984

Skinner HA, Holt S, Sheu WJ, et al: Clinical versus laboratory detection of alcohol abuse: the alcohol clinical index. Br Med J 292:1703–1708, 1986

Sobell LC, Sobell MB: Outpatient alcoholics give valid self-reports. J Nerv Ment Dis 161:32–42, 1975

Stockwell T, Hodgson R, Edwards G, et al: The development of a questionnaire to measure severity of alcohol dependence. Br J Addict 74:79–87, 1979

Svanum S, Levitt EE, McAdoo WG: Differentiating male and female alcoholics from psychiatric outpatients: the MacAndrew and Rosenberg alcoholism scales. J Pers Assess 46:81–84, 1982

Tabakoff B, Hoffman PL, Lee JM, et al: Differences in platelet enzyme activity between alcoholics and nonalcoholics. N Engl J Med 318:134–139, 1988

Wanberg KW, Horn JL: Assessment of alcohol use with multidimensional concepts and measures. Am Psychol 38:1055–1069, 1983

Wanberg KW, Horn JL, Foster FM: A differential assessment model for alcoholism: the scales of the Alcohol Use Inventory. J Stud Alcohol 38:512–543, 1977

Zung BJ: Psychometric properties of the MAST and two briefer versions. J Stud Alcohol 40:845–859, 1979

# Chapter 9

# Assessment of Organic Mental Disorders

**ROBERT M. BILDER, Ph.D.**
**JOHN M. KANE, M.D.**

# Chapter 9

# Assessment of Organic Mental Disorders

$T$he organic mental disorders occupy a unique position in DSM-III-R in that they are the only disorders for which pathophysiology is either "known or presumed" (American Psychiatric Association 1987). Despite this distinction, there are still no specific diagnostic tests for the most frequently encountered organic mental disorders, and the clinician must continue to evaluate these disorders through a careful review of history and phenomenology.

Fortunately for the clinician, advances in psychometric assessment have created new windows on brain function. These windows usually take the form of cognitive or behavioral tests that allow objective observation of the phenomenology associated with brain disease. Many tests are now available; those important for assessment of the organic mental disorders are often described as *neuropsychological* tests.[1]

The increasingly wide repertoire of neuropsychological tests has generally enhanced the evaluation of the organic mental disorders by increasing the range of functions assessed, improving reliability, and increasing validity. Despite the avail-

The authors thank Drs. Steven Roth and Bruce Saltz and an anonymous reviewer for their comments. The preparation of this chapter was supported in part by a grant from the National Institute of Mental Health (MH419960-02).

[1]The term *neuropsychological* should probably be reserved to describe tests for which a clearly defined relation exists between performance on the test and the integrity of some functional brain system or a circumscribed set of systems. In practice, more tests are described as neuropsychological than actually meet these criteria.

ability of these measures and the advantages of their use, they still do not see routine application in clinical evaluation. Instead, there is a tendency to perceive these measures as restricted to the domain of researchers and neuropsychological or psychometric specialists. This perception, born largely out of unfamiliarity with the methods, unduly limits the evaluation process, and deprives clinicians of potentially valuable tools for differential diagnosis, thorough characterization of their patients' assets and liabilities, and appropriate treatment planning.

This chapter familiarizes the reader with some of the major conceptual and methodological issues that pertain to the psychometric evaluation of organic mental disorders, and addresses topics of practical value for the clinician in either direct assessment or in the initiation of referrals for consultation.

## Conceptual Issues

### The Functional Organic Distinction

The functional/organic distinction persists in psychiatric nosology despite suggestions that it might create more problems than it solves. It has been argued that a mental disorder is by definition a brain disorder, and therefore the concept of functional mental disorders is unnecessary: "Physiological and pathological facts show us that this organ can only be the brain; we therefore primarily, and in every case of mental disease, recognise a morbid action of that organ" (Griesinger 1867, p. 1).

Others have argued for the validity of the functional/organic distinction. According to one view, functional disorders are those associated with (maladaptive) learning through normal brain mechanisms, while organic disorders disrupt brain physiology and thus interfere directly with the effects of experience or new learning (Geschwind 1975).

The DSM-III-R adopts a somewhat similar, pragmatic approach. Organic mental disorders are those for which there

186

is "brain dysfunction of *known* organic etiology," while nonorganic (functional) disorders are "more adequately accounted for by psychological or social factors . . . or because the presence of a specific organic factor has not been established" (American Psychiatric Association 1987, p. 98).

Among its advocates, it is the persistence of the functional/organic distinction that speaks most eloquently for its utility. Some other distinctions [such as that between reversible and irreversible disorders, or between treatable and (yet) untreatable disorders] may have even more practical significance, but these would constitute even poorer taxonomic devices. Thus, while it may be useful to consider alternatives, the functional/organic distinction still communicates information among clinicians. Moreover, the DSM-III-R definitions of functional and organic disorders appear to serve the majority of clinical needs given our present state of ignorance regarding the brain substrates of the mental disorders.

## Purposes of Assessment

We will distinguish between two major purposes of psychometric assessment: 1) differential diagnosis and 2) qualitative and quantitative characterization of neurocognitive function (cross-sectionally and/or longitudinally).

Psychometric techniques are now used less frequently for differential diagnosis, given the advent of sophisticated methods for structural and functional brain imaging and the availability of relevant laboratory tests. Nevertheless there are conditions for which psychometric methods may be superior to these hard laboratory measures. For example, the computed-tomography (CT) scan is better at detecting congenital cortical abnormalities, while neuropsychological methods are superior in the detection of persistent sequelae of closed head injury. Furthermore, the neuropsychological methods may detect impairment earlier in cases of vascular insufficiency or neoplasm (Hartlage and Telzrow 1982). The applications for characterization are, however, far more frequent and may find increasing value in the formulation and assessment of interdisciplinary treatment and rehabilitation plans. Given the differences between these purposes, they will be considered separately.

There are two types of differential diagnosis involving organic mental disorders. First is the differential diagnosis of a functional (or no disorder) versus an organic mental disorder (e.g., dementia vs. a mood disorder). Second is the differential of one organic mental disorder versus another (e.g., primary degenerative dementia of the Alzheimer type vs. multi-infarct dementia). Psychometric assessment may be useful in both types of differential.

Differentiating functional from organic disorders may sometimes be accomplished on the basis of absolute performance levels on psychometric tests. Thus, for example, a clinician may use psychometric evidence to demonstrate that criteria for dementia are satisfied. The DSM-III-R criteria for dementia include a number of cognitive impairments (including impairments of new learning, impaired remote memory, decreased capacity for engaging in abstract verbal behavior, along with impairments of higher cortical functions, poor judgment and planning, and personality changes). Psychometric measures that are sensitive to each of these cognitive disturbances are readily available. If very severe deficits are observed on enough of these psychometric measures, the clinician may conclude that criteria for dementia are satisfied (given the absence of contradictory clinical or historical data). This use of test scores is similar to the use of clinical laboratory values for the diagnosis of certain medical disorders.

Threshold scores to indicate abnormality or brain damage have been proposed. Any patient scoring below the predetermined threshold or cutoff score is classified as abnormal, brain damaged, or impaired, while a patient scoring above the cutoff is classified as normal, not brain damaged, or intact.

There are a number of problems with the use of such cutoff scores. First, cutoff scores are often derived from validation studies involving small samples, thereby limiting their reliability and generalizability. Moreover, the base rates of a given disorder may not be considered in reporting classification accuracy, leading to artificially inflated estimates of predictive validity.[2] As with any actuarial tool, there are also the usual caveats regarding the frequency and relative costs of making false-positive and false-negative classifications in individual cases. Despite these disadvantages, cutting scores continue to be used due to their superficial lack of ambiguity; the clinician must be alert to avoid misapplication of such classification strategies.

The pattern of deficit may be more important than the overall severity in indicating an organic mental disorder. The pattern of performance across a series of tests provides a much richer basis for neuropsychological inference. Moreover, information derived from a profile of neuropsychological tests may provide answers to diagnostic questions when simple, absolute deficit-level information does not.

In order to assess course of illness and the presence of deterioration, estimates of "premorbid" functioning must be made. Assessments of premorbid ability typically include measures of functions that are assumed to be resistant to deterioration even in the subacute phase following brain injury. Most widely used for this purpose are tests of general knowledge, vocabulary, and well-routinized skills, such as reading. These estimates of premorbid ability may be contrasted to overall performance levels, or to domains of specific deficit on tasks that are more sensitive to deterioration ("don't hold" tests), to constitute indexes of deterioration (Wechsler 1958). In certain populations it may be advantageous to estimate premorbid ability from demographic information (Wilson et al. 1979), although this is not a useful strategy when an illness interrupts educational achievement, which is the single best predictor of IQ.

---

[2]For example, a psychometric test that correctly identifies 85% of cases with dementia is not very useful in a clinic population where the base rate of dementia is 90%. The degree to which the instruments enhance prediction in a specific population is more meaningful.

Some neuropsychological pattern information is aimed at the identification of functional deficit patterns that may point to a specific diagnostic class. This type of neuropsychological pattern information can be useful in differentiating not only between organic and nonorganic disorders but also between different kinds of organic mental disorders. An example is the differential diagnosis of amnestic disorder from dementia, where the specificity of memory impairment must be evaluated to enable diagnosis. Functional assessment may also be critical in differentiating between different specific developmental disorders.

An additional kind of neuropsychological pattern information that may be useful in diagnosis is that concerning anatomic or physiologic localization of dysfunction in the brain. This use of psychometric tools is typically not important in making differentials between DSM-III-R diagnoses (although it may be possible to differentiate primary degenerative dementia of the Alzheimer type from multi-infarct dementia on the basis of neuropsychological pattern information). Neuropsychological assessment aimed at localization of dysfunction is more likely to be important as an aid to the differential diagnosis of Axis III disorders, or to specify the nature of a disorder within an Axis III disorder. Thus, for example, psychometric data may help in differentiating brain stem from cortical diseases, or in the localization of dysfunction before neurosurgical intervention in patients with intractable seizure disorders or intracranial neoplasms.

One important and underutilized purpose of psychometric assessment is monitoring response to treatment and/or the progression of the illness. Psychometric methods may offer advantages over other methods that are more widely used (e.g., subjective reports, informal interviews, global behavioral rating scales).

### Disorders Most Often Assessed

Among the organic mental disorders in DSM-III-R, the most

common are delirium, psychoactive substance induced disorders, and the dementias, but psychometric assessment techniques are most widely applied in the dementias. In delirium, impairment of attention is typically so severe as to obviate psychometric approaches. Informal qualitative assessments by a neurologist or neuropsychologist may nevertheless be valuable in some cases where focal pathology constitutes part of the differential diagnosis, but in general the characteristic symptoms and history suggest the diagnosis. Moreover, the resolution of delirium is typically rapid enough that detailed characterization of deficits (even if it were practical) is not useful. In the diagnosis of psychoactive substance induced disorders, symptomatic presentation, laboratory results, and history are usually conclusive, and the role of psychometric approaches is less salient. One key exception is alcohol amnestic disorder, in which both diagnosis and characterization of residual deficit may benefit from psychometric assessment (see also Chapter 8 regarding the assessment of alcohol abuse disorders).

A major role for psychometric approaches is found, however, in the assessment of dementias and organic mental disorders associated with Axis III physical disorders. Among the dementias, primary degenerative dementia of the Alzheimer type is so prevalent [more than 7% in those aged 65 or older (Gurland and Cross 1986)] and the role of cognitive assessment is so critical both for diagnosis and characterization of impairment, that a plethora of measures specifically designed for assessment of dementia now exist, a few of which will be discussed later in this chapter.

Less studied are the mental disorders associated with somatic illness. While the syndromes associated with physical illness may masquerade as virtually any one of the major mental disorders, psychometric evidence may be useful again in raising suspicion of a specific etiology or in characterizing the degree of functional impairment. Virtually every DSM-III-R diagnosis assumes that "it cannot be established that an organic factor initiated and maintained the disturbance." Despite the universality of this assumption, little emphasis is typically placed on the assessment of organic factors relative to other aspects of phenomenology that are also critical to accurate diagnosis. Is it because organic factors are so conspicuous that their identification is trivial? Or is it the case, as some have suggested (McIntyre and Romano 1975), that practitioners may underestimate somatic morbidity in psychiatric populations?

Some compelling evidence favors the latter interpretation. The incidence in psychiatric inpatient populations of physical illness requiring medical intervention may be as high as 80% (Johnson 1968; Hall et al. 1980). More disturbing are consistent findings that among those who are physically ill, these illnesses may remain undiagnosed in almost 50% of cases (Maguire and Granville-Grossman 1968; Koranyi 1979). In their analysis of 2,090 psychiatric clinic patients, Koranyi (1979) reported that, in many cases, somatic illness either directly caused (18%) or aggravated (51%) the psychiatric disturbance. While the frequency of undetected illness may be lower in outpatient settings (or in populations excluding patients of lower socioeconomic classes) there are nevertheless significant rates of undetected morbidity even in these populations (Hall et al. 1978). The significance of these findings is obvious when one considers the high proportion of patients who show rapid amelioration of psychiatric symptoms when the physical illness is treated [28% of all patients screened in one study (Hall et al. 1980)].

Given the magnitude of this clinical problem it is clear that efforts should be made to improve the rate of detection and subsequent treatment of somatic illness in syndromes that may present solely as psychiatric disorders. The major issues facing the clinician in a psychiatric setting, as in other branches of medicine, include the appropriate selection of differential diagnostic questions and the administration of (or referral for) the appropriate range of assessment procedures.

Narrowing the differential to the list of likely suspects can offer a real challenge to the clinician. The number of diseases of known etiology with prominent neurobehavioral consequences is so large that simply offering a list would occupy most of the pages allocated for this chapter. The reader is referred to more comprehensive discussions of the organic mental disorders that are available elsewhere (Lishman 1978; McEvoy 1981).

The incidence and types of organic factors that are likely to be encountered in the psychiatric setting do appear to vary in some systematic ways. Thus, cardiovascular diseases may be frequent but less often directly associated with psychiatric illness, while endocrine, nutritional, and metabolic disorders may more frequently masquerade undetected as psychiatric disorders. Added to these are less frequent but more often suspected disorders of the central nervous system including, for example, brain neoplasms, neurodegenerative disorders, temporolimbic seizure disorders, cerebrovascular insults, and sequelae of closed head injury. Adverse reactions to drugs also constitute an all-too-common source of psychiatric symptoms (Shader 1972). High rates of undetected diabetes mellitus may also be characteristic of psychiatric populations (Waitzkin 1966a, 1966b; Koranyi 1979) particularly when impotence is a presenting complaint (Goldman et al. 1970).

## Methodological Issues

### Overview of Assessment Procedures

The psychometric assessment of organic mental disorders has roots in two distinct traditions. On the one hand, there is a corpus of knowledge and techniques derived from neurology and neurosurgery. Informal techniques were developed for the clinical examination of patients with known brain lesions, aimed at the reliable identification of neurological syndromes. Some of these techniques have been formalized (typically through application in research) and have acquired the status of tests. An example of such a test would be the Kinsbourne-Warrington Tests for Finger Agnosia (Kinsbourne and Warrington 1962), and similar developments are described by Warrington as the analytical approach to neuropsychological assessment (McKenna and Warrington 1986).

A separate body of psychometric procedures has come from psychological laboratories. The early products of these schools came in the form of tests of intelligence and later in the form of tests of specific abilities. These tests often were carefully constructed and some showed excellent psychometric properties, but most were designed without consideration of brain function and very few were designed as tests of specific brain functions.

Nevertheless, the fact that these were psychometrically good tests, and often sensitive to a wide range of brain functions (albeit fortuitously) led to their survival as measures useful in psychometric assessment of brain disease. Moreover, in the course of their widespread application, these tests have often acquired a good deal of actuarial significance in the differential diagnosis and characterization of brain disorders. An example is the Wechsler Adult Intelligence Scale, which may be the most widely used test in neuropsychological assessment despite the fact that it was developed without any clear basis in brain-behavior theory.

It is worthwhile also to distinguish between different approaches to the interpretation of psychometric data, regardless of the source of that data. Actuarial or statistical methods are widely used; these methods are generally derived from studies contrasting patients with one diagnosis to those with another (or none). Based on the study data, test scores are calculated that best enable prediction of group membership.

Another approach involves the use of pathognomonic features or signs that may be used singly or in combination to identify a specific diagnostic group or syndrome. A similar clinical approach is embodied in the DSM-III-R, where conjunctions and disjunctions of criteria (signs) are employed to arrive at a diagnosis. As in the DSM-III-R, this pathognomonic-signs strategy typically employs a decision tree of diagnostic hypotheses.

The distinction between the actuarial and nonactuarial approaches is in some ways more practical than theoretical; in theory even elaborate decision patterns could be modeled and given a basis in actuarial statistics. Many of the rules of complex hypothesis testing and pattern detection can now be automatized, given the advent of powerful expert systems that use artificial intelligence techniques. Such systems are not yet in wide use. Furthermore, even if all relevant hypotheses and decisions could be modeled, further validation studies would be necessary to support the validity of the model. Thus the distinction between actuarial and nonactuarial methods persists in clinical practice.

The use of formal tests and quantitative techniques is critical to the application of actuarial interpretation methods and offers clear advantages in assessment of state change and in facilitating communication between professionals. These methods also offer the opportunity for the reliability and validity of methods to be assessed.

On the other hand, there is considerably more information that may be gleaned from a given assessment procedure than is captured in the typical test score. For this reason, investigators have developed approaches involving careful scrutiny of the qualitative characteristics of subjects' productions (or omissions) and have identified different strategies or paths to task solution that may yield similar outcomes. Such information may be considerably more useful in the identification not only of an individual's specific deficits but may also shed light on the fundamental mechanisms involved in task solution. Most familiar for this emphasis is the Boston process approach developed by Kaplan and colleagues (Milberg et al. 1986). Others have also emphasized the importance of integrating qualitative approaches with the interpretation of pathognomonic signs in a manner identifiably derivative from the neurological tradition (Luria 1980; Goldberg and Costa 1986; Reitan 1986).

This distinction between quantitative and qualitative methods is again, however, of more practical than theoretical weight.

Ostensibly qualitative performance features can, of course, be quantified once these have been identified as relevant to either diagnosis or characterization. Practically speaking, however, the progression from qualitative/observational to quantitative/scorable approaches may take years of refinement and research, and this merging of empirical and intuitive styles is one that continues to be advanced in sophisticated neuropsychological laboratories (McKenna and Warrington 1986). It may therefore be difficult for individuals without extensive experience or specific training in qualitative analysis to appropriately apply these techniques. These considerations suggest that nonspecialists may benefit more from the use of formal, structured techniques with known reliability and validity.

### Nonpsychometric Assessment

While the emphasis of this chapter is on psychometric assessment of the organic mental disorders, such methods are never diagnostic when used in isolation. Among the procedures necessary to comprise a neurodiagnostic workup, it is impossible to overestimate the importance of a detailed clinical history. No single source of information has greater significance in assessment of the organic mental disorders, and it could be argued that this is true for any disorder. In the organic mental disorders, however, the illness is more likely than in some other conditions to directly interfere with the patient's ability to render an accurate history. Thus, it becomes more salient to estimate the reliability of the history obtained, and when necessary to corroborate or directly obtain evidence from family members, friends, or other professionals who have long experience with the patient.

It is worthwhile to mention in this context that instruments have been developed specifically to assist in obtaining history relevant to the appropriate evaluation and treatment of organic mental disorders. Some include general formats and checklists for review of history and the elicitation of critical symptoms, such as the Neuropsychological Status Examination (Psychological Assessment Resources 1980). A particularly comprehensive system for the elicitation of neuropsychiatric history and symptoms is the Neurobehavioral Assessment Format (Siegal et al. 1980). Other scales are also available for the elicitation of history pertinent to a specific disorder, such as the scales for detecting risk factors suggestive of multi-infarct dementia (e.g., Hachinski et al. 1975).

Following history, the second most important component of a diagnostic workup is usually a comprehensive medical examination. In the detection of medical illnesses underlying or exacerbating changes in mental status, the most frequent positive findings may be revealed by detailed (34 panel) blood chemistry and a complete physical examination (Hall et al. 1980). Combined with a complete psychiatric history, a neurologic examination, electrocardiogram, complete blood count, urinalysis, and sleep deprived electroencephalogram, it has been suggested that 90% of cases with unrecognized medical illness would be identified (Hall et al. 1980).

It was already suggested that some of the purposes for which psychometric methods might be useful have been supplanted by breakthroughs in technology for the detection and characterization of structural and functional cerebral anomalies (e.g., CT, magnetic resonance imaging, brain electrical activity mapping, brain stem auditory evoked responses, cerebral blood flow, single photon emission CT, positron emission tomography, and super-conducting quantum interference devices). But the mental health clinician may in many cases be a provider of primary care. In some settings, moreover, exhaustive medical workup may be difficult to accomplish, and sophisticated brain-imaging techniques may be unavailable. In these circumstances, psychometric techniques may be convenient, inexpensive, yet sensitive measures to suggest an organic mental disorder and prompt further examination. Moreover, the role of psychometric examination in functional assessment and in the documentation of longitudinal course remains unique.

### Psychometric Assessment Methods

A multitude of psychometric assessment procedures are used in the assessment of organic mental disorders, and there are volumes dedicated to neuropsychological assessment. The interested reader should consult these sources for descriptions of individual tests (e.g., Lezak 1983). The focus here is the general approach to assessment of the organic mental disorders for the clinician. Some key examples are provided to give the clinician a start in applying these techniques.

There may be conflict over many issues in assessment methodology, but most experts would agree on one point: The clinician should learn and gain extensive experience in the administration of a comprehensive mental status examination. Norman Geschwind pointed out several common misimpressions concerning the mental status examination: 1) that conduct of such an examination is a "long and arduous task"; and 2) that such an examination "can be handed over to others." As to the former, he suggested that, as is true of any other examination procedure, "intimate knowledge of the examination and repeated practice" make possible the rapid identification of relevant data. As to the latter, he proposed that "the real measure of a physician's usefulness lies in his capacity to make critical decisions when he is alone with the patient in the small hours of the night" and further that effective screening, intelligent referral, and the adequate use of consultants' opinions depended critically on "[his] basic understanding of all aspects of his patient's problems" (Geschwind 1985, p. viii).

The essential elements of a comprehensive mental status examination are well articulated in texts such as the well-known book by Strub and Black (1985). Those authors advise that the full mental status examination be used routinely in the evaluation of psychiatric patients, given the frequent initial presentation of patients with neurologic disease to the mental health clinic. Following comprehensive history and behavioral observations, the formal mental status examination should include assessments of:

1. The level of consciousness;
2. Attention;
3. Language;
4. Memory;
5. Visuoperceptual/spatial and constructional ability;
6. Corporeal sensitivity;
7. Praxis;
8. Behavioral programming ability;
9. Concept formation and abstraction ability;
10. Basic academic skills (reading, writing, arithmetic);
11. Handedness and elementary sensorimotor function.

In addition to these cognitive, motor, and mnestic domains, the mental state examination should characterize the patient's emotional status (mood and affect), predominant ideation, unusual or idiosyncratic thought content, and level of insight into illness.

None of these neuropsychological or emotional domains is a unitary function, and even cursory assessment of a given function typically requires the use of multiple discrete procedures. For example, a quick and informal examination of language should minimally involve assessment of spontaneous speech (for fluency and prosody), verbal production, comprehension, repetition, naming, reading, and writing, along with higher-order language abilities such as verbal concept formation and abstraction. It should be made clear that the mental status examination may not, in and of itself, answer diagnostic questions or rule out organicity. Following a comprehensive mental status examination, however, the clinician will usually have sufficient information to point more clearly to specific diagnostic hypotheses and to direct appropriate referral questions to consultants.

The comprehensive mental status examination is to be advocated in the assessment of any patient for whom the diagnosis of an organic mental disorder is possible. But practical considerations may prohibit the use of a comprehensive examination that demands considerable clinical experience for rapid administration and interpretation. For this reason, some investigators have developed fully structured, quantitative examinations that are relatively brief and may be administered reliably by either professional or paraprofessional staff, usually after brief training (for a review of mental status scales used in the elderly, see Kochansky 1979 and Crook 1986).

Some examples of formal, structured mental status examinations that include many elements of a comprehensive examination as suggested above, include the Withers-Hinton Tests of the Sensorium (Withers and Hinton 1971) and the Mattis Organic Mental Syndrome Screening Examination (Mattis 1976). These examinations usually take from 20 to 30 minutes to administer and may be quite sensitive, though not specific, to dysfunction associated with organic mental disorders. Although the distinct subsections of these examinations may not be reliable enough to confidently specify a focal functional impairment (such as an isolated attentional or memory deficit), they may well raise specific hypotheses that can be tested through more detailed examination.

Further efforts have been made to reduce the time needed for the mental status examination, leading to the production, for example, of the "mini-mental-state" examination (MMSE). This test takes only 5–10 minutes for administration (scoring is simultaneous with administration) but shows acceptable reliability and validity in some applications (Folstein et al. 1975; DePaulo et al. 1980). Although the MMSE does little to aid in the characterization of patients' assets and liabilities, the capacity to reliably and rapidly raise suspicion of significant cognitive compromise and prompt further neurodiagnostic workup must be seen as a considerable asset in the routine assessment of neuropsychiatric disorders. The MMSE or a similar examination can also serve as a quantitative baseline measure for comparison to subsequent postintervention measures.

Comparable to the MMSE as a brief screening instrument for general cognitive change, there are also some special purpose screening instruments that are brief but more focused on specific diagnostic issues or functional domains. Some examples of this type of instrument include the Halstead-Wepman Aphasia Screening Test, which focuses on language disturbances (Reitan 1979); the Dementia Rating Scale, which focuses on memory, attentional, perseverative, constructional, and conceptual dysfunction common in primary degenerative dementia (Mattis 1976); and the Confabulation questionnaire, which focuses on the elicitation of confabulations typical of the organic amnestic syndrome associated with long-term alcohol use (Mercer et al. 1977).

These screening instruments comprise one approach to initial assessment of the organic mental disorders. As was pointed out, these tests have the advantage of being relatively brief, but the disadvantage of offering little to help characterize a patient's assets and liabilities. There are a diversity of more extensive approaches to the examination of organic mental disorders that can offer considerably more descriptive information, albeit at the expense of time.

The more elaborate, formal examinations and batteries of tests are not uniform in their contents, purposes, or in the types of information they convey. While the generalist clinician may not need to know the details of all these instruments, it is important to know the most widely used approaches in order to: 1) facilitate requests for consultation and 2) confidently interpret what the results do (and do not) indicate. The referring clinician enhances the odds of rapidly obtaining essential data by familiarity with the most common approaches to psychometric assessment.

The assessment of organic mental disorders frequently involves the application of nonspecific or general tests of intellectual or cognitive competence. Some of these general instruments have been so widely used that they have acquired neuropsychological significance despite the fact that they were developed without consideration of brain-behavior relationships. The best example is the Wechsler Adult Intelligence Scale–Revised (WAIS-R), for which there is now substantial actuarial evidence bearing on its validity in the discrimination of brain-damaged from non-brain-damaged individuals. Moreover, discrepancies between the verbal and performance scales, and specific patterns of subtest scores, may help to identify discrete neuropsychological deficits. In addition to these actuarially validated data, there are a variety of qualitative performance characteristics that may be useful in the identification of discrete neuropsychological syndromes (Kaplan et al., in press).

Similar trends have influenced the development of the Halstead-Reitan Battery, which was developed with the intent of assessing brain function, but without benefit of a modern knowledge of brain-behavior theory. The original tests of Halstead included several that would be considered polyfactorial from a functional-systems standpoint. The thrust of this original orientation is inherent in Reitan's concept of general indicators or higher-level central processing functions (Reitan 1986). These functions might be considered emergent properties of multiple functional systems. For this reason, the tests that measure polyfactorial functions tend to be the most sensitive to brain dysfunction. Composite indexes (such as the Halstead-Reitan average impairment index) are statistically more reliable than individual tests and not surprisingly have shown still greater actuarial validity in the discrimination of brain-damaged from control groups. In the use of either polyfactorial measures or composite indexes, one must consider whether the gain in sensitivity is worth the loss in specificity.

There are occasional tendencies for individual test scores to be used as psychometric Rosetta stones for the detection of organicity. While this approach may be valid in actuarial terms, and may sometimes assist the clinician in further raising suspicion of an organic mental disorder, it does nothing to characterize a patient's assets and liabilities. The use of psychometric test data simply to classify patients as "brain damaged" has been eloquently criticized: "the development of a procedure which permits only identification of individuals for whom use of the label is appropriate is equivalent to name-calling, especially when the label has adverse connotations" (Reitan 1986, p. 13).

Tests designed to assess more discrete functional systems have been developed, and continue to emerge as our knowledge of brain-behavior relationships advances. These methods vary from the measurement of quite discrete functions, such as finger-tapping speed, to the measurement of broader functional domains with multiple subcomponents, such as memory [e.g., Wechsler Memory Scale (Wechsler 1945); Boston Remote Memory Battery (Albert et al. 1979)] or language [e.g., Boston Diagnostic Aphasia Exam (Goodglass and Kaplan 1983); Illinois Test of Psycholinguistic Ability (Kirk et al. 1968)]. Such tests find appropriate application in the assessment of specific disorders, such as amnestic or aphasic disorders, and in the comprehensive assessment of neuropsychological functioning. The range of such measures is quite large and continues to increase, so that a listing of such tests, or even a description of the domains covered, would be beyond the scope of this brief chapter. The interested reader is referred to neuropsychology textbooks for introduction to these methods and descriptions of representative instruments (Lezak 1983).

Some psychometric measures have been developed to tap features specific to certain neurobehavioral syndromes, even though these features may not be clear correlates of any functional brain system. For example, an inventory was developed to assess characteristics of the hypothesized interictal personality profile of patients with temporal lobe epilepsy (Bear and Fedio 1977). There are also a number of assessment instruments designed specifically for the assessment of behavioral characteristics of patients with dementia (Blessed et al. 1968). These can be seen as comparable in purpose to the specialized screening instruments mentioned previously, but differ either in their length, or in their emphasis on general (noncognitive) adaptive characteristics. These measures may provide impor-

organic mental disorders, in addition to their role in raising suspicion of specific brain disease.

Finally, there are a variety of approaches to the assessment of organic mental disorders that utilize comprehensive batteries comprised of both general and special-purpose test instruments. Such assessments are typically conducted by or under the direct supervision of neuropsychologists. The composition of neuropsychological test batteries vary, but most comprehensive assessments include at least some measure of general intellectual functioning (typically the WAIS-R in native English-speaking adults who have no specific handicaps) along with an array of general and specialized instruments for the assessment of discrete functional brain systems.

Some clinicians prefer to use a fixed battery approach (i.e., the same set of instruments is administered to each patient). Others individually tailor the examination to raise key hypotheses or to answer specific referral questions. In either approach, a comprehensive evaluation will usually assess the integrity of general intellectual functioning and logical problem-solving ability; speech and language functions; vigilance, tracking, and attentional functions; behavioral programming and executive functions; visuospatial/constructional functions; learning and memory functions; sensory and motor functions; and basic academic skills.

Regardless of the instrumentation used, the overall goal of such a comprehensive assessment is usually not only to answer differential diagnostic or classificatory questions, but to provide the referral source with another picture of the patient as a whole, emphasizing the role that intact and compromised cerebral mechanisms may play in the mediation of the individual's current and future adaptive functioning.

# References

Albert MS, Butters N, Levin J: Temporal gradients in the retrograde amnesia of patients with alcoholic Korsakoff's disease. Arch Neurol 36:211–216, 1979

American Psychiatric Association: Diagnostic and Statistical Manual of Mental Disorders, Third Edition, Revised. Washington, DC, American Psychiatric Association, 1987

Bear DM, Fedio P: Quantitative analysis of interictal behavior in temporal lobe epilepsy. Arch Neurol 34:454–467, 1977

Blessed G, Tomlinson BE, Roth M: The association between quantitative measures of senile dementia and of senile changes in the cerebral grey matter of elderly subjects. Br J Psychiatry 114:797–811, 1968

Crook T: Overview of memory assessment instruments, in Clinical Memory Assessment of Older Adults. Edited by Poon LW. Washington, DC, American Psychological Association, 1986

DePaulo JR, Folstein MF, Gordon B: Psychiatric screening on a neurological ward. Psychol Med 10:125–132, 1980

Folstein MF, Folstein SE, McHugh PR: "Mini-Mental State": a practical method for grading the cognitive state of patients for the clinician. J Psychiatr Res 12:189–198, 1975

Geschwind N: The borderland of neurology and psychiatry: some common misconceptions, in Psychiatric Aspects of Neurologic Disease. Edited by Benson DF, Blumer D. New York, Grune & Stratton, 1975

Geschwind N: Foreword (1977), in The Mental Status Examination in Neurology, 2nd ed. Edited by Strub RL, Black FW. Philadelphia, F.A. Davis, 1985

Goldberg E, Costa LC: Qualitative indices in neuropsychological assessment: an extension of Luria's approach to executive deficit following prefrontal lesions, in Neuropsychological Assessment of Neuropsychiatric Disorders. Edited by Grant I, Adams KM. New York, Oxford, 1986

Goldman JA, Schechter A, Eckerling B: Carbohydrate metabolism in infertile and impotent males. Fertil Steril 21:397–401, 1970

Goodglass H, Kaplan E: The Assessment of Aphasia and Related Disorders, 2nd ed. Philadelphia, Lea & Febiger, 1983

Griesinger W: Mental Pathology and Therapeutics. New York, Hafner Press, 1965

Gurland BJ, Cross PS: Public health perspectives on clinical memory testing of Alzheimer's disease and related disorders, in Clinical Memory Assessment of Older Adults. Edited by Poon LW. Washington, DC, American Psychological Association, 1986

Hachinski VC, Iliff LD, Zilhka E, et al: Cerebral blood flow in dementia. Arch Neurol 32:632–637, 1975

Hall RCW, Popkin MK, DeVaul RA, et al: Physical illness manifesting as psychiatric disease. Arch Gen Psychiatry 35:1315–1320, 1978

Hall RCW, Gardner ER, Stickney SK, et al: Physical illness manifesting as psychiatric disease, II: analysis of a state hospital inpatient population. Arch Gen Psychiatry 37:989–995, 1980

Hartlage LC, Telzrow CF: Taxonomy of neuropsychological and CT scan comparisons. Paper presented at the annual meeting of the International Neuropsychological Society, Pittsburgh, February 1982

Johnson DAW: Evaluation of routine physical examination in psychiatric cases. Practitioner 200:686–691, 1968

Kaplan E, Fein D, Morris R, et al: The WAIS-R as a Neuropsychological Instrument. New York, Psychological Corporation (in press)

Kinsbourne M, Warrington EK: A study of finger agnosia. Brain 85:47–66, 1962

Kirk SA, McCarthy JJ, Kirk WD: Illinois Test of Psycholinguistic Abilities. Examiner's Manual, rev ed. Urbana, IL, University of Illinois Press, 1968

Kochansky GE: Psychiatric rating scales for assessing psychopathology in the elderly: a critical review, in Psychiatric

Symptoms and Cognitive Loss in the Elderly. Edited by Raskin A, Jarvik L. Washington, DC, Hemisphere, 1979

Koranyi EK: Morbidity and rate of undiagnosed physical illnesses in a psychiatric clinic population. Arch Gen Psychiatry 36:414–419, 1979

Lezak M: Neuropsychological Assessment, 2nd ed. New York, Oxford, 1983

Lishman A: Organic Psychiatry. Oxford, Blackwell, 1978

Luria AR: The Higher Cortical Functions in Man. New York, Basic Books, 1980

Maguire GP, Granville-Grossman KL: Physical illness in psychiatric patients. Br J Psychiatry 115:1365–1369, 1968

Mattis S: Mental status examination for organic mental syndrome in the elderly patient, in Geriatric Psychiatry. Edited by Bellak L, Karasu TB. New York, Grune & Stratton, 1976

McEvoy JP: Organic brain syndromes. Ann Intern Med 95:212–220, 1981

McIntyre S, Romano J: Is there a stethoscope in the house (and is it used)? Arch Gen Psychiatry 34:1147–1151, 1975

McKenna P, Warrington EK: The analytical approach to neuropsychological assessment, in Neuropsychological Assessment of Neuropsychiatric Disorders. Edited by Grant I, Adams KM. New York, Oxford, 1986

Mercer B, Wapner W, Gardner H, et al: A study of confabulation. Arch Neurol 34:429–433, 1977

Milberg WP, Hebben N, Kaplan E: The Boston Process Approach to neuropsychological assessment, in Neuropsychological Assessment of Neuropsychiatric Disorders. Edited by Grant I, Adams KM. New York, Oxford, 1986

Psychological Assessment Resources: Neuropsychological Status Examination. Odessa, FL, Psychological Assessment Resources, 1980

Reitan RM: Manual for Administration of Neuropsychological Test Batteries for Adults and Children. Tucson, AZ, Reitan Neuropsychology Laboratories, 1979

Reitan RM: Theoretical and methodological bases of the Halstead-Reitan neuropsychological battery, in Neuropsychological Assessment of Neuropsychiatric Disorders. Edited by Grant I, Adams KM. New York, Oxford, 1986

Shader RI (ed): Psychiatric Complications of Medical Drugs. New York, Raven Press, 1972

Siegal AW, Schechter MD, Diamond SP, et al: Neurobehavioral Assessment Format. Unpublished manuscript, 1980 (available from A.W. Siegal, Buffalo, NY)

Strub RL, Black FW (eds): The Mental Status Examination in Neurology, 2nd ed. Philadelphia, F.A. Davis, 1985

Waitzkin L: A survey for unknown diabetes in a mental hospital, 1: men under 50. Diabetes 15:97–104, 1966a

Waitzkin L: A survey for unknown diabetes in a mental hospital, 2: men from age 50. Diabetes 15:164–172, 1966b

Wechsler D: A standardized memory scale for clinical use. J Psychology 19:87–95, 1945

Wechsler D: The Measurement and Appraisal of Adult Intelligence, 4th ed. Baltimore, Williams & Wilkins, 1958

# Related Topics in Assessment

# Chapter 10

# Instruments for the Assessment of Family Malfunction

**JOHN F. CLARKIN, Ph.D.**
**IRA D. GLICK, M.D.**

# Chapter 10

# Instruments for the Assessment of Family Malfunction

**W**ith the advent of DSM-III (and its recent progeny, DSM-III-R), characterized by its generally explicit, behavioral, and time-referenced criteria for arriving at diagnoses of the individual patient, assessment instruments have been developed to reliably assess these criteria. Indeed, the number of instruments that subsequently arose stimulated the present volume. Inherent in this situation, however, is a dilemma for anyone wishing to measure the functioning of a family unit or even the individual's perception of his/her family unit, a social organism that is barely alluded to in DSM-III. While DSM-III hails itself as atheoretical, it is not entirely so (how could it be?). The DSM-III-R takes the stance that the locus of pathology and therefore the object of diagnosis is the individual. The family is conceptualized as a possible stressor to be rated on Axis IV. Little mention is given (only in V codes) to explicit family disruptions such as marital conflict.

A central question, then, is the relationship between diagnosed individual conditions on DSM-III-R Axis I and Axis II, and the family environment of these individuals. Is the family environment relevant at all, or only to some of these individual disorders? Is the family best conceived as a potential stressor affecting the individual (à la DSM-III-R), or as the all-important system context that gave rise to the individual behavior as often conceptualized by the family therapists?

Unfortunately, there is very little research information on these questions, and it is in this context that we explore some of the existing instruments to measure family functioning and malfunctioning.

It is precisely at the intersection of the individual pathology (as described phenomenologically in DSM-III-R) and the family environment that one of the inherent limitations of the current diagnostic system exists: its less than optimal relationship to treatment planning. Many have noted the imperfect relationship between the individual's diagnosis and the treatment needed (Clarkin and Perry 1987; Frances et al. 1984). For treatment planning, one must go beyond a phenomenological description of symptoms to a model of the disorder in question. Such a model would describe the relevant variables (including intrapsychic, interpersonal, and biological ones with their varying weights or degrees of importance) as they interact over time. Most such models give weight to one or more aspects of the family environment.

In this theoretical context, it should be noted that there are currently two types of family-instrument development: 1) instrument development that presupposes general areas of family functioning/malfunctioning that are central to the family as a whole and are hypothesized to be relevant whatever the diagnosis of the individual, or in situations where the chief complaint is family conflict with no one disordered individual, and 2) the development of family instruments given the fact that one individual in the family has a diagnosed DSM-III or DSM-III-R disorder. Both orientations are useful and may further empirical information on the relationship of the individual's pathology and the family system.

We hold several assumptions in guiding this task. The first assumption is that the diagnosed pathology of the individual has some potential relationship to the condition of the immediate family, thus leading to the need to assess the family when the individual resides with or is in constant contact with them. Most models of individual pathology suggest a role for the family environment, not necessarily as a causative agent in the pathology but as a mediating or maintaining cause that may affect the course of the disorder (e.g., models of schizophrenia and affective disorders). In addition there are other individual conditions (e.g., acting-out adolescents, phobias in married females) where the family environment can play a major role in controlling the individual's abnormal behavior if the right steps are taken. While many family therapists adhere to a basic position that all pathology does not reside in the individual but in the family system as a whole and that the diagnosis of the individual is a mistake, we find that position extreme and not supported by current research.

Second, we assume that family assessment instruments may assist in differential treatment planning in a number of ways: it may suggest the need for no family intervention, or simply psychoeducation; it may suggest the need for family therapy format due to the disrupted family environment; or it may indicate not only the need for family intervention, but also pinpoint a certain focus for the work. We have emphasized elsewhere (Glick et al. 1987) that the use of assessment instruments should be integrated with the clinical interview assessment and logically be related to the goals, strategies, and techniques of existing family interventions.

Our focus in this chapter will be on clinical assessment. Therefore, we will not cover those instruments that are being used primarily in research. Clinicians do not have independent raters available to observe and rate interactions. They are also trying to quickly assess and intervene, and thus have the cooperation of the family for a limited amount of assessment time. We will place most emphasis on self-report instruments, that is, paper and pencil instruments that are completed by the individual. Self-report instruments take little clinician time, are easy to administer and score, and provide the clinician with cost-effective information.

## Classification of Assessment Instruments

There are a number of ways to classify the existing family

and marital assessment instruments. We will briefly review these methods of classification here, as they help to clarify the intent and potential use of the instruments.

### Focus of Assessment Content

The instruments can be compared and contrasted by their focus (Table 1). For example, DSM-III-R Axis IV can be seen as an instrument that the clinician uses to rate the severity of stressors, including family and marital stressors, that are impinging on the patient. The underlying assumption here is that the individual is the site of the pathology and the family is a stressor. In contrast, instruments such as the Marital Satisfaction Inventory ask the individuals to report on their view of the family and marital interaction. The Family Assessment Measure is probably the most inclusive instrument; it asks the individual to report on self in relation to the family, self in key dyadic relations in the family, and family functioning as a whole.

**Table 1.**  Focus of Assessment Content

| Instrument | Focus |
|---|---|
| Diagnostic and Statistical Manual-III-R (DSM-III-R) | Individual pathology. Family is rated as stress factor on Axis IV. |
| Structural Analysis of Social Behavior (SASB) | Individual reporting on own interpersonal behavior. |
| Family Assessment Measure (FAM) | Self in relation to family. Dyadic relationship scale. Reporting on family as a whole. |
| Marital Satisfaction Inventory (MSI) | Individual reporting on marital interaction. |
| Camberwell Family Interview (CFI) | Family member reporting on a "patient" member. |

## Instrument Method

The method of gathering data is a common way to classify instruments. This would include the following methodologies: self-report, observer rating, semistructured interview, and completion of a standardized behavioral task. Each of these methods has its assets and liabilities. As mentioned previously, the self-report instruments are popular because they provide the patient's and family's points of view with little cost (time) to the clinician. The major threat to validity of a self-report instrument is its dependence on the individual's insight and honesty in reporting.

## Dimensions of Assessment

It is instructive to compare the family instruments on the dimensions of family functioning that they assess. In lieu of a generally accepted theory of family pathology and how this pathology relates to the different individual disorders in family members, this approach to instrument inspection provides a synopsis of the dimensions of family functioning that have some consensual face validity among family theorists.

Fisher (1976) identified five common dimensions in his review of family assessment: 1) structural descriptors such as role boundaries, 2) controls and sanctions, 3) emotions and needs such as affective expression, 4) cultural aspects, and 5) developmental aspects. Elsewhere, we (Clarkin et al. 1983) surveyed a number of existing family assessment instruments and arrived at five dimensions that were emphasized in many of the scales. These dimensions included 1) communication, negotiation, and conflict; 2) affectivity; 3) system and boundary issues; 4) individuation; and 5) behavior control. Bloom (1985) has approached this issue empirically by factor-analyzing the item pool from three commonly used family self-report instruments (Family Environment Scale, Family Assessment Scale, and the Family Adaptability and Cohesion Evaluation Scales).

He derived a 75-item scale composed of 15 dimensions of family functioning.

### Family and Marital Assessment

The existing family assessment instruments typically have items relating to the family as a group, including the interactions of spouses, parents, and children (see Table 2). In contrast,

**Table 2.** Family and Marital Assessment Measures

| Instrument | Dimensions |
| --- | --- |
| **Family Instruments** | |
| Family Adaptability and Cohesion Evaluation Scales (FACES) | Cohesion and adaptability |
| Family Assessment Device (FAD) | Communication, problem solving, role for coalition, affective responsiveness, affective involvement, behavioral control |
| Family Assessment Measures (FAM) | Task accomplishment, role performance, communication, affective expression, involvement, control, values and norms, overall rating |
| Family Environment Scale | Relationship dimension (cohesion, expressiveness, conflict), personal growth dimension (independence, activity orientation, intellectual/cultural orientation, active recreational, morale/religious emphasis), system-maintenance dimension (organization, control) |
| **Marital Instruments** | |
| Dyadic Adjustment Scale (DAS) | Satisfaction, cohesion, consensus, and affectional expression |
| Marital Satisfaction Inventory (MSI) | Conventionalization, global distress, affective communication, problem solving, disagreement about finances, sexual dissatisfaction, disaffection and disharmony, role orientation, family history of distress, dissatisfaction with children, conflict over child rearing |

the marital inventories focus principally on the interaction between spouses, including areas not typically covered in the family scales such as spousal sexual behavior and satisfaction. In addition, the marital inventories may make reference to children by items on parenting behaviors and satisfaction.

### Psychiatric Patient and Family Interaction

Traditionally, the family field has been opposed to diagnosing the individual patient and has focused instead on the interactions of the whole family system, which are seen as stimulating and governing the behavior of the individuals in the system. From this point of view, individual diagnosis is at best misleading in attempting to understand the individual's behavior, and, at worst, contributes to further scapegoating of the individual and impedes change.

In more recent years, however, it has become clear that some individual disorders (e.g., schizophrenia and bipolar disorder) have a prominent biological component such that the total, or even the predominant, control of the abnormal behavior cannot be attributed to the family system. Extensive research has been conducted on individuals with schizophrenia, and the differential effects of the family environment on the course of the disorder. This research has given rise to several instruments that assess the particular dimension of family life—termed *expressed emotion* (EE)—that has proved to be relevant to the course of schizophrenia. The Camberwell Family Interview (CFI) (Brown and Rutter 1966) is a semistructured interview of a significant family member and his/her attitudes and behavior toward the family member with schizophrenia. Unfortunately, this instrument requires extensive training in reliably rating dimensions of criticality, hostility, and overinvolvement, and therefore is not available to the average clinician. A striking clinical need is for a self-report instrument that correlates well with the CFI.

In addition to the measurement of EE, the psychoeducational approach to the schizophrenic patient and family has gained prominence recently (Anderson et al. 1986). It has been hypothesized that information about the symptoms, causes, course, and treatment of the disorder would be instrumental in helping the family cope by reducing specific environmental stress. A number of researchers have utilized simple questionnaires to assess the family's knowledge of schizophrenia before and after psychoeducational intervention (see Clarkin, in press, for a review). It is quite conceivable that family clinicians would want to use one or more of these instruments before psychoeducational intervention to assess the extent of family information and thus focus their psychoeducation.

Likewise, there has been some specific work with patients with depression and family/marital intervention (see Clarkin et al. 1988). When the patient presents with depression, for example, it may be clinically helpful to combine instruments for the assessment of depression in the individual and instruments for the assessment of marital and family discord by all family members. Depression in the context of marital discord is treated differently than depression without such family discord.

## Review of Specific Family Instruments

We will briefly review some of the most utilized and researched family assessment instruments that have clinical relevance. This review is not intended to be exhaustive or totally extensive, but to simply raise the most salient issues in instrument selection for the clinician. Hopefully, the clinician who uses not only family/marital treatment formats but also individual treatment formats will find these instruments relevant for treatment planning.

### Family Environment Scale (FES)

Developed by Rudolph Moos, who has a long history of studying and measuring different environments, the Family Environment Scale (Moos and Moos 1981) is a 90-item (true/false) self-report scale that assesses three family dimensions: relationship dimensions (cohension, expressiveness, and conflict), personal growth dimensions (independence, achievement orientation, intellectual-cultural orientation, active-recreational orientation, and moral-religious emphasis), and system maintenance dimensions (organization and control). By using three different forms of the instrument, one can assess the individual's perceptions of the actual family environment, the individual's perception of the ideal family environment, and the individual's expectations about family settings.

The scales have good internal consistency. There is extensive normative data on normal and distressed families, including those from diverse cultural groups. The scale has enjoyed extensive use in clinically relevant research, including derivation of treatment relevant family types (Billings and Moos 1982), evaluation of treatment outcome for alcoholism (Finney et al. 1980), and case studies using information from the scale to focus intervention (Moos and Fuhr 1982).

### The Family Assessment Device (FAD)

This is a 53-item self-report scale based on the McMaster model of family functioning (Miller et al. 1985). It assesses seven different dimensions of family functioning: problem solving, communication, roles, affective responsiveness, affective involvement, behavior control, and a general rating of health pathology (e.g., "When someone is upset, the others know why"; "In this time of crisis, we can turn to each other for support").

The seven scales have internal consistency estimates ranging from .72 to .92. The FAD has a low correlation with the Marlow Crowne Social Desirability Scale. The instrument shows good test-retest reliability. Concurrent validity is shown by its appropriate correlation with the Family Unit Inventory. More importantly, six of the seven scales (minus behavior control) have significant correlation with clinician's rating.

### The Family Assessment Measure (FAM)

This is a self-report instrument that yields measures on the following dimensions: task accomplishment, role performance, communication, affective expression, involvement, control, and values and norms (Skinner et al. 1983).

The latest and third version of the instrument (FAM III) (Skinner 1987) has 134 true/false items on three scales: 1) the general scale, measuring health and pathology of family functioning (e.g., "We spend too much time arguing about what our problems are"; "We have the same views on what is right and wrong"), and the response set of the individual taking the test; 2) a dyadic relationship scale, which focuses on specific dyads in the family (e.g., "I know what this person means when he/she says something"; "This person takes what I say the wrong way"); and 3) a self-rating scale, which focuses on the individual's perception of his/her functioning in the family ("My family expects too much of me"; "I do my share of duties in the family").

There is extensive normative data for both normal and clinical families. The scales have good internal consistency and are at times so highly correlated with one another as to suggest substantial scale overlap.

### The Marital Satisfaction Inventory (MSI)

This self-report instrument (Snyder 1979) contains 280 true/false items that cover marital relations, and a section for couples with children. The instrument yields $t$ scores on 11 scales: conventionalization, global distress, affective communication, problem-solving communication, time together, disagreement about finances, sexual dissatisfaction, role orientation, family history of distress, dissatisfaction with children, and conflict over child rearing. Sample items are: "My spouse and I don't have much in common to talk about"; "My spouse has no difficulty accepting criticism"; "Our children often manage to drive a wedge between my spouse and me."

Coefficients of internal consistency for the individual scales are quite good, as is test-retest reliability (average of .89). The instrument not only discriminates between clinic couples and matched controls, but has also been shown to discriminate between sexually dysfunctional couples and a matched clinical sample of couples with more general complaints of marital distress.

In a subsequent study (Snyder et al. 1981), couples applying for marital treatment were interviewed conjointly and rated on a 61-item checklist of relevant clinical criteria. Numerous significant MSI scale by criterion correlations supported the convergent and discriminant validity of the MSI scales.

Two additional scales, disaffection and disharmony, have been derived from factor analysis (Snyder and Regts 1982). Both these scales discriminated between normative and clinical populations. Furthermore, criterion-related validity was demonstrated by documenting the relationship of the scales to clinicians' ratings of couples entering marital therapy.

### Structural Analysis of Social Behavior (SASB)

Benjamin's (1974) Structural Analysis of Social Behavior (SASB) is a circumplex model of interpersonal relations and their intrapsychic representations. In this model, three circumplex surfaces (two focus on interpersonal transactions and a third on intrapsychic experiences) and two orthogonal dimensions of affiliation and interdependence are hypothesized to sufficiently describe systemic and interpersonal events. In addition to a set of rating scales and an observational coding system based on the SASB model (which are too time consuming to be clinically relevant), there are also index questionnaires that can be used to describe raters' perceptions of themselves and their relations with other people including current family members and the family of origin.

### Family Adaptability and Cohesion Evaluation Scales (FACES)

Olson and colleagues (Olson et al. 1979, 1983) developed the Family Adaptability and Cohesion Evaluation Scales (FACES) as a self-report measure of two central themes they found in the family therapy literature. Family cohesion is the emotional bonding between family members, and family adaptability is the ability of the family members singly and as a unit to change their interaction patterns in response to stress. The two dimensions of cohesion (low to high) and adaptability (from rigid to chaotic) form a circumplex model that defines 16 types of marital and family systems.

FACES has undergone extensive development, and the current version (FACES III; Olson and Killorin 1985) has 20 items, 10 items each for the adaptability and the cohesion scales. There is good scale internal consistency and low correlation with a social desirability response set. There are extensive norms from earlier versions of the instrument from a national survey.

## Summary

While some instruments (e.g., FAM, FAD) claim to be based on a model of family functioning, these models are at a very primitive level of development. They provide little explication of constructs that relate to the development, maintenance, and prognosis of pathology either in the individual or in the family system. Furthermore, these models seem to assume that the same areas of family functioning are relevant to all individual pathology, regardless of the specific diagnosis. The one major exception to this is the measurement of EE as it relates to schizophrenia and at times to mood disorders. Constructs of family functioning may or may not be applicable across different diagnostic groups (e.g., family constructs such as EE, which have been very useful with patients with schizophrenia, may or may not prove useful with patients with major affective disorder).

There is some increasing attention to the use of instruments to pinpoint foci of intervention (Benjamin 1977; Moos and Fuhr 1982). However, this work has been on a single-case basis. The field needs the generation of large-sample studies with specification of homogeneous patient groups of important subtypes of families that would have relevance for treatment planning in terms of *treatment format*, e.g., need for family versus individual and group treatments; *treatment strategies*, e.g., optimal use of behavioral systems, dynamic techniques, and strategies; and *optimal focus on family problem areas* that are appropriate targets for intervention. This third area has had the most attention, but authors who have focused on this have made little attempt to relate specific problem areas to specific individual patient pathology.

Probably the most effort is being put into self-report measures. There are, of course, problems with self-report methodology. Defensiveness and lack of insight by the reporter are a few obvious ones. The lack of correlation between the husband and wife reports on the same family at the same time with many of these self-report instruments is probably related to this problem.

## References

Anderson CM, Reiss DJ, Hogarty GE: Schizophrenia and the Family. New York, Guilford Press, 1986

Benjamin LS: Structural analysis of social behavior. Psychol Rev 81:392–445, 1974

Benjamin LS: Structural analysis of a family in therapy. J Consult Clin Psychol 45:391–406, 1977

Billings AG, Moos RH: Family environments and adaptation: a clinically applicable typology. American Journal of Family Therapy 10:26–38, 1982

Bloom BL: A factor analysis of self-report measures of family functioning. Fam Process 24:225–239, 1985

Brown GW, Rutter ML: The measurement of family activities and relationships. Human Relations 19:241, 1966

Clarkin JF: Family education, in A Clinical Guide for the Treatment of Schizophrenia. Edited by Bellack A. New York, Plenum (in press)

Clarkin JF, Perry S (eds): Differential therapeutics, in Psychiatry Update, Volume 6. Washington, DC, American Psychiatric Press, 1987

Clarkin JF, Frances A, Perry S: Family classifications and DSM-III, in Group and Family Therapy 1983. Edited by Wolberg LR, Aronson ML. New York, Brunner/Mazel, 1983

Clarkin JF, Haas G, Glick ID (eds): Affective Disorder and the Family. New York, Guilford Press, 1988

Finney JW, Moos RH, Newborn CR: Posttreatment experiences and treatment outcome of alcoholic patients six months and two years after hospitalization. J Consult Clin Psychol 48:17–29, 1980

Fisher L: Dimensions of family assessment. Journal of Marital and Family Counseling 2:367–382, 1976

Frances A, Clarkin JF, Perry S: Differential Therapeutics in Psychiatry: The Art and Science of Treatment Selection. New York, Brunner/Mazel, 1984

Glick ID, Clarkin JF, Kessler D: Marital and Family Therapy, 3rd ed. New York, Grune & Stratton, 1987

Miller IW, Epstein NB, Bishop BS, et al: The McMaster family assessment device: reliability and validity. Journal of Marital and Family Therapy 11:345–356, 1985

Moos R, Fuhr R: The clinical use of social-ecological concepts: the case of an adolescent girl. Am J Orthopsychiatry 52:111–122, 1982

Moos R, Moos B: Family Environment Scale Manual. Palo Alto, CA, Consulting Psychologists Press, 1981

Olson DH, Killorin E: Clinical Rating Scale for the Circumplex Model. St. Paul, Family Social Science, University of Minnesota, 1985

Olson DH, Sprenkle DH, Russell CS: Circumplex model of marital and family systems, 1: cohesion and adaptability dimensions, family types, and clinical applications. Fam Process 18:3–28, 1979

Olson DH, Russell CS, Sprenkle DH: Circumplex model of marital and family systems, 6: theoretical update. Fam Process 22:69–83, 1983

Skinner HA: Self-report instruments for family assessment, in Family Interaction and Psychopathology. Edited by Jacob T. New York, Plenum, 1987

Skinner HA, Steinhauer PD, Santa-Barbara J: The Family Assessment Measure. Canadian Journal of Community Mental Health 2:91–105, 1983

Snyder D: Multidimensional assessment of marital satisfaction. Journal of Marriage and the Family 41:813–823, 1979

Snyder D, Regts JM: Factor scales for assessing marital disharmony and disaffection. J Consult Clin Psychol 50:736–743, 1982

Snyder D, Wills RM, Keiser TW: Empirical validation of the Marital Satisfaction Inventory: an actuarial approach. J Consult Clin Psychol 49:262–268, 1981

## Chapter 11

# Ethnocultural Issues in the Assessment of Psychopathology

**ANTHONY J. MARSELLA, Ph.D.**
**VELMA A. KAMEOKA, Ph.D.**

# Chapter 11

# Ethnocultural Issues in the Assessment of Psychopathology

*T*he purpose of this chapter is to discuss ethnocultural issues in the assessment of psychopathology. For many years, the cultural determinants of psychopathology were largely ignored among psychiatrists and psychologists because of the belief that the etiology, expression, course, and outcome of mental disorders were largely universal in nature and therefore independent of cultural variation. However, recent research within the fields of transcultural psychiatry, medical anthropology, and cross-cultural psychology has posed serious challenges to the universalist position by demonstrating numerous ethnocultural variations in psychopathology (Draguns 1980; Marsella 1979, 1980, 1982, 1984; Marsella and White 1982; Kleinman and Good 1985; Triandis and Draguns 1980).

The literature indicates that cultural factors influence all aspects of psychopathology by 1) determining standards of normality and abnormality (Katz et al. 1978); 2) fostering stressors that exceed individual and group coping tolerances (Marsella and Scheuer 1987; Marsella et al. 1971); 3) creating personality configurations that have poor fit with environmental demands (Marsella 1984); 4) encouraging particular models of disease

Portions of this paper were presented at the workshop on "Depression and Suicide in Minorities," sponsored by the Division of Clinical Research, National Institute of Mental Health, Bethesda, Maryland, December 7–8, 1987.

perceptions, causality, and control (Serota 1986); and 5) conditioning particular patterns of disease expression and experience (Kleinman 1977; Marsella et al. 1973; Murphy et al. 1967). Transcultural psychiatric research is clear and unequivocal in demonstrating that cultures vary in the rates, diagnostic patterns, expression, and course and outcome of psychopathology. These variations demand that our assessment methods be responsive to cultural nuances in all aspects of the assessment endeavor.

While there have been many reviews of this research literature on cross-cultural variations in psychopathology, there have been relatively few articles that have focused specifically on the cross-cultural assessment of psychopathology (e.g., Butcher 1987; Marsella 1987). In light of this gap, this chapter will address the implications of cross-cultural research in psychopathology for assessment by discussing six basic topics: 1) the concept of culture, 2) cultural considerations in the assessment of psychopathology, 3) methodological strategies for valid comparisons in cross-cultural research, 4) cultural issues in epidemiology and clinical practice, 5) the importance of ethnic identity, and 6) closing comments and suggestions.

## The Concept of Culture

### The Definition of Culture

While the term *culture* is often used by researchers, clinicians, and laymen, there is little agreement on its definition. Kluckhohn and Kroeber (1952) reviewed 150 definitions of the term in their book. They pointed out that efforts to develop a single definition have been hampered by particular theoretical and conceptual predilections of authors. We favor a definition that represents an elaboration of a definition first advanced by Ralph Linton (1945), the famous cultural anthropologist.

Linton defined culture as shared, learned behavior transmitted from one generation to another. We agree with Linton's emphasis on culture as a behavior rather than a static entity. We also agree that culture is something that is learned or acquired, and that it is something transmitted across generations. However, we also believe that this definition of culture would be strengthened by adding a purpose dimension to the definition and by adding statements on the external and internal referents of culture. Thus, we would redefine culture in the following way:

> Culture is shared learned behavior that is transmitted from one generation to another for purposes of human adjustment, adaptation, and growth. Culture has both external and internal referents. External referents include artifacts, roles, and institutions. Internal referents include attitudes, values, beliefs, expectations, epistemologies, and consciousness.

This definition highlights the fact that culture is something that goes beyond clothes, food, buildings, arts, and the other referents so often associated with the term by laymen. Culture is something that mediates and shapes virtually all aspects of human behavior. It is the way in which human beings define and experience reality. It includes their sense of time, space, and causality; it is their sense of morality and personhood. It includes the very way that they experience consciousness.

These dimensions of human behavior are not inborn but rather are shaped by the socialization process. All socialization processes reflect the cultural context in which they exist and are promulgated. An ethnocultural group's language and its religious, economic, political, and social systems are institutional reflections of culture and help shape the internal referents as part of a reciprocal or interdependent system. For example, an agrarian socioeconomic system that includes an extended family organization, such as commonly exists in many parts of the developing world, both shapes and is shaped by the values, attitudes, and cosmologies of its cultural group members. As children are reared, they are conditioned directly and indirectly to think, feel, and act in certain ways. These ways constitute their reality. Their language helps shape this reality and is in turn shaped by it.

All of this affirms the simple fact that culture is a critical determinant of human behavior. To the extent that culture varies, human behavior must also vary. A white Anglo-Saxon male growing up on a farm in midwestern America does not experience the world in the same way as a Masai male growing up in Kenya, Africa. The difference between these two males is not only in the superficial referents of their appearance, dress, food, and rituals but also in the very way they define reality.

Thus, it is critical that any effort to assess something as complex as psychopathology must consider ethnocultural variations and must accommodate to these variations. All of the basic elements of assessment, including the languages used in instruments, the interpersonal relations involved in obtaining information, the questions asked, the tasks required, the norms, the scales, and the very concepts being explored are influenced by cultural factors. Cultural factors cannot be ignored in psychiatric assessment without risking serious validity and reliability problems.

### Culture as a Determinant of Human Behavior

While culture has long been recognized to be an important determinant of human behavior, psychiatrists and psychologists have generally favored biological or psychological factors in most of their theoretical and conceptual formulations. This has resulted in simplistic conceptions of both normal and abnormal behavior.

In our opinion, human behavior is a function of a variety of determinants that are in simultaneous interaction. The most important of these determinants are biological, psychological, cultural, and environmental. At any given moment, an individual is the representative product of all these determinants. Behavior then emerges as the continuous and ongoing adjustment and adaptation to those forces within the individual and

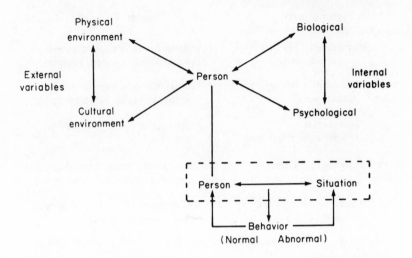

**Figure 1.** General interactional model of human behavior.

the setting (Marsella 1984, 1987). Figure 1 presents this conceptualization of human behavior.

Yet another way to portray the importance of culture as a determinant of human behavior is to arrange the critical elements within a hierarchical framework that highlights their interdependency. Figure 2 demonstrates the interactional relationship across macrosocial, microsocial, psychosocial, behavioral, and biological levels of analysis. Events at the macrosocial level (e.g., poverty, social change, war) ultimately exercise an influence on human behavior via the mediation of the other levels. Hormonal changes, neurotransmitter levels, and related biological substrates reflect the events and experiences from other levels and do not simply occur independent of them. Thus, culture impacts even the most complex biochemical structures and processes of our body.

*Cultural Variability in Human Behavior*

The broadest range of variability in human behavior is in

| Systems level | Typical variables |
|---|---|
| I. Macrosocial (Political, social, economic) | I. Westernization, Industrialization, sociotechnical change, poverty |
| ↓↑ | |
| II. Microsocial (Family, school, work) | II. Family relations, general social relations, social networks |
| ↓↑ | |
| III. Psychosocial (Personality, situations) | III. Psychological needs and motives, stressors |
| ↓↑ | |
| IV. Biobehavioral (Individual functioning) | IV. Basic sensory/motor functions, cognitive processes (attention, memory) |
| ↓↑ | |
| V. Biopsychosocial (Cells, chemistry, organs) | V. Neurotransmitters, immune systems, hormones, structures |

**Figure 2.** Hierarchical systems in human adaptation and psychopathology.

the spectrum of normal behavior. As noted earlier, there are tremendous variations in the behavior of a white Anglo-Saxon farmer living in Kansas and a Masai warrior living in Kenya. These differences are not merely superficial but extend to the deepest levels of human experience. However, as one continues to focus on behavior that is determined by increasing penetration of biological substrates, the spectrum of cultural variability narrows, though never to the point of exact similarity.

Figure 3 presents this formulation of cultural variability. As Figure 3 indicates, the spectrum of cultural variability decreases from normal behavior to neurological disease. But even within the spectrums of neurotic and psychotic behavior, there is sufficient cultural variation to require that careful attention be given to cultural considerations in assessment.

## Some Cultural Considerations in the Assessment of Psychopathology

### Assessment Alternatives

Only a few decades ago, the assessment of psychopathology

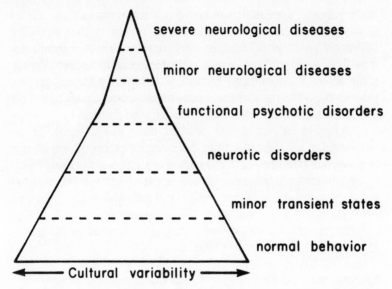

**Figure 3.** Symptom variability across normal behavior/neurological disease spectra.

was limited to a few psychometric instruments. Today, assessment instruments number in the hundreds, including structured interviews, ratings scales, personality scales, projective tests, intelligence and interest tests, neuropsychological tests, and performance tests.

All of the assessment instruments have one thing in common. They were developed by Western professionals, using Western concepts and scale formats, and, with few exceptions, were based on Western norms and expectations. When we cross cultural boundaries a number of serious problems are encountered in the use of these assessment alternatives (Butcher 1987).

The major problem that continues to plague our research and practice is the inappropriate use of these measures in cross-cultural contexts. For example, the assessment instruments are commonly used to determine ethnocultural differences in prevalence rates of specific disorders. Such cross population use of assessment tools begs a fundamental question that must be addressed before valid comparisons can be made. Are the meanings that we infer from scores on assessment measures comparable across ethnocultural groups? Alternatively stated, can we infer that scores on these assessment measures mean the same thing for the ethnocultural populations of interest?

Whether or not scores derived from our assessment instruments mean the same thing for different ethnocultural groups is a serious problem that requires empirical verification. Minimally, unless empirical evidence is provided for the equivalence of measurement properties and equivalence of a measure's meaning (e.g., construct validities) across cultural groups of interest, cross-cultural comparisons are seriously questionable (Irvine and Carroll 1980).

### Equivalence: The Key to Valid Cross-Cultural Assessment

Within the context of the assumptions about the nature and importance of culture for human behavior that were discussed previously, it is important to discuss some of the cultural requirements for the valid and reliable assessment of psychopathology. There are four cultural considerations that must be recognized and attended to by any clinician or researcher engaged in psychiatric assessment.

All of these considerations center around the concept of equivalence. *Equivalence* is a term that has gained fashion and popularity in cross-cultural studies because of its obvious importance. Quite simply, equivalence refers to the extent to which a word, concept, scale, or norm structure may be considered relevant and applicable to cultural groups other than the one in which these elements were developed. Equivalence means comparability.

In cross-cultural assessment, there are four types of equivalence: 1) linguistic, 2) conceptual, 3) scale, and 4) norm equivalence. Unless the assessment instruments applied to a particular patient are equivalent for his/her ethnocultural background and experience, it is doubtful that the conclusions will be valid and reliable. If the latter requirements are not met, then even the minimal requirements of good science are not being met, and the findings may end up having pernicious consequences for all involved [see Brislin et al. (1973), and Lonner (1979) for excellent discussions of these concepts].

**Linguistic equivalence.** Linguistic equivalence refers to the extent to which the content and grammar have a similar connotative and denotative meaning across cultures. Simple translation of material from one language to another has proven inadequate. Complex concepts often cannot be adequately translated. To help solve this problem, researchers have developed the technique of "back translation" (Brislin et al. 1973).

In back translation, a sentence or word is translated from language A to language B by one person and then translated back into language A by another person to ensure that the translation was accurate. Thus, one back translation technique involves the following: language A → language B → language A. If there are variations from the original then the translators can work toward a common term or meaning. There are various options that have been used, which go beyond the purposes of this paper. However, all of the techniques emphasize the importance of making sure that what is translated is equivalent in the different languages. In some cases, the problem of linguistic equivalence is simply one of content. For example, the opening question in the Minnesota Multiphasic Personality Inventory (MMPI) is "Do you like mechanics magazines?" Try that on a Masai warrior and see what reply you will obtain!

Sometimes the problem is not one of denotative meaning but one of connotative meaning. Tanaka-Matsumi and Marsella (1976) asked American subjects to associate to the word *depression* and Japanese subjects to associate to the word *yuutsu*, the closest Japanese equivalent word derived from back translation. The results indicated that the Americans replied with words reflecting internal subjective referents such as "blue, sad, down, despair, dejection." In contrast, the Japanese replied with "mountains, rain, storms, dark," terms reflecting an external referent. These findings raised questions about the connotative meaning of depression for the two groups and also questions about the very nature of personhood across these two cultures. Results such as these lead us to the second type of equivalence.

**Conceptual equivalence.** Conceptual equivalence refers to similarities in the conceptual meaning of the concepts used in assessment. For example, the term *dependence* has a very negative connotation in our Western society. It implies immaturity, excessive needs for nurturance and support, and personal incompetence. In American culture, dependency is devalued because we value independence, autonomy, personal strength, and individuality. To rely on others for help is considered to be a sign of weakness and vulnerability.

But as Doi (1973) pointed out in his book, *The Anatomy of Dependence*, dependency is very highly valued in Japan because it creates interdependency. *Amae* or dependency has a positive connotation in Japanese culture which values conformity and going along with others rather than individuality. Individuality threatens the collective identity of Japanese culture and is a danger to the very nature of the Japanese self. Thus, if you are studying dependency in Japan using American instruments, you may find that the questions are inappropriate and may lead to many negative and erroneous conclusions about Japanese character.

There are many other concepts that may not be conceptually equivalent across cultures, including anxiety, aggression, anger, jealousy, death, love, suicide, and person. Ethnocultural variations in these concepts have many implications for valid and reliable assessment of psychopathology since so many interview schedules, questionnaires, and tests attempt to assess these concepts. Marsella (1987) described a series of methodological procedures that can be used to study subjective experience across cultures to determine the conceptual equivalence of different terms.

Marsella stated that researchers should first elicit the domain of a particular concept through domain definition interviews. Then the items in the domain can be categorized and organized through sorting, ranking, and scaling. This is followed by efforts to understand meanings through the use of word associations, antecedent-consequent statements, semantic differentials, and implication grids. Last, behavioral observations, behavior differentials, and the assessment of behavioral baselines can be used to determine the behavioral referents of the concept. These procedures can help a researcher understand whether a concept is equivalent across cultures.

**Scale equivalence.** Even after linguistic and conceptual equivalence has been attained, there is still a need to consider scale equivalence. Scale equivalence requires that the scales used be culturally relevant and applicable. In Western culture, individuals are frequently exposed to various interview and survey formats such as Likert scales, Thurstone scales, and true/false scales. Very early in life, they come to scale events by the degree to which they may agree or disagree with them. But in many non-Western cultures, these formats are unfamiliar, and individuals may not be accustomed to selecting among a limited group of options. Further, they may be inclined out of social propriety to simply give an answer that they feel will please the interviewer or examiner.

Marsella once asked a Filipino man living in the slums of Manila to rate the degree of personal satisfaction with life on a five-point scale designed to look like a set of stairs. A stick figure on the top step was rated as very satisfied, and a stick figure on the bottom step was rated as very dissatisfied. The Filipino man was told: "Juan, the man on the top step is very satisfied and the man on the bottom step is very dissatisfied with his life; what step would you place yourself on?" Juan thought for a long while and then said he placed himself on the bottom step.

Marsella was pleased since the man lived under a bridge with an open sewer floating by his doorstep, and he had no money with which to feed his family. He should have been very dissatisfied. However, when he was asked why he chose the bottom step, the Filipino man said, "Doctor, I did not want to fall down the steps and hurt myself." A scale is not a scale everywhere in the world. Similarly, many non-Western people will have difficulty with true/false questions because they are too categorical and do not provide enough situational relevance. Things are not simply good or bad all of the time.

**Norm equivalence.**   The last type of equivalence that needs to be considered when assessment involves individuals from different cultures is norm equivalence. Because norms are the basis of most evaluations of normality and abnormality, it is critical that normative standards that are developed for one cultural group are not applied indiscriminantly to another cultural group. This is most obviously the case for intelligence tests but is as critical in personality and psychopathology scales. Cultures differ in behavioral expectations and standards. They also differ in standards of morality.

If an individual is judged against standards that are not culturally relevant, it is obvious that deviancy will be a risk. One way to deal with this problem is for researchers to establish baselines for the frequency, duration, and severity of clinical symptoms so that individuals can be evaluated against culturally applicable norms. If we simply determine that a patient experiences headaches, sadness, poor sleep, and so forth without knowing what acceptable cultural norms are, we may reach erroneous conclusions.

In sum, the need to ensure equivalence and comparability in cross-cultural assessment has posed major theoretical questions regarding the universality of mental health concepts across cultures, as well as major methodological difficulties for the cross-cultural investigator. Given the requirements for good science, no single strategy can adequately resolve problems inherent in cross-cultural assessments. However, as we discuss in the following section, methodological strategies have been operationalized in attempts to maximize cross-cultural comparability and minimize errors of inference in cross-cultural research.

## Methodological Strategies for Valid Comparisons in Cross-Cultural Research

Two methodological approaches that are typically used to examine ethnocultural variations in psychopathology have included 1) use of standard assessment tools in different ethnocultural populations (following appropriate translation procedures) and 2) development and use of culture-syntonic or "emic" measures in different ethnocultural populations. In this section, we address methodological criteria for valid cross-cultural comparisons when data are obtained using these approaches.

### Use of Standard Assessment Tools Across Cultures

There have been many efforts to assess psychopathology across cultural boundaries through the use of translated versions of a number of clinical instruments including structured interviews (e.g., Present State Examination; Diagnostic Interview Schedule) and rating scales (e.g., MMPI; Zung Self-Rating Depression Scale; Beck's Depression Inventory; Katz Adjustment Scale). Given the assumption that these measures assess "universal" characteristics of disorders, ethnocultural comparisons of scores are typically made by researchers to identify cultural differences in psychopathology. If mean differences between cultural groups are found on these instruments, investigators generally infer that the groups differ in psychopathology, despite the fact that many of these instruments were derived based on Western psychiatric conceptions of pathology. As we indicated earlier, an alternative explanation for the differences we observe between groups is that the instruments may be measuring different things in the cultural groups of interest and, thus, scores on these instruments may not be cross-culturally comparable.

One methodological approach to resolving this problem is an examination of the psychometric properties of instruments across ethnocultural groups (Berry 1980; Irvine and Carroll 1980; Kameoka 1985; Poortinga 1975). At the very least, when instruments are transported across ethnocultural boundaries, investigators must provide evidence for the equivalence of psychometric properties across the populations sampled before quantitative mean level comparisons are warranted.

Kameoka (1985) indicated that when standard rating scales are used across ethnocultural groups (subsequent to appropriate translation procedures), cross-cultural measurement equivalence can be evaluated by examining the factorial invariance of measures using confirmatory factory analytic methods formulated by Jöreskog (1971) and others (Alwin and Jackson 1981; Sörbom 1974). Confirmatory factor analytic methods involve testing a series of hypotheses about an instrument's measurement model across groups. These hypotheses are tested by evaluating the fit and presumed equality of different components of the scale's measurement structures including covariance structures of item responses, factor pattern matrix, covariance structure of error, and covariance among factors. This approach is superior to the conventional single-group exploratory-factor analytic strategy because it provides a confirmatory, hypothesis-testing framework for simultaneously testing statistical differences between measurement models across multiple populations. Basically, if these analyses indicate that the measurement model is invariant across cultural groups, then quantitative comparisons are justified.

Other psychometric approaches including identification of item bias have been suggested by cross-cultural methodologists (Van der Flier 1982) for the evaluation of measurement equivalence. However, Kameoka (1983) noted that these methods, including the evaluation of factorial invariance, are inadequate for resolving questions concerning construct interpretations or meanings of measures in different ethnocultural groups. Equivalence of a measure's meanings across populations should be determined through construct validation approaches that simultaneously examine construct interpretations within and between populations.

## Use of Indigenous Assessment Tools

Despite the usefulness of the above statistical procedures, statistical solutions do not address the fundamental problem regarding the data-gathering methods themselves. What is questionable here is the common practice of transporting assessment tools across ethnocultural groups. As we discussed earlier, in transporting assessment tools to other cultures, researchers virtually ignore indigenous meanings and perspectives on psychopathology that are inextricably imbedded in a sociocultural system that differs from the system in which the assessment tools were originally developed.

We believe that if substantial progress is to be made to reduce the apparent ethnocentricity of mental health concepts, theories, and assessment methods, researchers must begin to pay special attention to the development and testing of assessment technologies that are consistent with the way in which specific cultures define and order reality. The development of culture-syntonic assessment tools must be consistent with a culture's conceptual system, and every aspect of the assessment process should be consistent with indigenous experiences and perspectives. In this regard, the study of subjective experiences of psychopathology across cultures as described by Marsella (1987) constitutes a necessary first step in the development of culturally appropriate assessment tools.

The development and use of such emic assessment instruments, however, poses another methodological dilemma in cross-cultural research. Since the use of emic assessment instruments implies using different measures developed for different ethnocultural populations, how can we proceed to make cross-cultural comparisons when emic measures with different item content are used in the different populations? Various cross-cultural methodologists (Davidson et al. 1976; Hui and Triandis 1983; Irwin et al. 1977; Poortinga and Van de Vijver 1987) have suggested that answers to this question involve theory testing in the form of basic construct validation work both within and between cultures. When emic assessment instruments are used in research, cross-cultural comparisons should involve comparisons of construct interpretations (i.e., validities) of emic measures.

Specifically, this effort should begin with the specification of a theoretical model that explains the particular construct of interest in our assessment. This theoretical model defines the hypothesized relations between the construct and other theoretically relevant variables. These relationships constitute what Cronbach and Meehl (1955) refer to as the construct's "nomological network." This initial step in defining the construct's nomological network may not be acceptable to the cultural purist since the theoretical model itself may be ethnocentric. If, however, we are able to give the model tentative universal status, then we may proceed to develop culture-syntonic methods to operationalize variables in the model.

Cross-cultural comparisons may proceed by testing the extent to which the theoretical model is generalizable across different ethnocultural populations. If it can be shown that the disorder is related to other variables as predicted by the model within each culture, and that the interrelationships among these variables are the same across cultures, then it can be inferred that the meaning of the disorder, as measured by emic measures, is cross-culturally comparable. Further, various causal relations hypothesized in the theoretical model may be found to be invariant across cultures while other causal relations may be found to vary across cultures. Points of similarity and difference can be uncovered by tests of the model across populations. In identifying similarities and differences, such model-testing procedures will contribute to less ethnocentric biases in our efforts at developing theoretical conceptualizations of psychopathology.

The cross-cultural generality of construct interpretations of emic measures and underlying theoretical models can be evaluated statistically by the use of causal modeling technologies. As discussed by Kameoka (1985), recent statistical developments (Jöreskog 1977; Bentler 1980) in the area of latent variable causal modeling provide data-analytic approaches (e.g., LISREL analysis; Jöreskog and Sörbom 1981) for the evaluation of competing theoretical models within and between ethnocultural populations. Despite its statistical complexities, latent variable causal modeling provides a set of promising statistical techniques for evaluating culturally relevant assessment tools and, simultaneously, in testing the generality of our theoretical conceptualizations of psychopathology.

The previous analysis of the conceptual and technical requirements of cross-cultural research assumes great importance when applied to epidemiological and clinical activities. The next section discusses some of the steps that must be considered for these activities. It is clear that the human and economic costs that have been generated by our failure to be responsive to cultural factors are enormous.

## Cultural Issues in Epidemiology and Clinical Practice

### Epidemiology

Although there have been many cross-cultural epidemiological studies, variations in measurement strategies and instruments have made it extremely difficult to reach conclusions about comparative differences in rates of psychopathology (see reviews by Barrett and Rose 1986; Eaton 1986; and Marsella 1980, for summaries of research findings). Marsella et al. (1985) proposed a series of criteria for valid cross-cultural or comparative epidemiological studies.

Marsella et al. (1985) proposed that researchers should 1) use relevant anthropological data to determine clinical patterns and experiences; 2) develop glossaries and definitions for symptoms; 3) derive symptom patterns using multivariate statistical methods as well as a priori clinical experiences and acumen; 4) use similar case identification methods; 5) use culturally appropriate assessment methods with special consideration to linguistic, conceptual, and scale equivalence; and 6) establish frequency, duration, and severity baselines for both indigenous and medical symptoms. The use of these criteria would greatly improve cultural comparability and validity.

Since many decisions on the delivery of mental health services are made on the basis of epidemiological data, it is necessary that the results of epidemiological surveys be both valid and reliable. There are obvious implications for minority groups if epidemiological surveys either overestimate or underestimate true prevalence and incidence rates. In spite of the fact that thousands of psychiatric epidemiological studies have been conducted, there are relatively few findings that can withstand rigorous scientific review and scrutiny. Too often, case identification methods and diagnostic category assignment are ethnoculturally biased. In many instances, culture-specific disorders are ignored and not counted. Further, culturally normative hallucinatory and delusional behaviors are often considered only within the context of Western culture, resulting in labels such as schizophrenia being assigned indiscriminantly. These same problems are found throughout a clinician's practice.

### Clinical Practice

A clinician engages in clinical interviews, conducts psychological and neurological tests, renders a diagnosis, recommends a therapeutic plan, and evaluates the patient's progress. All of these activities are subject to ethnocultural bias. Any clinician who is insensitive to the fact that members of different cultural traditions vary in their communication style and content, hold different assumptions about the nature of their illness and their capacity to control it, and have different expectations about treatment and therapist behavior will make a significant number of errors in their clinical practice. This will result in risks for the patient and in possible lawsuits for the clinician.

It is now quite clear that clinicians have a professional and a moral responsibility to understand the importance of ethnocultural factors in clinical practice and to seek consultation and support if they are incapable of understanding the patient's problems within the context of the patient's culture. There is no need to say more on this matter since even professional organizations like the American Psychological Association are now considering the implications of this fact for ethical standards and guidelines.

## The Importance of Ethnic Identity

Too often when we conduct cross-cultural research or engage in cross-cultural clinical activities, we assume that the individual(s) we are interacting with are normative representatives of a particular ethnic group. This, of course, is unfortunate because most American minority groups have tremendous variability in ethnic identity. While some members may continue to behave according to traditional cultural patterns, others may be highly Westernized. Thus, it is absolutely necessary that efforts be made to assess the ethnic identity of research subjects and clinical patients.

Efforts to assess ethnic identity have not been totally successful because ethnic identity is a complex variable that has many dimensions. In our experience, it is necessary to assess individuals' attitudes and values and their behavioral practices. The latter can frequently be accomplished through the use of a behavioral checklist. For example, the individuals can indicate whether they speak a language, eat foods, read newspapers, belong to social organizations, dress, engage in religious practices, or participate in social activities that are associated with a particular cultural tradition. On the basis of attitudinal scores and behavioral activity scores, it is possible to generate an index of ethnic identity that can be used in research and clinical practice.

The extent to which an individual embraces his/her cultural tradition is the key for cross-cultural research and clinical practice. It is not the person's racial appearance or his or her generation. Some third and fourth generation members in the United States may still be closely affiliated with their traditional culture. Thus, we advocate that more use be made of ethnic identity indices in research and clinical practice. Indeed, it would be very useful to have research data on comparisons of psychopathology among groups with differing levels of ethnic identity. For example, imagine a $3 \times 3$ factorial research design in which generation (first, second, third) and ethnic identity (weak, medium, strong) are the marginal variables. Such a design could enable us to partition the variance that is attributed to generation and ethnic identity. Profiles of symptomatology, concepts of illness and health, and expectations for therapy could all be generated from this type of sampling design, which is sensitive to intracultural variations.

## Closing Comments and Suggestions for Future Research

### Culture and Assessment: Some Thoughts and Guidelines

It is critical that any assessment yield valid and reliable conclusions. Anything less could have pernicious consequences for both the patient and the professional. Because a patient's cultural background is such a potent determiner of human behavior, every effort must be made to ensure that culture is carefully considered across the entire assessment endeavor.

Ethnocultural minority groups in America have a growing sense of pride in their cultural heritage and new awareness of the ethnocentricity of many of the assumptions within the mental health professions, especially the bias present in psychiatric and psychological tests and assessments. There is a growing risk of litigation. But more important, there is simply the question of sound professional practice and the meeting of ethical standards. Pedersen and Marsella (1982) have raised a number of questions about the possible bias and conflict inherent in the American Psychological Association Code of Ethics and have argued that clinicians should be trained in cultural knowledge and awareness before engaging in clinical activities with patients from different cultural groups.

In light of these concerns, we suggest the following guidelines for clinicians conducting psychiatric assessments:

1. Be thoroughly familiar with the instrument, technique, or methodology used in the assessment, including research and publications that can attest to the validity of applying the assessment instruments to members of different ethnocultural groups.
2. Be familiar with the ethnocultural traditions of the patient you are assessing. If possible, determine the degree of ethnic identity that the patient has with his or her reference group. Factors that can be considered include the patient's preferences for food, dress, entertainment, residential neighborhood, language, attitudes, values, religion, and so forth.
3. Debrief the patient after the assessment to determine his or her perceptions of what occurred and evaluations of its relevance for him or her.
4. Take detailed notes of your perceptions and experiences during the assessment activities with special attention given to possible ethnocultural biases.
5. Whenever possible, use an examiner who is familiar with the ethnocultural background of the patient.
6. Participate in culture-awareness training to heighten sensitivities to the importance of culture as a determinant of human behavior.

### Culture and Human Variability

More than 200 years ago, Jean-Jacques Rousseau, the famous

French philosopher, claimed that "Mankind is by nature good, and only our institutions have made him bad" (Durant and Durant 1967, p. 19). These words altered the course of Western social and intellectual history because they introduced the notion that culture was a major determinant of human behavior. In the last few decades, there has been a constantly increasing interest in the role that culture plays in the etiology, distribution, and expression of psychopathology.

Cultural variability is a major biosocial force for preserving individual and group heterogeneity. Thus, it serves well the purposes of evolution because it constantly provides a broad spectrum of options in the face of pressing environmental demands. It is important for psychiatrists and psychologists to understand the important role of culture in psychopathology and in the larger effort after human progress and development. Octavio Paz (1961), the famous Mexican author and poet, stated:

> What sets worlds in motion is the interplay of differences, their attractions and repulsions. Life is plurality, death is uniformity. By suppressing differences and peculiarities, by eliminating different civilizations and cultures, progress weakens life and favors death. The idea of a single civilization for everyone, implicit in the cult of progress and technique, impoverishes and mutilates us. Every view of the world that becomes extinct, every culture that disappears, diminishes a possibility of life.

Let us seek similarities and let us seek differences, and let us always recognize that both are reflections of life.

## References

Alwin D, Jackson D: Applications of simultaneous factor analysis to issues of factorial invariance, in Factor Analysis and Measurement in Sociological Research. Edited by Jackson D, Borgatta E. Beverly Hills, CA, Sage, 1981

Barrett J, Rose R (eds): Mental Disorders in the Community: Progress and Challenge. New York, Guilford Press, 1986

Bentler P: Multivariate analysis with latent variables: causal modeling. Annual Review of Psychology 31:419–456, 1980

Berry J: Introduction to methodology, in Handbook of Cross-Cultural Psychology: Methodology, Vol 2. Edited by Triandis H, Berry J. Boston, Allyn & Bacon, 1980

Brislin R, Lonner W, Thorndike R: Cross-Cultural Research Methods. New York, John Wiley, 1973

Butcher J (ed): Special series: cultural factors in understanding and assessing psychopathology. J Consult Clin Psychol 55:459–512, 1987

Cronbach LJ, Meehl PE: Construct validity in psychological tests. Psychol Bull 52:281–302, 1955

Davidson A, Jaccard J, Triandis H, et al: Cross-cultural model testing: toward a solution of the etic-emic dilemma. International Journal of Psychology 11:1–13, 1976

Doi T: The Anatomy of Dependence. Tokyo, Kodansha International, 1973

Draguns J: Psychological disorders of clinical severity, in Handbook of Cross-Cultural Psychology: Psychopathology, Vol 6. Edited by Triandis H, Draguns J. Boston, Allyn & Bacon, 1980

Durant W, Durant A: The Story of Civilization. Volume 10: Rousseau and Revolution. New York, Praeger, 1967

Eaton W: The epidemiology of schizophrenia, in Handbook of Studies on Schizophrenia, Volume 1: Epidemiology, Etiology, and Clinical Features. Edited by Burrows G, Norman T, Rubinstein G. New York, Elsevier, 1986

Hui C, Triandis H: Multistrategy approach to cross-cultural research. Journal of Cross-Cultural Psychology 14:65–83, 1983

Irvine S, Carroll W: Testing and assessment across cultures: issues in methodology and theory, in Handbook of Cross-Cultural Psychology: Methodology, Vol 2. Edited by Triandis H, Berry J. Boston, Allyn & Bacon, 1980

Irwin M, Klein R, Engle P, et al: The problem of establishing validity in cross-cultural measurements. Ann NY Acad Sci 285:308–325, 1977

Jöreskog KG: Simultaneous factor analysis in several populations. Psychometrika 36:409–426, 1971

Jöreskog KG: Structural equation models in the social sciences: specification, estimation, and testing, in Applications of Statistics. Edited by Krishnaiah PR. Amsterdam, North-Holland, 1977

Jöreskog KG, Sörbom D: LISREL: Analysis of Linear Structural Relationships by Maximum Likelihood and Least Squares Methods. Chicago, International Education Services, 1981

Kameoka VA: Multivariate strategy to determine cross-cultural comparability of psychological constructs, in Cross-Cultural Psychology's Contributions to Ethnic Minority Research: Recommendations. Symposium conducted at the American Psychological Association Convention, Anaheim, CA, August 26–30, 1983

Kameoka VA: Construct validation of psychological measures in cross-cultural research: analysis of linear structural relationships, in Crosscultural and National Studies in Social Psychology. Edited by Diaz-Guerrero R. Netherlands, North-Holland, 1985

Katz M, Sanborn K, Lowery A, et al: Ethnic studies in Hawaii: on psychopathology and social deviance, in The Nature of Schizophrenia. Edited by Wynne L, Matthyse S, Cromwell R. New York, John Wiley, 1978

Kleinman A: Depression, somatization, and the "new" cross-cultural psychiatry. Culture, Medicine, and Psychiatry 6:1–39, 1977

Kleinman A, Good B (eds): Culture and Depression. Berkeley, CA, University of California Press, 1985

Kluckhohn C, Kroeber T: Culture. New York, Vintage Press, 1952

Linton R: The Cultural Background of Personality. New York, Appleton-Century-Crofts, 1945

Lonner W: Cross-cultural research issues, in Perspectives on Cross-Cultural Psychology. Edited by Marsella AJ, Tharp R, Ciborowski T. New York, Academic Press, 1979

Marsella AJ: Cross-cultural studies of mental disorders, in Perspectives on Cross-Cultural Psychology. Edited by Marsella AJ, Tharp R, Ciborowski T. New York, Academic Press, 1979

Marsella AJ: Depressive experience and disorder across cultures, in Handbook of Crosscultural Psychology: Psychopathology, Vol 6. Edited by Triandis H, Draguns J. Boston, Allyn & Bacon, 1980

Marsella AJ: Culture and mental health, in Cultural Conceptions of Mental Health and Therapy. Edited by Marsella AJ, White G. Boston, D. Reidel Publishing, 1982

Marsella AJ: An interactional theory of psychopathology, in Ecological Models in Clinical and Community Psychology. Edited by Lubin B, Connor W. New York, John Wiley, 1984

Marsella AJ: The measurement of depressive experience and disorders across cultures, in The Measurement of Depression: Biological, Psychological, Behavioral, and Social Aspects. Edited by Marsella AJ, Hirschfeld R, Katz M. New York, Guilford Press, 1987

Marsella AJ, Scheuer A: Coping across cultures: an overview, in Healthy Human Development: Applications from Cross-Cultural Psychology. Edited by Dasen P, Berry J, Sartorius N. Beverly Hills, CA, Sage, 1987

Marsella AJ, White G (eds): Cultural Conceptions of Mental Health and Therapy. Boston, D. Reidel Publishing, 1982

Marsella AJ, Escudero M, Gordon P: Stresses, resources, and symptom patterns in urban Filipino men, in Transcultural Research in Mental Health. Edited by Lebra W. Honolulu, University Press of Hawaii, 1971

Marsella AJ, Kinzie D, Gordon P: Ethnic variations in the expression of depression. Journal of Cross-Cultural Psychology 4:435–458, 1973

Marsella AJ, Sartorius N, Jablensky A, et al: Depression across cultures, in Culture and Depression. Edited by Kleinman A, Good B. Berkeley, University of California Press, 1985

Murphy HBM, Wittkower E, Chance N: Cross-cultural inquiry into the symptomatology of depression: a preliminary report. Int J Psychiatry 3:6–15, 1967

Paz O: The Labyrinth of Solitude. New York, Grove Press, 1963

Pedersen P, Marsella AJ: The ethical crisis in cross-cultural counselling and psychotherapy. Professional Psychology 13:492–500, 1982

Poortinga Y: Some implications of three different approaches to intercultural comparison, in Applied Cross-Cultural Psychology. Berry J, Lonner WJ. Amsterdam, Swets & Zeitlinger, 1975

Poortinga Y, Van de Vijver F: Explaining cross-cultural differences: bias analyses and beyond. Journal of Cross-Cultural Psychology 18:259–282, 1987

Serota C: Demographic and clinical variations in the perception of causality and control among first-episode psychotic patients in Hawaii. Ph.D. dissertation, University of Hawaii, 1986

Sörbom D: A general method for studying differences in factor means and factor structures between groups. Br J Math Stat Psychol 27:229–239, 1974

Tanaka-Matsumi J, Marsella AJ: Cross-cultural variations in the phenomenological experience of depression: word association. Journal of Cross-Cultural Psychology 7:379–396, 1976

Triandis H, Draguns J (eds): Handbook of Cross-Cultural Psychology, Vol 6: Psychopathology. Boston, Allyn & Bacon, 1980

Van der Flier H: Deviant response patterns and comparability of test scores. Journal of Cross-Cultural Psychology 13:267–298, 1982

# Chapter 12

# Assessment of Psychopathology in Minorities

**BRUCE L. BALLARD, M.D.**

# Chapter 12

# Assessment of Psychopathology in Minorities

*T*he assessment of psychopathology in minorities has become increasingly complex as the field of psychiatry has embraced a biopsychosocial model. To apply this model requires attention to possible genetic and other biological issues, all of which are difficult to elucidate among differing ethnic groups. Psychosocial issues involve consideration of a range of environmental factors as well as developmental psychological factors that may have somewhat similar or different manifestations across several minority populations. At the same time, there is diversity within minorities that indicates the need to assess psychosocial issues within subgroups, such as all patients within a certain age range or all within a certain social class.

In the clinical setting one hopes to assess each individual patient as accurately as possible, and assessment of cultural issues is important in clarification of the diagnosis as well as in appropriate treatment interventions. There have been progressive attempts made to deepen our understanding of psychopathology and treatment approaches in patients from minority groups. In the psychoanalytic literature, Bernard (1953) and Kennedy (1952) noted issues of cultural style plus attitudes of therapists that must be considered in the treatment of black patients. Schachter and Butts (1968) noted transference and countertransference issues when patient and therapist are from different racial groups. Ticho (1971) noted the necessity of sensitization toward one's own cultural background and the manifestations of countertransference phenomena. She observed this in her own adaptation to a South American culture and South American patients and in adapting to the United States and black American patients. Bradshaw (1978) noted problems of therapists in dealing with anger and aggression in black patients and mistaken views that psychopathology must exist in poor black families. Pierce (1986) has noted the factor of multiple microaggressions experienced by blacks. Spurlock and Lawrence (1979) have elucidated developmental issues in black children. More recently, Jones (1984) has reiterated the importance of noting the patient's feelings about racial and cultural differences, and he has noted the critical roles of empathy and of countertransference.

Foulks et al. (1977) surveyed a range of issues and approaches that should be considered when an anthropological perspective is included in the examination of cultural issues in psychiatry. In my view, a major contribution has been made by those investigators who have alerted us to the emic and etic approaches, that is, the differences between examining the internal characteristics of only one culture (emic) and comparing multiple cultures from a perspective outside the system (etic).

Recognizing both the broad view of the anthropologist and the sophisticated observations of clinicians treating patients is essential in assessing psychopathology in patients from minority groups. Additional data would enhance our diagnostic capacities, and psychometric assessment might provide that data.

There have been some comparisons of different populations who have taken the Minnesota Multiphasic Personality Inventory (MMPI). Noting that prior studies have maintained that there are differences between blacks and whites, with blacks scoring higher in psychopathology, Bertelson et al. (1982) studied 462 patients. They noted that no significant differences on the MMPI were found when black and white populations were matched in key demographic variables—sex, age, socioeconomic status, rural or urban residence, employment, years of education, marital status, hospital status, and date of testing.

Montgomery and Orozco (1985) note that in a comparison of 365 Anglo-American and Mexican American college students, Anglo-Americans scored differently on 10 of 13 MMPI scales, but scored differently on only 2 of 13 if acculturation and age were statistically controlled. They concluded that differences are due to levels of acculturation. Greene (1987) notes that there is no simple relationship between ethnic group membership and MMPI performance and finds that moderator variables such as social class, education, and type of setting play an important role in determining the specific pattern of scores that are found. Jones and Thorne (1984) raise questions about establishing new norms in order for the MMPI to be appropriately used in the clinical assessment of patients from minority groups, noting problems in assuming minorities are homogeneous. They also note the necessity of comprehension of the direct experiences of minority subjects in understanding psychological assessment.

Dana (1986) notes the importance of scrutinizing cross-cultural attitudes in interpreting psychological test data. Abel et al. (1987) advise caution in the use of projective techniques in the study of culture and psychopathology.

There have been attempts to establish normative data for various minority group populations. Jackson (1986) attempts this in her study of black infant attachment behaviors. She used a rating of behaviors based on an experimental play session and noted that behavior seen in healthy black infants would have been labeled as pathological if assessed in terms of behavior patterns described in the general infant attachment literature. In my view, there would have to be studies noting psychological test results and correlating those results with careful clinical observation of patients from minority groups.

It is useful to note Gibbs's (1986) use of the Beck Depression Inventory to study the incidence of depression in non-clinical populations, specifically black adolescent girls. She noted the implications for early intervention as evidence of depression was found in a number of the subjects.

While the two studies just cited did not use the traditional psychological test battery, they are an indication of the need for further specific studies of minority populations. Such studies would enable us to refine our clinical diagnoses. At this stage of inadequate knowledge of the complexities of biological, psychological, and social influences contributing to psychiatric problems in minority patients, the precise value of psychological testing needs to be demonstrated in additional research studies. Further studies are needed because of the following concerns.

First, the literature on specific psychometric assessment as applied to psychiatric patients from minority groups is sparse. There is considerable literature on the use of intelligence testing in school populations. As applied to minority children, the interpretation of intelligence tests has been controversial, with debates about whether sufficient social and environmental factors have been considered. At the same time, assessment of intelligence has implications in establishing treatment goals for children referred for psychiatric evaluation and possible treatment. The Wechsler Adult Intelligence Scale (WAIS) is also a part of the standard test battery that is given in psychiatric facilities, and the test results are again considered in diagnosis and treatment. Caution in the interpretation of test results is still warranted.

Second, there are questions about the statistical approaches used in assessing validity when comparative measurement techniques are used for different population groups. Drasgow (1984) raises that issue and doubts that certain studies can truly be cited as evidence that tests are "fair" to ethnic and cultural minority groups.

The use of psychometric assessment techniques in the determination of mental illness and psychopathology in patients from minority groups presents many problems. Which psychological tests are best utilized? Do such tests really help us in understanding cultural influences on mental phenomena and on behavior? What are the best ways to employ those tests to enhance our clinical understanding? Are there serious dangers in misapplication of gross test findings to behavioral phenomena in minority populations—especially since there remains a societal stereotyping of such populations?

All of the above issues must be raised, as we consider the contributions of clinicians who reiterate the need for recognition of cultural factors per se in the clinical assessment of patients. The data on testing of school populations, data from studies of various test batteries given to patients from minority groups, data from clinical studies of minority patients, and ongoing research data must be brought together to improve and to refine our diagnostic and treatment approaches to such patients. Standard tests must be interpreted with caution, and any new approaches that arise will require extensive studies to establish normative responses for patients from minority groups. Establishing normative responses will require careful investigation of factors that contribute to heterogeneity within minority groups (Jones 1987), and extensive work in this area is yet to be done. At the same time, proper assessment of psychiatric needs in minority populations is critical. That issue is urgent in light of studies that indicate the very poor medical care that minorities often receive. In 1984, the Secretary of the U.S. Department of Health and Human Services established a Task Force on Black and Minority Health. The report of that task force (U.S. Department of Health and Human Services, 1985) documented major disparities in key health indicators among various minority groups compared with whites. Sixty thousand excess deaths occur each year in minority populations, and six causes account for more than 80% of the excess mortality. Those six causes are cancer, cardiovascular disease and stroke, chemical dependency, diabetes, homicides and accidents, and infant mortality.

It is important to note that the presence of such serious medical conditions increases the likelihood of concomitant neurologic and psychiatric conditions. Questions are being raised about the incidence of preexistent psychiatric and/or neurologic illness in understanding the high incidence of homicide. Unfortunately, the report did not directly address issues of psychiatric illness in minority populations, but the data nevertheless point to the urgency of accurate psychiatric clinical assessment in patients from minority groups. The role of sophisticated neuropsychological testing could become increasingly important and useful. There is a need for substantial research in using those measures in minority patients.

Overall, the assessment of the medical, psychological, and social factors underlying psychiatric illness in minority patients involves consideration of a multitude of factors. Also, regardless of ethnic and/or cultural background, each patient has had an individual experience. Any data, including psychometric data, that currently shed light on problem areas are useful clinically if interpreted with caution. Only further research can help us to delineate more precisely the utility of psychometric assessment in understanding psychopathology in minorities.

## References

Abel TM, Metraux R, Roll S: Psychotherapy and Culture. Albuquerque, University of New Mexico, 1987

Bernard VW: Psychoanalysis and minority groups. J Am Psychoanal Assoc 1:256–267, 1953

Bertelson AD, Marks PA, May GD: MMPI and race: a controlled study. J Consult Clin Psychol 50:316–318, 1982

Bradshaw WH: Training psychiatrists for working with blacks in basic residency programs. Am J Psychiatry 135:1520–1524, 1978

Dana RH: Personality assessment and Native Americans. J Pers Assess 50:480–500, 1986

Drasgow F: Scrutinizing psychological tests: measurement equivalence and equivalent relations with external variables are the central issues. Psychol Bull 95:134–135, 1984

Foulks EF, Wintrob RM, Westermeyer J, et al: Current Perspectives in Cultural Psychiatry. New York, Spectrum, 1977

Gibbs JT: Assessment of depression in urban adolescent females: implications for early intervention strategies. Am J Soc Psychiatry 6:59–66, 1986

Greene RL: Ethnicity and MMPI performance: a review. J Consult Clin Psychol 55:497–512, 1987

Jackson JR: Characteristics of black infant attachment behaviors. Am J Soc Psychiatry 6:32–35, 1986

Jones EE: Some reflections on the black patient and psychotherapy. The Clinical Psychologist 37:62–65, 1984

Jones EE, Thorne A: Rediscovery of the subject: intercultural approaches to clinical assessment. J Consult Clin Psychol 55:497–512, 1987

Kennedy JA: Problems posed in the analysis of Negro patients. Psychiatry 15:313–327, 1952

Montgomery GT, Orozco S: Mexican Americans' performance on the MMPI as a function of level of acculturation. J Clin Psychol 41:203–212, 1985

Pierce CA: Solomon Carter Fuller Lecture. American Psychiatric Association Annual Meeting, May 1986

Schachter JL, Butts HF: Transference and countertransference in interracial analyses. J Am Psychoanal Assoc 16:792–808, 1968

Spurlock J, Lawrence LE: The black child, in Basic Handbook of Child Psychiatry. Edited by Noshpitz JD, et al. New York, Basic Books, 1979

Ticho GR: Cultural aspects of transference and countertransference. Bull Menninger Clin 35:313–334, 1971

U.S. Department of Health and Human Services: Report of the Secretary's Task Force on Black and Minority Health. Washington, DC, U.S. Department of Health and Human Services, 1985

# Chapter 13

# Legal and Ethical Aspects of Psychometric Testing

**ROBERT D. MILLER, M.D., Ph.D.**

# Chapter 13

# Legal and Ethical Aspects of Psychometric Testing

*P*sychometric evaluation has developed into a powerful tool for clinical evaluation and legal assessment in the past half century. Ours has become a society devoted to technology, cost-effectiveness, and specialization, and psychological tests appear to promise rapid, impersonal, reliable evaluations based on scientific methodology rather than on subjective clinical evaluations.

In the 1960s, criticism of the medical model approach to the mentally disordered coalesced from several sources. The ability of psychiatrists to diagnose or to predict the future behavior of their patients came under attack from clinicians and also from legal scholars who based their arguments on published reports in the clinical literature (Ennis and Litwack 1974; Morse 1978). The developing professions of clinical psychology, sociology, and social work challenged psychiatry's hegemony over the mentally disordered and offered their own concepts and methods as alternatives to the biological and psychoanalytic models provided by psychiatry (Grob 1983).

Most of the current psychological tests have come out of a tradition quite different from the conventional medical model, which has traditionally been based on subjective clinical assessments derived largely from a small number of patients evaluated intensively. The psychometric approach comes from a statistical approach based on relatively brief experience with a large number of individuals. Unlike clinical assessments, many psychological tests have little content validity—that is, it is not possible to predict accurately how individual subjects would respond to particular items on a given test from the items themselves.

The American Psychiatric Association (1987) responded to these criticisms with the development of the latest Diagnostic and Statistical Manual of Mental Disorders, which attempts to render the diagnostic process more objective and therefore more reliable. All of these trends represented a growing rejection of the value of individual expertise, particularly opinions put forward on the basis of subjective personal experience, without some objective-appearing, "scientific" evidence to support it (Kaplan and Miller 1986).

At the same time, a general economic downturn made time-consuming clinical evaluations unfeasible, and the influx of minorities into schools and the job market caused a demand for efficient and objective methods for measuring aptitudes and abilities. The climate was ideal for the increased use of objective-appearing tests (Wigdor and Garner 1982).

As long as tests were used chiefly for assessments of psychopathology as part of voluntary individual psychological evaluation and treatment, there were few challenges of their reliability or validity. But when their use spread to group administration for educational or job placement, where subjects had not sought psychological evaluation, had no choice about taking the tests, and could have their futures significantly affected by the test results, criticism mounted. Although most psychometric tests used for placement evaluation do not measure psychopathology per se, the legal and ethical issues have been most thoroughly examined in these areas, and will be discussed in some detail.

## Ethical Aspects of Psychometric Testing

The American Psychological Association (1985) has promulgated specific standards for the development, dissemination, and use of psychological tests. Those standards explicitly require that test administrators be familiar with a test's research basis, use tests only in contexts in which they have been shown to be reliable and valid, and not go beyond their expertise or the test's empirically demonstrated applicability. Alleged abuses of testing that are lodged against psychologists concern going beyond the test's established capacity or using tests without proper training (Hall and Hare-Mustin 1983). Bray (1982) and Lanyon and Goodstein (1971) argue that the standard of care expected of psychologists using tests includes using them only in situations for which they have been validated. Kahn and Taft (1983) agree and point out that such common practices as using outdated versions of tests, failure to use complete tests, and drawing conclusions on the basis of a single test (Bigler and Ehrfurth 1981) are ethically (and legally) questionable. But several surveys of practicing psychologists revealed that most based their interpretations of tests on their clinical experience rather than on the research data or published scoring systems (Wade and Baker 1977). And Rogers and Cavanaugh (1983) demonstrated that few psychiatrists requesting testing as part of a forensic evaluation were aware of how the tests had been administered or scored.

The intimate nature of many test questions has the potential to invade subjects' privacy, and the results must be handled with strict confidentiality (American Psychological Association 1985; Ewing 1977; Fersch 1980; Graham and Lilly 1984; Westin 1967). London and Bray (1980) and Mirvis and Seashore (1979) point out the significant problems of double agency involved when psychologists are employed to further an organization's goals rather than those of its employees. Problems also occur when courts require disclosure of test data.

A number of studies have demonstrated that characteristics of test administrators may significantly affect their results. Examiner reaction to the socioeconomic class of test takers (Levy and Kahn 1970), demand characteristics of the testing situation (Harvey and Sipprelle 1976), the examiner's sex (Binder et al. 1957; Ferguson and Buss 1960; Sarason and Harmatz 1965) or hostility (Hammer and Piotrowski 1953), and other examiner characteristics (Meehl 1956; Mintz 1957) have been shown to affect test results.

### Test Biases

There is still considerable controversy about whether particular tests inherently discriminate against certain classes of subjects. Some authors argue that tests designed to assist in placement of students in particular classes are biased against those already culturally disadvantaged (Goldman and Hartig 1976), while others argue that they are in fact sufficiently accurate predictors of future performance to be used in such situations (Cleary et al. 1975). These arguments will be discussed more fully in the context of litigation on testing.

Several authors have emphasized that the appearance of objectivity of many psychological tests may cause those not familiar with their appropriate use to grant them more validity and reliability than they deserve (Task Force 1980). This problem becomes particularly important when tests are used for group placements or as part of forensic assessments. Other authors have argued that test results indicating psychopathology may cause problems in coercive systems if no treatment is available for the problems uncovered (Brodsky 1980; Fersch 1980; Task Force 1980).

### Computerized Testing

Because of their automated nature, the growing number of psychological tests that can be administered and scored by computer pose additional problems, since they do not appear to require an experienced clinician to evaluate, are thus less expensive to administer, and appear even more "objective" than clinician-administered tests (Butcher 1987; Kahn and Taft 1983). The American Psychological Association (Committee on Professional Standards 1986) has applied the same standards for computerized tests as for psychological tests in general. They emphasize (Guideline 9) that "Computer-generated interpretive reports should be used only in conjunction with professional judgement."

### Applied Testing

Psychological tests to be used for group placements should be specifically designed and validated for those settings (Mann 1980). When tests created for individual clinical evaluation are used for school or job placements, significant problems of reliability, validity, and confidentiality result. These problems have been thoroughly debated in the context of litigation.

## Legal Aspects of Testing

Many of the ethical issues discussed above have found their way into the courtroom. Because of their impact on greater numbers of people, the two major series of cases, almost all in the federal courts, have dealt with tests used to make school and employment placement decisions.

### Educational Testing

Psychological tests have long been a part of evaluation and placement procedures at all levels of formal education. Two main types have been developed: aptitude tests (including intelligence) and achievement tests, including standardized tests for entrance to college and to various graduate programs. Such tests were originally developed to facilitate identification of children who needed special attention because of learning difficulties. The passage of laws restricting child labor and mandating education, and the tremendous increase in numbers of children in schools after 1900 called for more efficient methods of class placement (Wigdor and Garner 1982). After the Supreme Court's landmark desegregation decisions, there was growing criticism that placement tests were being used to maintain segregation, both by keeping minority students out of previously all-white schools, and by relegating minorities to lower tracks within nominally integrated schools (Bersoff 1979). In the first series of cases, there was a clear trend for the federal courts to rule that any tests on which minorities scored lower than whites were impermissibly discriminatory. Initially, courts concentrated more on the results of the tests than their construction or validity, despite extensive expert testimony on both sides.

Courts in the District of Columbia (*Hobson* 1967) and Louisiana (*Moses* 1972) held that educational systems in which lower tracks contained predominantly blacks, with aptitude tests used as part of the assignment system, were discriminatory. The courts held that the tests measured cultural preparation rather than innate ability. Although ability grouping was not held to be discriminatory per se, the existing track systems were barred because of the use of tests, although neither court examined the tests themselves.

In *Diana* (1970), the state of California entered into a consent decree, promising to provide equal opportunities for ethnic minorities when it was shown that lower scores on intelligence tests were responsible for lower class placement of Chinese and Spanish children; additional evidence revealed increases in test scores of up to 40 points when the children were retested by bilingual psychologists. Another California federal court (*Larry P.* 1980) held that black students were being discriminated against by the use of tests to place them disproportionately in special education classes. Evidence was presented indicating that scores rose to above the cutoff point for the special classes when testing took cultural backgrounds into account. The district court assumed that intelligence was randomly distributed along all races, and held that since the effect (even if not the intent) of the testing was discriminatory [which was disputed by expert witnesses, (Lambert 1981)], testing was not permissible. And in *Debra P.* (1981), a federal district court in Florida held tests to be valid and reliable, even though 78% of blacks initially failed literacy tests required for high school graduation compared to 25% of whites; but the appeals court, while admitting that the tests were valid, held that they might have contained material not covered in class ("curricular validity") and sent the case back to the district court for further fact finding.

This trend toward barring tests on constitutional grounds if their use resulted in discrimination along racial or ethnic lines was slowed by two U.S. Supreme Court decisions. In *San Antonio Independent School District* (1973), the Court held that education was not a fundamental constitutional right. And in a case dealing with alleged employment discrimination (*Washington* 1976) the Court held that discriminatory results were not sufficient to establish constitutional violations without demonstration of discriminatory intent. Subsequent federal court decisions have tended to follow this lead; for example, in *PASE* (1980) the court for the northern district of Illinois held that the WISC, WISC-R, and Stanford-Binet intelligence tests were not discriminatory and could be used as part of a placement system.

### Employment Testing

Litigation concerning the use of tests in employment and advancement decisions has involved arguments similar to those in educational placement, except that there has typically been more specific examination of the tests themselves by the courts. Many of the decisions have been based on federal laws (such as Title VII of the Civil Rights Act of 1964) and regulations [such as the Equal Employment Opportunities Commission Guidelines (EEOC)] rather than on constitutional protections (Bersoff 1979; Booth and Mackay 1980).

In the first major federal case (*Griggs* 1971), in which black employees alleged that the use of general ability tests for advancement unfairly discriminated against them, the Supreme Court, basing its decision on the 1964 Civil Rights Act and the EEOC Guidelines, ruled that the results of such tests must have a proven correlation with specific job performance in order to be acceptable, but did not specify how to demonstrate such correlation. In *Albemarle* (1975) the Court went further by rejecting the testing procedures used because the tests had been validated on populations that were not representative of the pool of job applicants and because they had been validated only for upper-level jobs, not the entry-level jobs for which their use was under challenge. Several authors predicted that these decisions heralded the "death of employment testing" (Johnson 1976). But in *Washington* (1976), the Court, basing its decision on equal protection grounds rather than on federal guidelines, ruled against the claims from the District of Columbia that aptitude tests disproportionately discriminated against black applicants for the police department, holding that there had been no demonstration of discriminatory intent. The courts have generally ignored the argument that no matter how subjective or poorly validated the tests are, they are still probably better than other available methods (Booth and Mackay 1980; Tenopyr 1981).

Another issue of even greater potential significance to psychologists was raised in *Detroit Edison* (1979). The union alleged discrimination in promotion based in part on results of aptitude tests and argued that their grievances could not properly be addressed without access to the test scores themselves. The Supreme Court ruled that the privacy interests of the test takers was sufficient to bar the union's requested access to the scores and ignored arguments that access to test scores would destroy the validity of the tests. This "truth-intesting" movement (Graham and Lilly 1984; Robertson 1980) has led to the passage in New York and California of legislation requiring disclosure of test scores and correct answers for some educational aptitude tests, such as the Scholastic Aptitude Test, despite strenuous objections from testing companies and organized psychology.

### Personality Tests

There have been fewer court cases involving the use of personality tests. In *Merriken* (1973), a federal court ignored the validity of tests in agreeing with plaintiffs that mandatory personality tests used to identify students at risk for drug abuse in order to place them in mandatory counseling programs violated their *parents'* privacy rights because of lack of informed consent. In *Aronson* (1981) a student challenged her dismissal from college on the basis of high scores on the paranoia scales of personality tests. Because of procedural problems, no constitutional issues were before the Illinois appeals court, which ruled that the admission contract signed by the plaintiff (which specified that students would be required to take personality tests and might be dismissed based on their results) was valid.

The major legal examination of personality tests came during Congressional hearings on the use of such tests for federal employment. Proponents of the tests suggested that they served as a convenient focus for growing public concern over a general erosion of privacy (Amrine 1965). Fueled by several popular books critical of personality testing (Gross 1962; Guion 1965; Hoffman 1962; Packard 1964) and testimony from outspoken critics (Smith 1965), committee members had a field day in attacking individual questions on the tests. Although proponents of appropriate use of personality tests explained in great detail how the tests were designed, validated, and interpreted, much was made of questions involving attitudes toward religion and sexuality, expressing concern (which was shared by many of the psychologists who testified) about the fact that the score sheets were kept on file, where answers to personal questions would be available to supervisors. Representatives of federal agencies that used personality tests assured the committees that the tests were not used in shotgun fashion and that the precautions recommended by the expert witnesses were already in place. No significant changes in the use of tests came out of the hearings.

### Testing for Forensic Purposes

All the usual psychological tests have been used as part of evaluations of competency to stand trial and criminal responsibility. When expert witnesses rely on test results under cross-examination, they should expect to have test responses dissected, question by question (Slovenko 1979; *United States v. Alexander & Murdock* 1972). Such an approach is particularly hard to counter when nonexpert juries, judges, or committees attempt to understand the relevance of non-face-valid questions on tests such as the MMPI.

In addition to the use of standard tests as part of the evaluation of criminal responsibility or competency to stand trial, there has been an attempt to develop specific rating scales to measure these capacities. Such tests are not direct measures of psychopathology per se, but attempt to measure the impact of mental functioning on the ability to perform legally relevant behavior.

The first widely used competency tests were developed at Bridgewater State Hospital in Massachusetts to permit nonprofessional staff to perform competency evaluations with some degree of consistency (Robey 1965; Lipsitt et al. 1971). There was little attempt to standardize or to validate these tests, which were designed to ensure that the evaluation was sufficiently comprehensive rather than to provide a quantitative measure of competency.

Subsequently, a major effort was made by the Harvard Laboratory of Community Psychiatry (Laboratory of Community Psychiatry 1973) to provide both a screening test (the Competency Screening Test; CST) and a more thorough evaluation instrument (the Competency Assessment Instrument; CAI) for which some efforts were made at validation (Nottingham and Mattson 1981). Schreiber and associates (1987) criticized the CAI because its focus was almost entirely on legal questions. And Brakel (1974) severely criticized both the CST and the CAI because the scoring systems were not only quite subjective, but also significantly biased in a pro-establishment fashion.

A major difficulty with all of these tests is that they provide a final global numerical score. While, with the exception of the CST, the tests' authors did not designate a particular cutoff score as indicative of incompetency, the scales lend themselves too readily to such a use in the hands of clinicians and judges alike. While scores on the disordered ends of the scales might well correlate with conditions sufficiently severe to indicate incompetency, the reverse is not necessarily true. False negatives (incompetent patients who appear to be competent on the basis of their scores) are quite likely in the case of defendants with incapacities limited to one area, such as the defendant with intact cognition who delusionally believes that all defense attorneys are part of a conspiracy against him.

Roesch and Golding (1980) and Golding and colleagues (1984) have developed the Interdisciplinary Fitness Interview (IFI), which covers the same areas as its predecessors. It differs in requiring evaluators not only to rate a subject's functioning in each area, but also to indicate the weight of that score in terms of its effect on competency. The IFI was designed to be administered jointly by a lawyer and a clinician in order to provide better balance between legal and clinical questions. The IFI is provided with detailed instructions for evaluators and designed to be used after extensive training with the instrument.

Schreiber and associates (1987) compared the CST, the CAI, and the IFI with assessments done by hospital staff under field conditions, with assessments by a panel of experts, and with ultimate court decisions. They found that while the CST had low correlation with any of the other measures, both the CAI and the IFI correlated well with each other and with hospital and court determinations.

Grisso (1986) also reviewed each of these instruments; like Brakel, he noted (but was less bothered by) the subjectivity of the CAI, and pointed out that the meager instructions left much to evaluators' judgment. He also pointed out that the CST was developed with an inpatient population and was not standardized with the general outpatient population for which it was designed. He noted with approval the detail with which the IFI manual was devised and agreed with its authors that it shows promise. Brodsky (in press) recently developed an instrument for use in evaluating an inmate's competency for execution; because of the small number of such cases at this time, it has not been field tested.

Unlike tests designed to predict job or school performance, the effectiveness of competency tests are usually measured against court decisions, which are not independent of the expert opinions under investigation. Grisso (1986) and Schreiber and associates (1987) pointed out that judges and evaluators gradually adjust their behavior to each other's opinions.

There have also been recent efforts to develop instruments to provide standardized evaluations of criminal responsibility (insanity). Both instruments are organized interviews rather than checklists. Slobogin and associates (1984) developed the Mental State Evaluation (MSE) as a screening test for defenses involving mental states, such as insanity and diminished capacity; like the CST, it is biased in favor of false positives. Preliminary data suggest that trainees using the MSE accurately identify defendants without valid insanity defenses while recommending further evaluation for other defendants, half of whom are ultimately found sane. Rogers (1986) points out the lack of reliability and validity studies done with the MSE and discusses his Rogers Criminal Responsibility Assessment Scale (R-CRAS), which was also designed to enable evaluators to organize their assessments and to provide criterion validity. Rogers reported (1986) that the validity of individual factors in the R-CRAS was moderate but that final agreement with court disposition was 97%. Melton and colleagues (1987), who believe that clinicians should not address ultimate legal issues such as insanity, predictably criticize the R-CRAS because it attempts to do just that. In a more balanced review, Grisso (1986) acknowledges that it will probably never be possible to devise objective measures of such elusive concepts as the inability to conform one's behavior to legal requirements, and commends the instrument for its logical and comprehensive approach.

In the civil area, rating scales have also been developed in response to a need for objective and standardized evaluations. Perhaps the most common problem so addressed has been the prediction of dangerousness, which figures in a variety of evaluations from involuntary civil commitment to release decisions for both civil and criminal patients. As the literature indicates that predictions made on clinical grounds are highly inaccurate (Ennis and Litwack 1974; Morse 1978), Wexler (1981) has suggested that an actuarial approach be adopted under which predictions would be made on statistical tables, for which specific statistical confidence limits can be given. Megargee (1970) has pointed out that research into prediction of dangerousness through tests is fraught with ethical problems; and that even postdiction cannot be accomplished satisfactorily with current methods. He reviewed a variety of uses of tests to predict dangerousness, and concluded that while no existing test can predict dangerousness, it is possible that experienced clinicians using a variety of methods including tests may be able to make useful contributions pending development of new methods.

## Conclusions

When psychometric tests are used for the clinical indications for which they were developed and standardized, and the results are handled according to professional guidelines, few ethical problems exist. But when such tests are applied to situations for which they were not designed, and particularly when they are used coercively to determine school or job placement, the potential for significant abuse exists. Those who develop and use tests for such purposes must be very careful to standardize the tests with appropriate populations, to consider the many sources of errors (such as variations based on tester or subject characteristics), not to overestimate the power of the tests, and to guard the confidentiality of all results.

## References

Albemarle Paper Company v. Moody, 422 U.S. 405 (1975)
American Psychiatric Association: Diagnostic and Statistical

Manual of Mental Disorders, Third Edition, Revised. Washington, DC, American Psychiatric Press, 1987

American Psychological Association: Standards for Educational and Psychological Testing. Washington, DC, American Psychological Association, 1985

Amrine M: The 1965 congressional inquiry into testing: a commentary. Am Psychol 20:859–870, 1965

Aronson v. North Park College, Ill. App., 418 N.E.2d 776 (1981)

Bersoff DN: Regarding psychologists testily: legal regulation of psychological assessment in the public schools. Maryland Law Review 39:27–120, 1979

Bigler ED, Ehrfurth JW: The continued inappropriate singular use of the Bender Visual Motor Gestalt Test. Prof Psychol 12:562–569, 1981

Binder A, McConnell D, Sjoholm N: Verbal conditioning as a function of experimenter characteristics. Journal of Abnormal and Social Psychology 55:309–314, 1957

Booth D, Mackay JL: Legal constraints on employment testing and evolving trends in the law. Emory Law Journal 29:121–194, 1980

Brakel SJ: Presumption, bias, and incompetency in the criminal process. Wisconsin Law Review 1974:1105–1130, 1974

Bray DW: Job, school choices call for valid tests. APA Monitor, May 1982, p 5

Brodsky SL: Ethical issues for psychologists in corrections, in Who Is the Client? Edited by Monahan J. Washington, DC, American Psychological Association, 1980, pp 63–92

Brodsky SL: An assessment of competence for execution: guidelines for ethics and quality. Journal of Psychiatry and Law (in press)

Butcher JN: The use of computers in psychological assessment: an overview of practices and issues, in Computerized Psychological Assessment: A Practitioners' Guide. Edited by Butcher JN. New York, Basic Books, 1987, pp 3–14

Cleary TA, Humphries TG, Kendrick SA, et al: Educational uses of tests with disadvantaged students. Am Psychol 30:15–41, 1975

Committee on Professional Standards and Committee on Psychological Tests: Guidelines for Computer-Based Tests and Interpretations. Washington, DC, American Psychological Association, 1986

Debra P. v. Turlington, 474 F.Supp. 244 (1979); 644 F.2d 397 (1981)

Detroit Edison v. NLRB, 440 U.S. 401 (1979)

Diana v. State Board of Education, C.A. No. C–70–37 R.F.P. (N.D. Cal., filed Feb. 3, 1970)

Ennis BJ, Litwack TJ: Psychiatry and the presumption of expertise: flipping coins in the courtroom. California Law Review 62:693–752, 1974

Ewing DW: Freedom Inside the Organization: Bringing Civil Liberties to the Workplace. New York, Dutton, 1977

Ferguson DC, Buss AE: Operant conditioning of hostile verbs in relation to experimenter and subject characteristics. Journal of Consulting Psychology 24:324–327, 1960

Fersch EA Jr.: Ethical issues for psychologists in court settings, in Who Is The Client? Edited by Monahan J. Washington, DC, American Psychological Association, 1980, pp 43–62

Golding SL, Roesch R, Schreiber J: Assessment and conceptualization of competency to stand trial: preliminary data on the interdisciplinary fitness interview. Law Hum Behav 8:321–334, 1984

Goldman RD, Hartig LK: The WISC may not be a valid predictor of school performance for primary grade children. Am J Ment Defic 80:583–587, 1976

Graham JR, Lilly RS: Psychological Testing. Englewood Cliffs, NJ, Prentice-Hall, 1984, pp 347–416

Griggs v. Duke Power Company, 401 U.S. 424 (1971)

Grisso T: Evaluating Competencies: Forensic Assessments and Instruments. New York, Plenum, 1986

Grob GN: Mental Illness and American Society, 1875–1940. Princeton, NJ, Princeton University Press, 1983

Gross ML: The Brain Watchers. New York, Random House, 1962

Guion RM: Personnel Testing. New York, McGraw-Hill, 1965

Hall JE, Hare-Mustin RT: Sanctions and the diversity of ethical complaints against psychologists. Am Psychol 38:714–729, 1983

Hammer EF, Piotrowski Z: Hostility as a factor in the clinician's personality. J Proj Tech 17:210–217, 1953

Harvey MA, Sipprelle CN: Demand characteristics on the subtle and obvious subscales of the MMPI. J Pers Assess 40:539–543, 1976

Hobson v. Hansen, 269 F.Supp. 401 (D.D.C. 1967)

Hoffman B: The Tyranny of Testing. New York, Crowell-Collier, 1962

Johnson JG: Albemarle Paper Company v. Moody: the aftermath of Griggs and the death of employee testing. Hastings Law Journal 27:1239–1262, 1976

Kahn M, Taft C: The application of the standard of care doctrine in psychological testing. Behavioral Sciences and the Law 1:71–84, 1983

Kaplan LV, Miller RD: The courtroom psychiatrist: expertise at the cost of wisdom? Int J Law Psychiatry 9:451–468, 1986

Laboratory of Community Psychiatry: Competency to Stand Trial and Mental Illness. New York, Jason Aronson, 1973

Lambert NM: Psychological evidence in Larry P. vs. Wilson Riles: an evaluation by a witness for the defense. Am Psychol 39:937–952, 1981

Lanyon RI, Goodstein LD: Personality Assessment, 2nd ed. New York, Wiley, 1971

Larry P. v. Riles, 343 F.Supp. 1306 (N.D. Cal. 1972), aff'd, 502 F.2d 963 (9th Cir. 1974) [Riles I]; No. C-71-2270 R.F.P. (N.D. Cal., Oct. 16, 1979), appeal docketed, No. 80-4027 (9th Cir., Jan. 17, 1980) [Riles II]

Levy MR, Kahn MW: Interpreter bias on the Rorschach test as a function of patients' socioeconomic class. Journal of Projective Techniques and Personality Assessment 34:106–112, 1970

Lipsitt PD, Lelos D, McGarry AL: Competency for trial: a screening instrument. Am J Psychiatry 128:105–109, 1971

London M, Bray DW: Ethical issues in testing and evaluation for personnel decisions. Am Psychol 35:890–901, 1980

Mann PA: Ethical issues for psychologists in police agencies, in Who Is the Client? Edited by Monahan J. Washington, DC, American Psychological Association, 1980, pp 18–42

Meehl PE: Wanted—a good cookbook. Am Psychol 11:262–272, 1956

Megargee EI: The prediction of violence with psychological tests, in Current Topics in Clinical and Community Psychology, Vol 2. Edited by Spielberger CD. New York, Academic Press, 1970

Melton GB, Petrilla J, Poythress NG, et al: Psychological Evaluations for the Courts: A Handbook for Mental Health Professionals and Lawyers. New York, Guilford Press, 1987

Merriken v. Cressman, 364 F.Supp. 913 (E.D. Pa. 1973)

Mintz EE: Personal problems and diagnostic errors of clinical psychologists. Journal of Projective Techniques and Personality Assessment 21:124–128, 1957

Mirvis PH, Seashore SE: Being ethical in organizational research. Am Psychol 34:766–780, 1979

Morse S: Crazy behavior, morals, and science: an analysis of mental health law. South California Law Review 51:527–654, 1978

Moses v. Washington Parish School Board, 300 F.Supp. 1340 (E.D. La. 1971), aff'd, 456 F.2d 1285 (5th Cir. 1972)

Nottingham EJ, Mattson RE: A validation study of the Competency Screening Test. Law and Human Behavior 5:329–335, 1981

Packard V: The Naked Society. New York, McKay, 1964

PASE v. Hannon, 506 F.Supp. 831 (N.D. Ill. 1980)

Robertson DF: Examining the examiners: the trend toward truth in testing. Journal of Law and Education 9:167–199, 1980

Robey A: Criteria for competency to stand trial: a checklist for psychiatrists. Am J Psychiatry 122:616–623, 1965

Roesch R, Golding SL: Competency to Stand Trial. Urbana, IL, University of Illinois Press, 1980

Rogers R: Conducting Insanity Evaluations. New York, Van Nostrand Reinhold, 1986

Rogers R, Cavanaugh JL: Usefulness of the Rorschach: a survey of forensic psychiatrists. Journal of Psychiatry and Law 11:55–67, 1983

San Antonio Independent School District v. Rodriguez, 411 U.S. 1 (1973)

Sarason IG, Harmatz MG: Test anxiety and experimental conditions. J Pers Soc Psychol 1:499–505, 1965

Schreiber J, Roesch R, Golding SL: An evaluation of procedures for assessing competency to stand trial. Bull Am Acad Psychiatry Law 15:187–203, 1987

Slobogin C, Melton GB, Showalter CR: The feasibility of a brief evaluation of mental state at the time of the offense. Law and Human Behavior 8:305–320, 1984

Slovenko R: Psychological testing as a basis for expert testimony. International Journal of Medicine and Law 1:21–41, 1979

Smith KU: Testimony before the Senate Subcommittee on Constitutional Rights of the Judiciary Committee. Am Psychol 20:907–915, 1965

Task Force on the Role of Psychology in the Criminal Justice System: Report, in Who Is the Client? Edited by Monahan J. Washington, DC, American Psychological Association, 1980, pp 1–17

Tenopyr ML: The realities of employment testing. Am Psychol 36:1120–1127, 1981

United States v. Alexander & Murdock, 471 F.2d 969 (D.C. Cir. 1972)

Wade TC, Baker TB: Opinions and use of psychological tests: a survey of clinical psychologists. Am Psychol 32:874–882, 1977

Washington v. Davis, 426 U.S. 229 (1976)

Westin AF: Privacy and Freedom. New York, Atheneum, 1967, pp 133–157

Wexler DB: Mental Health Law: Major Issues. New York, Plenum Press, 1981

Wigdor AK, Garner WR (eds): Ability Testing: Uses, Consequences, and Controversies. Part I: Report of the Committee. Washington, DC, National Academy Press, 1982

# Appendix

# List of 100 Assessment Instruments

# Appendix

# *List of 100 Assessment Instruments*

The following list of tests and instruments is by no means comprehensive:

## Self-Report Tests

### *Multidimensional Instruments*

1) Minnesota Multiphasic Personality Inventory (MMPI)
2) Millon Clinical Multiaxial Inventory
3) Clinical Analysis Questionnaire
4) Symptom Checklist 90–R
5) Eysenck Personality Questionnaire

### *Personality Tests*

6) California Personality Inventory
7) Jackson Personality Inventory
8) Guilford-Zimmerman Temperament Survey
9) Lazare Klerman Personality Scales
10) Personality Diagnostic Questionnaire
11) MMPI Personality Disorder Scales

### *Mood Scales*

12) Profile of Mood States
13) Emotions Profile Index

### *Depression Instruments*

14) Beck Depression Inventory

15) Center for Epidemiological Studies–Depression Scale
16) Zung Depression Scale
17) Geriatric Depression Scale
18) Hopelessness Scale
19) Attributional Style Questionnaire
20) Automatic Thoughts Questionnaire

### Hypomania Instrument

21) General Behavior Inventory

### Anxiety Instruments

22) State-Trait Anxiety Inventory
23) Fear Questionnaire
24) Social Avoidance and Distress Scale
25) Maudsley Obsessional Compulsive Inventory
26) Fear Survey Schedule

### Hostility Instrument

27) Buss Durkee Hostility Inventory

### Schizophrenia Instruments

28) Magical Ideation Scale
29) Perceptual Aberration Scale
30) Physical Anhedonia Scale

### Drug and Alcohol Instruments

31) Michigan Alcoholism Screening Test
32) Drug Abuse Screening Test
33) Alcohol Use Questionnaire
34) Alcohol Dependence Scale

### Social Behavior Instruments

35) Structural Analysis of Social Behavior
36) Family Assessment Measure
37) Family Environment Scale
38) Marital Satisfaction Inventory
39) Social Adjustment Scale–Self-Report
40) Derogatis Sexual Functioning Inventory

### Life Events Instrument

41) Social Readjustment Rating Scale

# Structured Interviews

### Axis I

42) Structured Clinical Interview for DSM-III-R
43) Schedule for Affective Disorders and Schizophrenia
44) Diagnostic Interview Schedule
45) Present State Examination
46) Inpatient Multidimensional Psychiatric Scale
47) Anxiety Disorders Interview Schedule–Revised

### Axis II

48) Structured Clinical Interview for DSM-III-R Axis II
49) Personality Disorder Examination
50) Structured Interview for DSM-III Personality Disorders
51) Diagnostic Interview for Borderlines
52) Personality Interview Questions
53) Schedule for Schizotypal Personalities
54) Psychopathy Checklist

### Miscellaneous

55) Role Activity Performance Scale

56) Camberwell Family Interview

## Observer Rating Scales

### Psychiatric Rating Scales

57) Hamilton Anxiety Scale
58) Hamilton Rating Scale for Depression
59) Montgomery Asberg Depression Rating Scale
60) Clinical Anxiety Scale
61) Manic State Rating Scale
62) Brief Psychiatric Rating Scale
63) Scale for the Assessment of Thought, Language, & Communication
64) Scale for the Assessment of Positive Symptoms
65) Scale for the Assessment of Negative Symptoms
66) Suicidal Ideation Scale

### Nurse's Rating Scales

67) Psychotic Inpatient Profile
68) Ward Behavior Inventory
69) Nurses' Observation Scale for Inpatient Evaluation

### Adjustment Scales

70) The Performance Test of Activities of Daily Living
71) Katz Adjustment Scale—Relative
72) Social Adjustment Scale—Interview
73) Phillips Scale of Premorbid Adjustment in Schizophrenia
74) Global Assessment Scale
75) Hollingshead-Redlich Index of Social Position

### Side Effects Scales

76) Abnormal Involuntary Movement Scale

77) Extrapyramidal Symptom Rating Scale
78) Simpson-Angus Parkinsonism Scale
79) van Putten & May Akathisia Scale
80) Rockland Dyskinesia Scale

## Neuropsychological Tests

81) Neuropsychological Status Examination
82) Neurobehavioral Assessment Format
83) Dementia Rating Scale
84) Withers-Hinton Tests of the Sensorium
85) Mini-Mental State Exam
86) Halstead Reitan Battery
87) Luria Nebraska Neuropsychological Battery
88) Wisconsin Card Sorting Test
89) Purdue Pegboard Test
90) Ravens Coloured Progressive Matrices
91) Wechsler Adult Intelligence Scale–Revised
92) Shipley Institute of Living Scales
93) Peabody Picture Vocabulary
94) Wechsler Memory Scale–Revised
95) California Verbal Learning Test
96) Benton Visual Retention Test
97) Boston Remote Memory Battery
98) Boston Diagnostic Aphasia Exam
99) Illinois Test of Psycholinguistic Ability
100) Confabulation Questionnaire

## References

1) Hathaway S, McKinley J: Minnesota Multiphasic Personality Inventory. Minneapolis, National Computer Systems, 1943
2) Millon T: Millon Clinical Multiaxial Inventory Manual, 3rd ed. Minneapolis, National Computer Systems, 1983
3) Krug S, Cattell R: Clinical Analysis Questionnaire Man-

ual. Champaign, IL, Institute for Personality and Ability Testing, 1980

4) Derogatis L: SCL-90-R Manual-II. Towson, MD, Clinical Psychometric Research, 1983

5) Eysenck H, Eysenck S: Psychoticism as a Dimension of Personality. New York, Crane-Rusak, 1976

6) Gough H: Manual for the California Personality Inventory. Palo Alto, CA, Consulting Psychologists Press, 1975

7) Jackson D: Jackson Personality Inventory Manual. Los Angeles, Western Psychological Services, 1983

8) Guilford J, Zimmerman W, Guilford J: The Guilford-Zimmerman Temperament Survey Handbook: 25 Years of Research and Applications. San Diego, CA, Educational and Industrial Testing Services, 1976

9) Lazare A, Klerman G, Armor D: Oral, obsessive and hysterical personality patterns: replication of factor analysis in an independent sample. J Psychiatr Res 7:275–290, 1970

10) Hyler S, Rieder R, Spitzer R, et al: Personality Diagnostic Questionnaire. New York, New York State Psychiatric Institute, 1984

11) Morey L, Waugh M, Blashfield R: MMPI scales for DSM-III personality disorders: their derivation and correlates, J Pers Assess 49:245–251, 1985

12) McNair D, Lorr M, Droppleman L: Profile of Mood States (Manual). San Diego, Educational and Industrial Testing Services, 1971

13) Plutchik R, Kellerman H: Emotions Profile Index Manual. Los Angeles, Western Psychological Services, 1974

14) Beck A, Ward C, Mendelson M, et al: An inventory for measuring depression. Arch Gen Psychiatry 42:667–675, 1961

15) Radloff L: The Center for Epidemiological Studies–Depression Scale: a self-report scale for research in the general population. Applied Psychological Measurement 1:385–401, 1977

16) Zung W: A self-rating depression scale. Arch Gen Psychiatry 12:63–70, 1965

17) Yesavage J, Brink T, Rose T, et al: Development and validation of a geriatric depression screening scale. J Psychiatr Res 17:37–49, 1983

18) Beck A, Weissman A, Lester D, et al: The measurement of pessimism: the hopelessness scale. J Consult Clin Psychol 42:861–865, 1974

19) Peterson C, Semmel A, von Baeyer C, et al: The Attributional Style Questionnaire. Cognitive Therapy Research 6:287–300, 1982

20) Hollon S, Kendall P: Cognitive self-statements in depression: development of an Automatic Thoughts Questionnaire. Cognitive Therapy Research 4:383–396, 1980

21) Depue R: General Behavior Inventory. Minneapolis, University of Minnesota, 1985

22) Spielberger C, Gorsuch R, Lushene R: Manual for the State-Trait Anxiety Inventory. Palo Alto, CA, Consulting Psychologists Press, 1970

23) Marks IJ, Mathews AD: Brief standard self-rating for phobic patients. Behav Res Ther 17:263–267, 1979

24) Watson D, Friend R: Measurement of social-evaluative anxiety. J Consult Clin Psychol 33:448–457, 1969

25) Hodgson R, Rachman S: Obsessional-compulsive complaints. Behav Res Ther 15:389–395, 1977

26) Lang PJ, Lazovik AD: Experimental desensitization of a phobia. Journal of Abnormal and Social Psychology 66:519–525, 1963

27) Buss A, Durkee A: An inventory for assessing different kinds of hostility. Journal of Consulting Psychology 21:343–349, 1957

28–30) Chapman L, Chapman J: Scales for rating psychotic and psychoticlike experiences as continua. Schizophr Bull 6:476–489, 1980

31) Selzer M: The Michigan Alcoholism Screening Test: the quest for a new diagnostic instrument. Am J Psychiatry 127:1653–1658, 1971

32) Skinner H: The drug abuse screening test. Addict Behav 7:363–371, 1982
33) Horn J, Wanberg K, Foster F: The Alcohol Use Inventory. Baltimore, Psych Systems, 1983
34) Skinner H, Horn J: Alcohol Dependence Scale User's Guide. Toronto, Addiction Research Foundation, 1984
35) Benjamin L: Structural analysis of social behavior. Psychol Rev 81:392–445, 1974
36) Skinner H, Steinhauer P, Santa-Barbara J: The Family Assessment Measure. Canadian Journal of Community Mental Health 2:91–105, 1983
37) Moos R, Moos B: Family Environment Scale Manual. Palo Alto, CA, Consulting Psychologists Press, 1981
38) Snyder D, Wills R, Keiser T: Empirical validation of the Marital Satisfaction Inventory: an actuarial approach. J Consult Clin Psychol 49:262–268, 1981
39) Weissman M, Bothwell S: Assessment of social adjustment by patient self-report. Arch Gen Psychiatry 33:1111–1115, 1976
40) Derogatis L: Psychological assessment of the sexual disabilities, in Clinical Management of Sexual Disorders. Edited by Meyer J. Baltimore, Williams & Wilkins, 1976
41) Holmes TH, Rahe RH: The social readjustment scale. J Psychosom Res 11:213–218, 1967
42) Spitzer R, Williams J, Gibbon M: Structured Clinical Interview for DSM-III-R. New York, Biometrics Research Department of New York State Psychiatric Institute, 1986
43) Endicott J, Spitzer R: A diagnostic interview: the Schedule for Affective Disorders and Schizophrenia. Arch Gen Psychiatry 35:837–844, 1978
44) Robins L, Helzer J, Croughan J, et al: National Institute of Mental Health Diagnostic Interview Schedule: its history, characteristics and validity. Arch Gen Psychiatry 38:381–389, 1981
45) Wing J, Cooper J, Sartorius N: The Description and Classification of Psychiatric Symptoms: An Instructional

Manual for the PSE and CATEGO System. London, Cambridge University Press, 1974

46) Lorr M, McNair D, Lasky J: Inpatient Multidimensional Psychiatric Scale. Palo Alto, CA, Consulting Psychologists Press, 1962

47) DiNardo P, Barlow D, Cerny J, et al: Anxiety Disorders Interview Schedule–Revised. Albany, NY, Center for Stress and Anxiety Disorders, 1985

48) Spitzer R, Williams J: Structured Clinical Interview for DSM-III-R Personality Disorders. New York, Biometrics Research Department of New York State Psychiatric Institute, 1985

49) Loranger A, Susman V, Oldham J, et al: The Personality Disorder Examination: a preliminary report. Journal of Personality Disorders 1:1–13, 1987

50) Pfohl B, Stangl D, Zimmerman M: Structured Interview for DSM-III Personality Disorders, 2nd ed. Iowa City, University of Iowa College of Medicine, 1981

51) Gunderson J, Kolb J, Austin V: The diagnostic interview for borderline patients. Am J Psychiatry 138:896–903, 1981

52) Widiger T: Personality Interview Questions. Lexington, University of Kentucky, 1985

53) Baron M, Asnis L, Gruen R: The Schedule for Schizotypal Personalities: a diagnostic interview for schizotypal symptoms. Psychiatr Res 4:213–228, 1981

54) Hare R: A research scale for the assessment of psychopathy in criminal populations. Personality and Individual Differences 1:111–117, 1980

55) Good-Ellis M, Fine S, Spencer J, et al: Development of a role activity performance scale. Am J Occup Ther 41:232–241, 1987

56) Brown GW, Rutter M: The measurement of family activities and relationships. Hum Rel 19:241–263, 1966

57) Hamilton M: The assessment of anxiety states by rating. Br J Med Psychol 32:50–55, 1959

58) Hamilton M: Rating depressive patients. J Clin Psychiatry 41:21–24, 1960
59) Montgomery S, Asberg M: A new depression scale designed to be sensitive to change. Br J Psychiatry 134:382–389, 1979
60) Snaith R, Baugh S, Clayden A, et al: The Clinical Anxiety Scale: a modification of the Hamilton Anxiety Scale. Br J Psychiatry 141:518–523, 1982
61) Beigel A, Murphy D, Bunney W: The Manic State Rating Scale: scale construction, reliability and validity. Arch Gen Psychiatry 25:256–262, 1971
62) Overall J, Gorham D: The Brief Psychiatric Rating Scale. Psychol Rep 10:799–812, 1962
63) Andreasen N: Scale for the Assessment of Thought, Language, and Communication. Iowa City, University of Iowa College of Medicine, 1979
64) Andreasen N: Scale for the Assessment of Positive Symptoms. Iowa City, University of Iowa College of Medicine, 1984
65) Andreasen N: Scale for the Assessment of Negative Symptoms. Iowa City, University of Iowa College of Medicine, 1983
66) Beck A, Kovacs M, Weissman A: Assessment of suicidal intention: the Scale for Suicide Ideation. J Consult Clin Psychol 47:343–352, 1979
67) Lorr M, Vestre N: The Psychotic Inpatient Profile: a nurse's observation scale. Journal of Consulting Psychology 25:137–140, 1969
68) Burdock E, Hardesty A: Manual of the Ward Behavior Inventory. New York, Springer, 1968
69) Honigfeld G, Klett C: The Nurse's Observation Scale for Inpatient Evaluation. J Clin Psychol 21:65, 1965
70) Kuriansky J, Gurland B: The Performance Test of Activities of Daily Living. Int J Aging Hum Dev 7:343–352, 1976
71) Katz M, Lyerly S: Methods for measuring adjustment and social behavior in the community, I: rationale, de-

scription, discriminative validity and scale development. Psychol Rep 13:503–535, 1963

72) Weissman M, Sholomskas M, John K: The assessment of social adjustment: an update. Arch Gen Psychiatry 38:1250–1258, 1981

73) Phillips L: Case history data and prognosis in schizophrenia. J Nerv Ment Dis 117:515–525, 1963

74) Spitzer R, Gibbon M, Endicott J: Global Assessment Scale. New York, New York State Psychiatric Institute, 1973

75) Hollingshead R: Two-Factor Index of Social Position, in ECDEU Assessment Manual for Psychopharmacology. Edited by Guy W. Rockville, MD, Department of Health, Education, and Welfare, 1976

76) National Institute of Mental Health: Abnormal Involuntary Movement Scale, in ECDEU Assessment Manual. Edited by Guy W. Washington, DC, Department of Health, Education, and Welfare, 1976

77) Chouinard G, Annabele C, Ross-Chouinard A, et al: Ethopropazine and benzotropine in neuroleptic-induced parkinsonism. J Clin Psychiatry 40:73–81, 1979

78) Simpson G, Angus J: Drug induced extrapyramidal disorders. Acta Psychiatr Scand (Suppl 212) 45:11–19, 1970

79) van Putten T, May P: Subject response as a predictor of outcome in pharmacotherapy: the consumer has a point. Arch Gen Psychiatry 35:477–480, 1978

80) Simpson G, Lee J, Zoubok B, et al: A rating scale for tardive dyskinesia. Psychopharmacology 64:171–179, 1979

81) Schinka J: Neuropsychological Status Examination. Odessa, TX, Psychological Assessment Resources, 1980

82) Siegel A, Schechter M, Diamond S, et al: Neurobehavioral Assessment Format. (Available from author, Buffalo, NY)

83) Mattis S: Mental status examination for organic mental syndrome in the elderly patient, in Geriatric Psychiatry. Edited by Bellak L, Karasu T. New York, Grune & Stratton, 1976

84) Withers E, Hinton J: Three forms of the clinical tests of the sensorium and their reliability. Br J Psychiatry 119:1–8, 1971

85) Folstein M, Folstein S, McHugh P: Mini-mental state exam: a practical method for grading the cognitive state of patients for the clinician. J Psychiatr Res 12:189–198, 1975

86) Reitan R: Manual for Administration of Neuropsychological Test Batteries for Adults and Children. Tucson, AZ, Reitan Neuropsychological Laboratories, 1979

87) Golden C, Hammeke T, Purisch A: Manual for the Luria-Nebraska Neuropsychological Battery. Los Angeles, Western Psychological Services, 1980

88) Heaton R: Wisconsin Card Sorting Test Manual. Odessa, TX, Psychological Assessment Resources, 1985

89) Purdue Research Foundation: Examiner's Manual for the Purdue Pegboard. Chicago, Science Research Associates, 1948

90) Raven J: Guide to Using the Coloured Progressive Matrices. New York, Psychological Corporation, 1965

91) Wechsler D: Wechsler Adult Intelligence Scale–Revised Manual. New York, Psychological Corporation, 1981

92) Zachary R: Shipley Institute of Living Scale Manual. Los Angeles, Western Psychological Services, 1986

93) Dunn L: Expanded Manual for the Peabody Picture Vocabulary Test. Minneapolis, MN, American Guidance Service, 1965

94) Wechsler D: Wechsler Memory Scale–Revised. New York, Psychological Corporation, 1986

95) Delis D, Kramer J, Fridlund A, et al: California Verbal Learning Test. New York, Psychological Corporation, 1986

96) Benton A: The Revised Visual Retention Test, 4th ed. New York, Psychological Corporation, 1974

97) Albert M, Butters N, Levin J: Temporal gradients in the retrograde amnesia of patients with alcoholic Korsakoff's disease. Arch Neurol 36:211–216, 1979

98) Goodglass H, Kaplan E: The Assessment of Aphasia and Related Disorders, 2nd ed. Philadelphia, Lea & Febiger, 1983

99) Kirk S, McCarthy J, Kirk W: Illinois Test of Psycholinguistic Abilities, Examiner's Manual, rev ed. Urbana, University of Illinois Press, 1968

100) Mercer B, Wapner W, Gardner H, et al: A study of confabulation. Arch Neurol 34:429–433, 1977